THE BERKSHIRE-LITCHFIELD LEGACY:
Litchfield, Ancram, Salisbury, Stockbridge, Lenox

by
Willard A. Hanna

Photographs by Mary Lou Estabrook

CHARLES E. TUTTLE COMPANY
Rutland, Vermont & Tokyo, Japan

REPRESENTATIVES:

For Continental Europe:
BOXERBOOKS, INC., Zurich

For the British Isles:
PRENTICE-HALL INTERNATIONAL, INC., London

For Australasia:
BOOKWISE (AUSTRALIA) PTY. LTD., Sydney

Published by the Charles E. Tuttle Company, Inc.
of Rutland, Vermont and Tokyo, Japan
with editorial o(ces at
Suido 1-chome, 2-6, Bunkyo-ku, Tokyo

Library of Congress Card No.   84-51028

International Standard Book No.   0-8048-1480-5

First Tuttle edition 1984

Printed in USA

Map of Mid-Housatonic Region

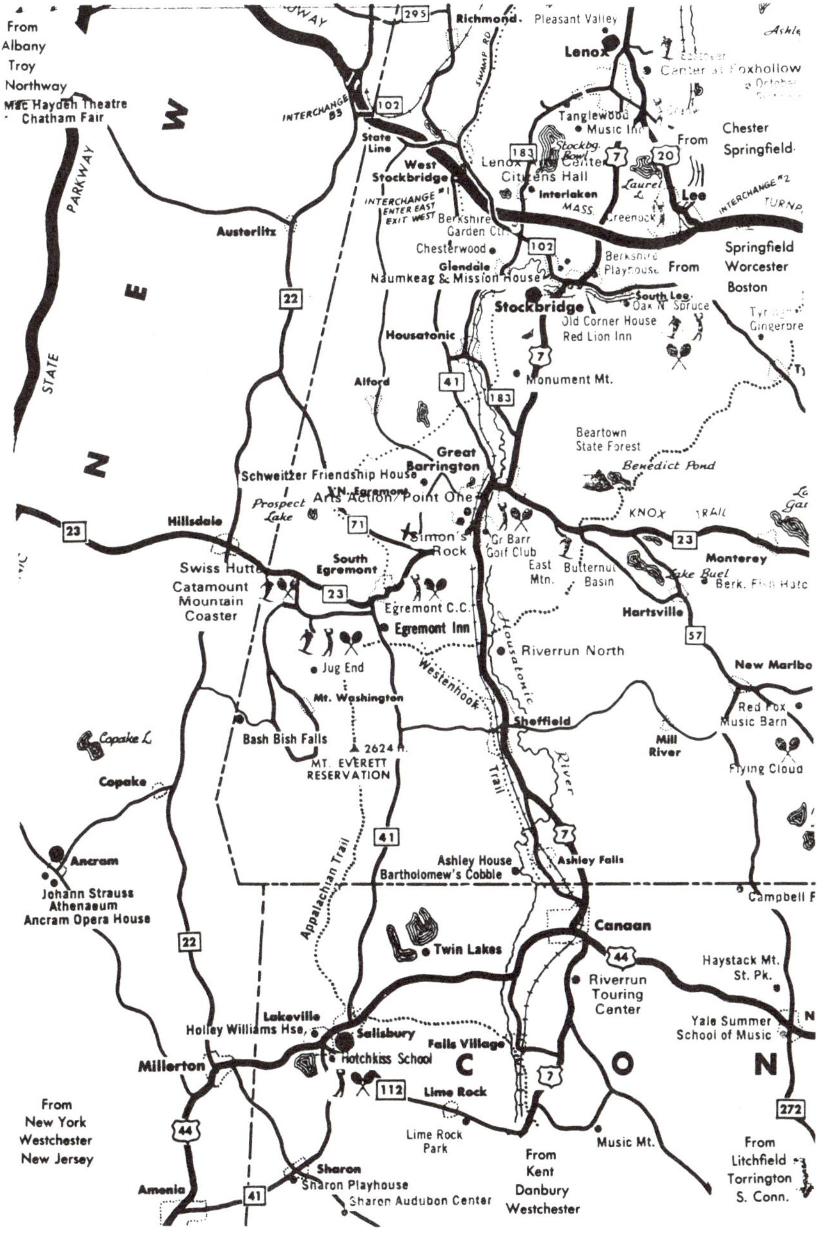

Parade of Young Ladies of Mrs. Pierce's School with
Mr. Reeve's Law Students as Spectators.

TABLE OF CONTENTS

Part I

Historical Sketches

Part II

One Day Itineraries

Foreword

Berkshire County, Massachusetts, and Litchfield County, Connecticut, which are justly celebrated for their historical, cultural, and scenic splendors, have earned the reputation of being sheltered enclaves of refuge from the urban and industrial disfigurations of recent times. In the early period of their development some of the towns and villages of the region were rivals to Boston and Hartford as centers of population and industry. Somehow they have achieved the miracle of remaining pleasant and prosperous while conceding to other areas the wages of growth, doing so, moreover, in a manner conducive at once to nostalgia for the distant past and confidence in the future.

The Berkshire-Litchfield legacy, the topic of this inquiry, is one of outstanding human achievement, which, like the more comprehensive Yankee spirit and character, is the more readily divined than defined. One especially agreeable area in which one can lay through personal study and experience to this common legacy is the fifty-mile stretch of the mid-Housatonic River valley in which are located the key towns (i.e., New England townships) of Litchfield and Salisbury, Connecticut; Lenox and Stockbridge, Massachusetts; and Ancram, New York (Columbia County).

Here lived such prominent American figures as Ethan Allen and Oliver Wolcott of revolutionary wartime fame, the eminent divines Jonathan Edwards and Stephen West, the Holleys and the Cushings (magnates of the original American iron industry), the Fields (Cyrus, the layer of the Atlantic cable and his numerous distinguished kinsmen), the Beechers (one of them Harriet Beecher Stowe), the Hopkinses (Mark the Teacher and Mark the Forty-niner), William Cullen Bryant and Herman Melville, and generations of Williamses, Sedgwicks, Ashleys, and other very important families. Many of their homes, which classify as gems of early American architecture, are still standing in wonderfully well preserved villages within an exhilarating natural environment. Their presence can still be felt as a reminder of an era of greatness and graciousness that is not necessarily past. This report on the Berkshire-Litchfield legacy is focused, therefore, upon localities, personalities, and activities which are among the richest elements of the American national heritage.

PART I

HISTORICAL SKETCHES

CHAPTER 1

Early History of the Mid-Housatonic River Towns

Prior to the influx of a few especially venturesome settlers in about the year 1715 the mid-Housatonic river valley constituted a buffer enclave almost devoid even of Indians. The Connecticut and Massachusetts Yankees, having established their "plantations" on the Connecticut River, were pausing to recharge their energies and clarify their claims to lands to the west. The New York *patroons*, having laid out their great manors along the Hudson, lacked the resources and the motivation to push very vigorously eastward. The French of Montreal postured and probed but hazarded no real drive southward. The Mohawk Indians, who created the formidable Six Nations league and allied themselves intermittently with the French, made life so hazardous at the English frontier settlement of Deerfield, Mass., for instance, that for several decades it seemed quite foolhardy for settlers to penetrate beyond already established frontiers. The indigenous Housatonic Indians, the mere remnants of the once important Mohegan Tribe, seemed few and inoffensive, but no one could be quite sure.

In the early days the mid-Housatonic valley was visited only by occasional explorers, traders, soldiers, and government agents, one of the latter of whom, Rev. Benjamin Wadsworth of Boston, wrote of his observations in terse, testy terms much quoted then and later. It was a region, he said, of "hideous, howling wilderness" and "hideous high mountains," in all "woody, rocky, mountainous, swampy" terrain — "extremely bad for riding." The first episode of recorded history occurred when Major John Talcott (or, according to variorum account, Colonel William Whiting) was reconnoitering with a party of soldiers in a campaign of the war against King Philip. Either Major Talcott surprised and massacred a singularly unwary party of Indians then disporting themselves in the river and along its bank, or Colonel Whiting laid an ambush which the suddenly alerted Indians almost broke through. In any event, at some point very close to the present Connecticut-Massachusetts boundary line (the extreme northeast corner of Salisbury Town is commonly mentioned), the palefaces killed or captured forty-five redskins. Notwithstanding, indeed perhaps because of this unprovoked outrage, for the victims seem not to have been Housatonic Indians but hostile interlopers, the valley Indians were disposed to be friendly toward their subsequent white visitors. The first of these to be clearly documented did not arrive until the second decade of the eighteenth century.

The original white settlers found themselves in juridical as well as an environmental wilderness. Certain grants conferred upon the Hudson River valley *patroons* by the Dutch or the English colonial administration, the most commonly cited of them the 1705 Patent of Westerhook (the Dutch version of   Housatonic), which was never actually activated, stated that their lands extended eastward to the Connecticut River or at least to the Connecticut or Massachusetts border, neither of which, unhappily, was as yet clearly defined.

Certain royal charters granted to English colonists made it appear that they could claim all lands westward to the Pacific. There gradually emerged a tentative compromise to the effect that the Massachusetts and Connecticut state lines would be drawn possibly 10 miles, perhaps 20 miles east of the Hudson with some still to be devised allowance for the river's perverse deviations from true North-South course. A provisional accord was worked out in 1734 to be clarified and reclarified still later after continuing trespasses. Such were the imprecisions both of early treaties and later surveys that even in the 1850s there remained, at the point where the New York, Masachusetts, and Connecticut state lines all intersected, one little lawless enclave, the infamous Boston Corners, a resort of horse thieves, ruffians, and fanciers of the more lethal style of prize fighting.

While officials asserted claims and entered protests—Connecticut, for instance, in 1727 ordered New Yorkers to desist from trespass and Massachusetts in 1731 did likewise—a few private citizens took direct action. They parleyed with the Indians for rights which might apply to as little as a few scores of acres of grass covered valley land suitable for pasture or planting. In return for the irresistible lure of guns, rum, blankets, coins, baubles, and trinkets, the Indians affixed their marks to rude documents which the interlopers regarded as title deeds and the Indians as ceremonial indications of conditional welcome. Early or late, the state authorities worked out similar ententes with the Indians or just collected and filed away the settlers' compacts while issuing their title deeds, there having to be some documentary evidence how the world of nature passed from God to man. The settlers soon established homes, farms, and trading posts, engaged in a brisk and complex series of land deals among one another and with equally venturesome newcomers, and soon squeezed out the Indians. The earliest of the settlers came from or through the Hudson River valley; they were mainly Dutchmen and their families who sought greater freedom and opportunity than the *patroons* could ever tolerate on the part of mere menials. Then came much greater numbers of English colonists from the Connecticut valley, propelled westward by land hunger or the fever of land speculation. The pattern of development on the west side of what eventually became the New York state boundary, where the *patroons* held enormous fief-like patents, was quite different from that which prevailed within Massachusetts and Connecticut and will be discussed in the sketch of Ancram Town. What follows relates primarily to the "Western lands," that is, the border towns (i.e., townships) of the new Berkshire County (Mass.) and Litchfield County (Conn.)

Massachusetts began to regularize matters in the year 1722 by monitoring a venture whereby a group of private citizens acquired from the Indians 98 square miles of terrain inclusive of most of the present day Berkshire townships of Sheffield, Great Barrington, and Stockbridge. For a consideration of "460 Pounds, 3 Barrels of Sider, and 30 quarts of Rum", Chief Konkapot, Chief Umpachenee and a score of their followers (virtually the total adult male population of a couple of clusters of wigwams on the banks of the Housatonic between present day Great Barrington and Stockbridge) signed away far more rights than they very soon even suspected. Reserving only a couple of small enclaves for themselves for planting and hunting, they conceded (the settlers said they ceded in perpetuity) the use of a tract of land approximately 4 miles wide on either side of the Housatonic for a distance of about 12 to 15 miles north of the present Connecticut-Massachusetts border. The 55 original participants in this land transaction thus acquired the southwest portion of present day Berkshire County for an original outlay of perhaps £550 in toto, i.e., about 2½ cents per acre.

Connecticut, slowed down by dispute whether its Western lands belonged to the colony proper or to the towns of Hartford and Windsor, to which they had been assigned for safekeeping during a prolonged quarrel with England over the interpretation and application of the royal charters, delayed until 1731. It then dispatched agents to explore, survey, and treat with the early settlers and the Indians. Chief Tacconoc, the sachem of Weatogue (the riverside section of today's Salisbury Town) had already more or less alienated rather extensive parcels of land, the inducement in one instance having been "80 pounds and diverse victuals and clothes" preceded, it seems certain, by unstinting quantities of firewater. He was later to lodge formal changes that he had been defrauded but was to be appeased by certain modest gratification — once, for instance, as winter set in, by the gift of two warm new blankets.

Its dubious royal charters being duly reinforced by specious contracts negotiated with the Indians, the Connecticut General Assembly ordered its surveyors to lay out various new towns approximately six miles square (the standard township) but some larger, some smaller, depending upon the terrain. Beginning in 1738 it put these new towns up for public sale in Hartford and elsewhere by inviting would-be settlers in each individual case to bid on some 25 to 50 "shares," a share signifying entitlement to a proportionate part of the 36 square miles, more or less, of town area. As sections of the town were presently opened up, the shareholders determined by lottery which plots of land would be assigned to whom, such "distributions" continuing until all the land was bespoken. Each of the original purchasers of the 60-square mile town of Salisbury thus acquired rights to some 1,550 acres of village, farm, mountain, and swampland by bidding, on the average, about double the reserve price of £30, i.e., about half a cent per acre. Reasonably good land sells today for $5,000 per acre. It must be remembered, however, that in terms at least of theoretical economics, the land was valueless until it was developed; and £30 banked in 1738 at compound annual interest of a mere 2 to 3 percent would have grown into a fortune which would tax the capacity of a pocket calculator to compute.

The original purchasers, known hereafter as the "proprietors," might or might not become actual settlers and virtually all were to some degree land speculators. Almost nobody refrained from taking big, quick profits by sale of plots to newcomers lacking the information, opportunity, or resources to bid in shares at public auction. According to the original provisions of purchase, the proprietors were required during the first three to five years to clear and fence six acres of land, to build and occupy a house, and to refrain from sale of any part of their holdings. The purchasers construed these conditions to signify that they could offer inducement to others to perform the more arduous chores of development, and could commit themselves, in return for labor and services, to transfer title to village and farm plots just as soon as it became legal to do so. Some of the proprietors of Litchfield, for instance, not only never worked their lands but never even visited them; they paid no

LENOX, FROM THE NORTHWEST.

STOCKBRIDGE, FROM THE NORTH.

Site of Salisbury Revolutionary Furnace

taxes and later, in certain cases, suffered confiscation. Others found circumstances sufficiently attractive that they took up residence and founded the very prosperous families which became most prominent in local affairs, soon to be known as the River Gods.

One entire six mile square area within the Berkshire region was designated as a distinctively indigenous settlement in which the scattered little bands of Housatonic Indians would be collected, together with such other Indian tribes as might be lured by the vision of civilization, Christianization, and democratization. Here they were to create a New England town typical in all respects save that the inhabitants, church-members, school-goers, and voters all, farmers, artisans, tradespeople, and eventually professionals, would be the heretofore savage, indolent, and wicked Indians. With the continuing moral and financial support of the London based Society for the Propagation of the Gospel in Foreign Parts and special donations from the Prince of Wales (20 guineas), the Duke of Cumberland (20 guineas), the Governor of Massachusetts (£500) among others, the youthful Rev. John Sergeant inspired the Indians to build a school, a church, a row of frame houses, to develop farms, to learn arts and crafts, and to begin to behave like sober, God-fearing, industrious citizens, rather more so, in fact, than some of their white neighbors. Rev. Sergeant invited in four white families to set the Indians a good example. Within the next several decades the white settlers, one of whose daughter Sergeant married, had set such a matchless example of land-grabbing and devious entrepreneurship that the Indians eventually sought shelter in distant reservations. They carried with them little more than a splendid velum Bible (the gift of Dr. Francis Ayscough, chaplain to the royal court) and a showy South Seas conch shell (the gift of a Boston congregation) as symbols of a utopia lost long before it was created. Meanwhile John Sergeant had died discouraged, his widow had joined the predators, and the eminent Jonathan Edwards had assumed the pastorate and leadership. Edwards devoted himself mainly, however, to preaching hell and damnation to the whites,   no doubt their their deserts, and to authorship of some of the most erudite and incomprehensible of mid-eighteenth century theological treatises, risking only occasional and tepid championship of Indian rights. Such was the most direct sequel to the cordial reception of the whites by Chief Konkapot, who died a senile Christian, and Chief Umpachenee, who accepted conversion but died a drunken debauchee, and such too, the early history of Stockbridge village, where the "Indian Mission" is proudly memorialized but the Indian Town for the most part conveniently put out of mind

The new towns developed with almost miraculous celerity. Little clusters of log cabins sprang up and the more easily cleared grasslands began to produce corn and wheat. Within a mere five to ten years, fine big frame houses of elegant design began to replace log cabins, farmyards harbored numerous poultry and livestock, and apple orchards supplied fruit and beverage—the cider to which the populace was addicted, its virtues being regarded as much enhanced if fermented or distilled. By reason of influx of persons with skills not only as farmers but also as artisans and craftsmen, very soon there were sawmills, gristmills, smithies, tanneries, and other service operations, also stores, inns, and taverns. A village of half a hundred to a hundred persons in the 1730s might grow into one of 500 or more in the 1740s. At the level of a thousand or so the growth rate almost always tapered off. The then already surplus population moved onward to create new towns and villages elsewhere, especially in New Hampshire and Vermont, where land grants became available on conditions almost as attractive as those of Massachusetts and Connecticut in earlier years and speculation was at times frenetic.

Each town emerged as a largely autonomous entity based upon a village sited insofar as possible at the geographical center with various other closely interrelated villages within an approximate three to five mile radius. Distances were short and communications between towns and villages were relatively easy along existing Indian trails or newly indicated six-yard wide town roads. The former were preferred until some of the latter became negotiable by a man mounted on horseback, a sled or wagon drawn by a team of oxen, eventually (within 50 years) a horse carriage. Even though trails and roads might become impassable, especially during winter blizzards and spring thaws, the towns and villages were never really isolated for long stretches of time, and movement between and among them was generally a matter of no more than a few hours. The Housatonic, unfortunately, was navigable only by canoes and shallow draft barges with numerous rapids and falls inhibiting any long trajects. It was first bridged close to present day Falls Village in 1744, but within a decade or two there were other bridges and always there were ferries and in winter thick ice.

The administration of the towns devolved upon the original "proprietors" and the later "inhabitants," persons who owned taxable property and were at the same time in good standing with but not necessarily members of the church. Other persons, that is, landless workmen, black slaves (of whom there were very few), and Indians (except in Stockbridge) were disenfranchised. Unless they were also "saints" (persons who had testified to the deep emotional experience of "salvation" and subscribed without reservation to the rigorous Calvinistic doctrines of the Congregationalist, the established church, even "proprietors" and "inhabitants" expereienced certain disadvantages. For the town was also ipso facto a parish, and the pastor, whom the townspeople chose, presided over it as a miniature theocracy, sometimes pursuing moral transgressors with rigidity of purpose rarely displayed by the town constable in his dealings with other offenders.

The vehicle of town administration was the annual, semi-annual, or specially called Town Meeting. The agents were the elected Moderator (Mayor), Clerk (Record Keeper), and three to five Selectmen (councilmen, some of the latter of whom doubled as constable, tax collector, or fence-watcher), performing various functions for which paid employees were eventually engaged. At Town Meetings the "inhabitants" voted on all administrative proposals including the levying of routine or special taxes. The former averaged at first about two cents on the dollar (a penny on the pound) of assessed property value for such projects as roads, bridges, and public buildings, plus another two cents on the dollar for school and church. At Town Meetings the "inhabitants" also elected a representative to send to the General Assembly, the colonial executive-legislative-juridiciary body, which, in theory, exercised strict control over town affairs but in practice relegated most matters to the town officials. No town was long without its lawyer, who functioned also as notary public and justice of the peace. Civil and criminal cases of any gravity, of which there were very, very few, were referred to the General Assembly. But most cases related to disorderly or immoral conduct or to disputes over land boundaries and inheritances. Minor offenses against state or church were dealt with by imposition of fines, exposure in the stocks, or — very rarely — chastisement at the whipping post, both stocks and whipping post being   situated on   permanent display in the village green.

If not the most prominent inhabitant, the pastor was almost always the most learned, almost certainly a graduate of Harvard or Yale, and commonly the most respected, the exact mix of reverence and apprehension with which he was regarded being, of course, difficult to determine. The town's first pastor normally received one free share of land as inducement to play shepherd to a wilderness flock and had control over another free share allotted to the church and yet another allotted to the school. Being thus a proprietor as well as a pastor he experienced little if any financial hardship. Rev. Jonathan Lee of Salisbury and Rev. Hezekiah Gold of Cornwall became known in fact as two of the richest men in the region. The pastor was also entitled to an annual salary on the order of £100 to £150 per annum, a sum which was not always promptly or gladly paid by his parishioners, who had the option of paying their "church tax" in cash or in kind but not infrequently skimped on both. He could ask his congregation to build him a manse, which, being at first a log cabin and serving also as meeting hall, he generally preferred very soon to vacate in favor of a house of his own. One entitlement to which he held his charges strictly accountable, given the severity of the New England winter, was a gigantic mound of firewood. He wasted none of it on the church, where the frigid air and the uncushioned benches were presumed to discourage drowsing during the hour-long sermon which he was expected to preach each Sunday morning and afternoon. He endeavored mightily to heat up at the least the minds and souls of the parishioners with visions of the fires of Hell and the blisses of Heaven and to explain how preordination to damnation or salvation made sinfulness no less an abomination. Indeed he explained, necessarily at great length, how the damned should glory in the obvious fact that only their consignment to Hell could insure to the saved their serene installation as saints in Heaven, neither Heaven nor Hell being possible without the other by way of contrast. "Would you not gladly be damned for the Glory of God?" Stephen Hopkins, first pastor of Great Barrington, used frequently to demand of his congregation, which, having perhaps made its decision, eventually suspended his salary and did not impede his departure to seek a new pulpit elsewhere.

The first half of the eighteenth century was a period of great intellectual and emotional turbulence among church-goers, which meant virtually all New England townspeople. Preoccupation with the more esoteric aspects of theology relating, for instance, to free will and divine grace, was not scheduled until the 1770s to yield precedence to considerations of liberty, equality, and fraternity. The harsher doctrines of Calvinism were alternatingly mellowed a bit and then reinforced as a degree of relaxation and indeed exhaustion with regard to the terrors or beatitudes of eternity would be succeeded by the passionately emotional revivalism of the Great Awakening. Three conflicting tendencies emerged. First (based on the Saybrook Platform of 1708) was a move to impose outside discipline upon the previously autonomous individual church and pastor by organizing a supervisory body to pass upon the pastor's qualifications and to enforce purity of doctrine. Second (based on the Half-way Convention of 1657) was a move to relax the criteria for full church membership—to accept statement of intent to lead the godly life rather than requiring convincing testimony of the experience of salvation. Third was the acceptance of the rights of Methodists, Baptists, Episcopalians, and Quakers, whose numbers were constantly growing as evangelicalism spread, to divert their church tax payments to support their own religious activities.

In 1825 the Congregational church was disestablished and a more liberal brand of theology became truly respectable. But the eighteenth century clash and crunch of churchmen is as revealing of New England life and thought as was the confrontation of Whigs and Tories, patriots and loyalists, Jeffersonians and Hamiltonians. This evolutionary process in ecclesiastical and hence social affairs at once electrified and paralyzed individual pastors and whole parishes and led to repeated schisms in which personalities and politics, naturally, were fully as important as polemics. The Reverend Gold, pastor of the Cornwall Church, was able to preach to his rebellious congregation one Sunday morning because a sedate lady in the front pew employed her footstool to knock the Bible from the hands of the Deacon, who was about to pre-empt the pulpit. This deplorable episode was merely symptomatic of a deep seated malaise which is the key to much of the history of early Cornwall Town.

The pastor's junior colleague in learning was the teacher, at first a wretchedly paid drudge earning about $5 per month and spending half of it to room and board with the families of his students. He underwent successive three to four month long seizures of drilling the youth of one village after another in the three R's and the catechism; but the quality of early education as doled out in bleak little one-room schoolhouses ofttimes built not on but in a roadway did not ordinarily make for truly functional literacy. The general Assembly reserved one free share of land in each new township for the support of schools and required the opening of at least one free primary school in each town. But the land endowment somehow got misplaced and village education did not really begin to flourish until the early nineteenth century. In Litchfield the school lands were leased for 99 years for a mere pittance. Certain indigent females might open private "Dame's Schools" which constituted a rebuke and a challenge to most free schools. The towns began at the same time to open academies in which, for payment of a few dollars per term in tuition, both boy and girl students could study languages (English, Latin, Greek), literature, history, geography, and natural science (the latter inclusive of philosophy). The pastor, for a fee, tutored boys for admission to Harvard and Yale. The pastor, the lawyer, and the physician commonly accepted understudies in theology, law, and medicine, such private professional apprenticeship beginning ordinarily after several years in college. The professions of pastor, lawyer, physician, it might be mentioned, were sometimes practiced seriatum or simultaneously. An incumbent village pastor was likely to join the continental army to serve concurrently as chaplain, surgeon, and judge advocate, and teachers sometimes relieved pastors of the burden of the second (afternoon) Sunday sermon.

The proprietors and the professional men indulged themselves from the first in their craving for style and luxury. They built and furnished the fine homes, many of which survive today as evidences of truly discriminating taste and a gracious manner of living. The secret of the superlative architecture is that skilled builders brought with them from the eastern seaboard towns the clear image of other mansions, also drawn or printed plans with suggestions of many alternatives of detailing for avoidance of tedious standardization. But it was not until about the year 1800 that the exteriors of the buildings began to be painted and the interiors to be decorated with wallpaper and ornate furnishings, and not until about half a century later that the villagers could bring themselves to replace the trees which had once been so laboriously destroyed.

The rows of immaculate white houses shaded by enormous elms (now vanishing) on well maintained lots spaced out along clean streets give rather a false impression today of what the early villages actually looked like. The nearby hills had been all but denuded of forests, which supplied wood for construction and fuel and timber to ship to distant markets. Bleak looking buildings clustered about the village green, which was not a park but a pasture and a subject for contention in that stray cows, goats, and pigs foraged at will unless rounded up and confined in the pound. The streets were pitted, rutted, muddy, dusty, filthy, and in winter time all but buried in snowdrifts. They were populated by scavaging dogs, pigs, and fowl and overgrown with weeds and brush. In Litchfield, for instance, famous today for its stately avenues, children were known to get lost when crossing over to a neighbor's and pedestrians were known to freeze to death while searching on a snowy winter night for a dimly lighted house within yards of their destination. Those who ventured out in spring or summer were tortured by mosquitoes and black flies. Bears, wolves, wild-cats, and other "varmints" were so numerous that they commanded a generous town bounty—long three shillings five pence for a wolf, one shilling for a "pizin serpant," a penny or more for a mere crow or squirrel. And there were recurrent rumors, especially upon receipt of report of a raid on some distant village, that bands of naked Indians were lurking nearby, poised to scalp, burn, and loot.

By frontier standards of the James Fenmore Cooper variety life in the Housatonic valley was remarkably safe and agreeable. There were no Indian raids and only a few not unprovoked Indian atrocities. There were no great famines, plagues, droughts, floods, or other widespread disasters. But neither was there much entertainment or recreation other than church-going, barn- and house-raising, and certain more or less innocent festivities associated with weddings, corn huskings, hunting, and winter sports such as sleigh-riding, ice skating, and bundling.

The all but universal and obligatory ritual of church-going was not as grim as it might sound. The trip to church provided occasion for a break in labor, a display of finery, the exchange of news and gossip, also the proof of status, for pews were assigned on the basis of wealth and influence. The sermon might be overly tedious — or terrifying; the music might be harrowing to sensitive ears, for the Deacon droningly "lined out" the psalms with each member of the congregation repeating them at a tempo and pitch of his own devising. But between morning and afternoon services in the uncushioned, unheated, badly ventilated church people gathered at the homes of friends, at the inn, or at specially constructed little "Sabbath-houses" where, in winter, there was always a good fire, and at all seasons of the year a bountiful table.

Barn-raising, house-raising, or church- or meeting house-raising, meant plentiful rum and cakes, the few occasions on which such events were scheduled on a tee-totalitarian and austerity basis being patronized by almost no volunteer helpers. Cider, not necessarily soft, flowed freely on other occasions as well, and there was no dearth of roasts, pies, and thick, rich soups. Although home comforts and amenities might seem to have been meager, the life was basically a healthy one. The ordinary diet, for instance, was much more than amply satisfying for those content with such simple fare as bread baked from newly ground grain, freshly churned butter and thick cream, venison, wild fowl, trout, salmon, smoked ham and turkey, and highly spiced sausage together with a great variety, in season, of fruits, berries, and vegetables. Of course, a single meal or even a whole series of meals might consist of nothing other than fried corn meal mush drenched with maple syrup, a combination which could become cloying, but one could always resort to a crock of sauerkraut in the cellar or black walnuts in the attic if one craved other sustenance. If the preachers are to be believed, one also resorted all too systematically to apple jack, apple brandy, and more classical fluids, the incidence of habitual inebriation even among the pastors themselves being quite shocking.

One very important factor in village social life and also, alas, in dissipation was the tavern, commonly operated in conjunction with or close to the inn. The inn and the tavern were to be found very close to the village center, often right on the green adjacent to the Meeting Hall, the Church, and the spacious properties (interlinked home, barn, workshop, office) of the leading tradespeople, professional men, artisans, and landed gentry. The innkeeper offered rooms and beds or at least mats on the floor to the very numerous traveling public which found overnight stops either necessary or pleasurable. He provided also barn space for horses and food for both man and beast. The quality of the accommodations, service, and food at the better inns drew favorable comment from knowledgeable visitors who were often quite astonished to discover that the townspeople were far from being rude frontiersmen. The tavern keeper too provided food, but more especially he served up drinks—whiskey, rum, gin, and brandy, plain or blended into the house formula for a grog, flip, toddy, punch, or a harmless sounding herbal infusion for the ladies. The tavern fetched in not only the traveling public but also the local citizenry for afternoons and evenings of spirited conversation in which local and distant events were critically and exhaustively analyzed. It was the tavern which linked the villages and villagers together in surprisingly close relations well before the privately built toll turnpikes of the early nineteenth century began to carry scheduled stagecoaches and the railways, which attracted the investment money several decades later, suddenly multiplied traffic ten to a hundred times over. The taverns also, as was all to often apparent, provided employment for the justices of the peace, who had to deal with tavern patrons charged, for instance, with "striking and quoriling in a tumultuous manner," the sort of complaint which was recurrently lodged against Ethan Allen.

The early settlers experienced remarkably little distraction from the labors of building a new life and livelihood. During the French and Indian Wars (1754-1763) the people of the Housatonic valley had occasional but false alarms about impending Indian attack and were called upon to supply soldiers, as they did to a total of at least one-third of all the able bodied men to serve in the campaigns against French outposts on Lake Champlain and their stronghold at Crown Point. The Housatonic volunteers served mainly under Colonel William Johnson, an eccentric Irish gentleman of the Hudson River valley who attracted also a following of lean and hungry Indian braves whom he entertained lavishly as honored relatives of his Indian wife. But Colonel Johnson relied upon intrepidity rather than strategy and his 1754 campaign against Crown Point was a disaster. So too was a second, English-commanded campaign (1755) in which the Housatonic volunteers also participated, and a third (1756), and a fourth (1757). From their experiences the volunteers derived an enduring detestation for the arrogant and obtuse English officers. They learned mainly how not to fight the French, the Indians, or later the English themselves, a lesson which few appreciated until about 15 years later.

The half century between 1720 and 1770 saw the rapid transformation of the mid-Housatonic region from primitive frontier into flourishing towns which carried real weight in colonial and presently also national affairs. The most significant of the new towns was Salisbury, which became the center of the nation's first really important iron industry. The early settlers and surveyors discovered that Salisbury had vast deposits of exceptionally high grade, easily worked ore. What was more, these deposits were located conveniently close to mountain forests which could provide timber and charcoal, quarries which could yield crushed limestone for flux, and streams which would serve for washing ore and powering machinery.

Mr. Thomas Lamb, the first English settler in Salisbury, was also the region's first great entrepreneur, shrewdly combining speculation in lands with development of industry. Systematically, and not too scrupulously, Mr. Lamb acquired a good 20 percent of the town lands including strategic sites on the three most important streams and ownership of two of the three most productive mines. In the year 1735 or 1736 he built and brought into operation on Salmon Kill (Creek) near present day Lime Rock Village the region's first furnace and forge. He employed a pair of black-smiths who used the puddling and blooming process to produce pig iron to work into nails, kettles, horseshoes, plows, and other necessities of farm and home. Mr. Lamb presently pocketed his massive profits and moved to New York.

In 1762, just a few years after Mr. Lamb's departure, a gigantic and belligerent young gentleman of many skills and more schemes, a certain Mr. Ethan Allan from nearby Cornwall, raised the capital to build a blast furnace which promptly moved the iron industry into a new scale of output and profit. Mr. Allen too soon moved on, leaving many cracked heads and outraged feelings (he drank, he cursed, he fought, he professed deism, he boldly espoused inoculation against smallpox). Later he was to become famous for taking Fort Ticonderoga and still later infamous for engaging in alleged land swindles in Vermont. Thanks to Ethan Allen and Thomas Lamb, how-ever, the mining and processing of iron became a boom industry throughout the entire mid-Housatonic valley, an infant industry which was to salvage and sustain the flickering fortunes of General George Washington's army and navy.

With the outbreak of the War of the Revolution the towns of the mid-Housatonic valley achieved their maturity. In Sheffield in 1773 the citizenry drew up a set of "resolves" curiously paralleling the language and content of the later Jeffer-sonian document which they were to call the Second Declaration of Indepen-dence—also, to be sure, of the English and French philosophers whom the drafters of the declaration diligently studied. Already in 1766 the representatives of various towns of Litchfield County had published a manifesto declaring the Stamp Act "unconstitutional, null, and void" and decreeing defiance of all such English abuses. And in 1774 at the Red Lion Inn in Stockbridge, prominent men from a score of nearby towns called for a boycott on all commerce with the English and the devel-opment of self-sufficiency in textiles and other necessities. Town after town adopted comparable resolutions and the local historians still debate whose "Declaration of Independence" came first. In Great Barrington there was one clear first, both for the region and the nation. At irate crowd of some 1,500 persons,   about half from Berkshire and half from Litchfield County, stopped the King's Court of Common Pleas from sitting and bid the judges bethink themselves of American rather than English type justice. Other townspeople soon did likewise.

It was not long until Committees of Correspondence were exchanging exhortations to action and Minute Men were drilling on the village greens. When word reached the region of English provocations on the seaboard, the Housatonic Valley Minute Men at once marched eastward. One large detachment under command of Colonel (later Major-General) John Patterson of Lenox, who distinguished himself later at Valley Force, Monmouth, Trenton, and Saratoga, arrived in Lexington just too late for the real battle but in plenty of time to be integrated into the gradually coalescing Continental Army and to fight in all the major campaigns of the coming war. Among the mid-Housatonic volunteers, early or late, were Indian scouts from Stockbridge and Kent and a body of cavalrymen recruited and commanded by Salisbury's Colonel Elisha Sheldon. At town meetings the villagers voted increasingly onerous taxes to pay bounties (up to £50-100 in addition to state bounty) to new volunteers, to subsidize their families, to purchase food, uniforms, and weapons, and later to help the disabled. Approximately one-half the able-bodied men of the region performed military service and hundreds were killed or wounded.

The region's most effective contribution to the war effort was not its men but its cannons. The Lakeville furnace, forge, and foundry was by far the largest and most important of half a dozen such establishments in the valley. It supplied George Washington with at least a thousand cannons, many of them relatively large 9, 12, and 18 pounders (the weight refers to the ball) which were shipped at enormous difficulty and expense, by ox-cart or ox-sled, to the armies in the fields and to the port cities. These were rather primitive weapons, to be sure, cast in earthen molds and bored by simple equipment. Flawed workmanship necessitated nicely calculated corrections in loading, aiming, and firing if the gunner were to score a hit or at least to avoid blowing himself up. But such cannon lent credibility and impact to otherwise ill-equipped regiments and real sting to mosquito fleets or privateers.

The percentage of officers was extraordinarily high among valley volunteers and some achieved considerable fame. General Oliver Wolcott became one of the best known by causing a statue of George III, deposed from its pedestal in New York City, to be dragged by ox-sled all the way to his backyard in Litchfield and there melted down by his daughters and cast into 42,088 bullets. Rev. Thomas Allen, "the fighting parson of Pittsfield," led a company of soldiers direct from church to the battlefield at Bennington. There, reportedly, he fired the first shots against General Burgoyne's army, the pastor himself later admitting to having "extinguished the flashes" of an English sharpshooter. But it was Ethan Allen whose feat was the most celebrated.

Ethan Allen was the agent of a plan hatched in Litchfield, Salisbury, Pittsfield or all three (local historians disagree) to seize British Fort Ticonderoga and, as was equally important, to dismantle its cannon for shipment to Boston in anticipation of the need which soon arose. With about a hundred of his rowdy Green Mountain Boys and a score or so of volunteers from Litchfield and Berkshire Counties, Ethan Allen succeeded very early one morning by stealth and audacity in penetrating the fort unchallenged (May 10, 1775), demanding and getting the unconditional surrender of the only half-aroused commander. Captain Knox's subsequent safe transport of the cannon by ox-sled in winter over all but impassable mountain roads was a feat of endurance which matched Ethan Allen's inspired caper. The people of the Great Barrington region, through which Knox's parade passed, were later to turn out again en mass to view the spectacle of Burgoyne's English and Hessian troops being marched off to prison camp after their surrender at Saratoga.

Burgoyne's troops, some still splendidly uniformed and others, the ordinary soldiers, shivering, dressed in tatters, and dragging   enormous cannon, attracted much sympathy and hospitality. Colonel Elijah Dwight of Great Barrington invited the officers to a lavish reception and the townspeople offered their barns for the soldiers to sleep in. The Hessians attracted mixed notices. Baroness van Riedesel, the wife of the commanding officer, was lionized wherever she went, riding, as she did, in a gilded carriage along with her two very attractive children under escort of handsome officers. The Baronness and the officers were entertained in Salisbury at a glittering ball attended by "25 belles" who could not get enough of dancing, and various of the gentry who made very indiscreet profession of Tory sympathies. But the cold, hungry soldiers slept in the fields and lived on quarter rations. Numerous of the soldiers decided to desert and found a cordial reception as skilled workmen—carpenters, masons, decorators, tailors, wagon makers, millers, the gristmill in Salisbury, for instance, being operated for years thereafter by a resettled Hessian.

The revolutionary Patriots predominated throughout the Housatonic region, but there were also Tories and rather shocking episodes of abuse and persecution of those suspected of being loyalists and royalists. In Sheffield the very authors of the famous Sheffield Resolves came under suspicion of lack of genuine revolutionary ardor. The leading merchant, Don Raymond, was publicly humiliated for having allegedly inspired a menial to cut down the Liberty Tree, said menial being tarred and feathered. Stockbridge Elijah Williams, the leading citizen of Stockbridge, felt it only prudent to carry an official certification of loyalty and even then, he was twice jailed as a Tory sympathizer. Timothy Edwards, son of Jonathan Edwards, was constantly harassed. Richard Smith, owner of the Lakeville Furnace, found it expedient to abandon his properties and spend the wartime years in Europe. Near Sharon there occurred a small pitched battle between bands of Tories and patriot vigilantes, and scores of fugitive royalists spent many a cold and weary month hiding out in caves near Great Barrington and Lenox.

The patriot-loyalist clashes of revolutionary days were in large part a manifestation of long-term friction between the gentry and the masses which the achievement of independence at first did little to lessen. The immediate postwar period in the Housatonic valley, as elsewhere, was marked by widespread hardship and outrage. The iron industry went into a recession. Returning soldiers found their lands and their homes suffering from prolonged neglect, themselves and their families deeply in debt, their labors little wanted and ill rewarded. Popular disaffection resulted in displays of animosity against the prosperous and the prominent and resistance to the as yet very insecure government.

The climax of this early populist protest movement occurred when the charismatic ex-Revolutionary officer Daniel Shays (was he a visionary or a demagogue?) led a little band of fighters (were they rabble or patriots?) in a forlorn attempt to seize the Springfield Armory. The anticlimax occurred one winter night on the Housatonic when a hundred of Shays' fugitives staged seriatum raids upon Stockbridge, Great Barrington, and outlying settlements, seizing "silk-stocking hostages," releasing prisoners, consuming looted stores of liquor, and at last surrendering to a few reluctantly recruited militiamen who generally shared their sentiments.

In the last decade of the century the Housatonic valley towns staged a rapid recovery, and by the turn of the century the villages were much more prosperous, beautiful, and animated than ever before. The regional iron industry was greatly expanded and it profited from an enormous new market. Salisbury and other towns produced the iron which was required not only for all traditional purposes but for the newly invented machinery of big industrial establishments, for the railway networks which multiplied rapidly all commerce and industry, and for the arsenals which required stockpiling of munitions before, during, and after the War of 1812, the Civil War, and the Spanish-American War. The growth of railways, which, by the mid-nineteenth century, linked the Housatonic valley towns with Albany, New York City, Hartford, Boston, and points much more distant, led to the exploitation of another great natural resource, especially the widespread deposits of high grade marble then much in demand for fine private and public buildings in urban centers. West Stockbridge, for instance, supplied 33,000 cubic feet of marble at $1.00 per foot for the New York City Hall, much of it in blocks 50 feet long.

Numerous other industries sprang up. In Lee the local financiers took advantage of remaining timber stands and abundant water power to manufacture paper for the ravenous New York City presses. Almost every town in the valley experimented with textile plants. The big Glendale mill just outside Stockbridge, for instance, employed 60 girls to convert local wool into many tens of thousands of yards annually of satinet. The more romantically minded socioeconomists began to point out great cultural as well as commercial advantage. The terms of employment, they mentioned , provided for generous pay of about 2 cents per hour for an easy 13-hour day, plus free bed and board in a discreetly supervised hostel (2 to a bed, 6 beds to a room, 50 to 60 girls at long, sparsely set tables in the dining hall). During their leisure time the girls attended programs of lectures, music, and miscellaneous studies. The mills thus spelled not only the emancipation of the New England "spinster" of ages between 18 and 35 from the dreary unpaid chores of home and farm but also her introduction into the world of art and culture.

In Stockbridge and elsewhere in the valley, whether or not suddenly emancipated and enlightened spinsters were a major factor, it was culture, not industry, which soon came to prevail. One by one the textile mills, the iron furnaces, the marble quarries, and many of the related industrial enterprises closed down. It was not, it would seem, for lack of minerals, fuel, wool, labor, or capital. People of the valley, who had pioneered in industrialization in the eighteenth century, seemed to have had their fill of it by the time the twentieth century rolled in. Big scale modern industrialization was relegated to towns well up or down river. In the mid-river valley, the exceptionally aggressive Hotchkiss and Sons, makers of the most advanced armaments, vacated little Sharon in favor of Hartford, Bridgeport, and other cities. Even Mr. Joseph Bostwick, inventor of a better mousetrap which fetched so many importunate customers to his door that his home town became known as the Mousetrap Capital of the Universe, suspended operations, inspired, perhaps, by a brighter vision of the Sharon future as the serenely beautiful little town it is todav.

The Housatonic River Gods of the eighteenth century were the proprietors, the pastors, the furnace operators, and the generals, a single deity ofttimes manifesting himself in several guises. In the nineteenth century there were enshrined lesser River Gods of the same descriptions and commonly the scions of the early families, conspicuous among them the Holly dynasty of iron magnates of Salisbury. But the era of divinities passed and the era of mere luminaries set in. The transition was signaled by widespread rejection of the harsher tenets of Calvinism and attraction to exponents of a new religious, social, economic, political, and literary order. Practitioners of law and letters played key roles and scientists and inventors revealed mysteries of the universe yet more engrossing than the old conundrums regarding Heaven and Hell. This development was by no means confined to the Housatonic valley, but in the nineteenth and twentieth centuries history of the valley it has been the regional contributions to this movement of modernization which have become most significant. In the eighteenth century Salisbury, for instance, was distinctive for its industry, Stockbridge for its Indian experiment, Ancram for its role in the manor system. What was most distinctive about the new towns was simply the character and the activities of the key individuals, or, to be more precise, the key families — the Sedgwicks, the Hopkinses, and the Fields.

Heirs of the old River Gods, these bright new luminaries left a whole new valley legacy, a new New England tradition which altered and enriched the old. It was a tradition of astonishing achievement on the part of highly gifted individualists who dared deliberately to reject and select the heirloom concepts. They did so in order to recreate or perhaps create the genuine New England spirit which had somehow become dimmed in the course of the revolutions against the King, Calvinism, and the River Gods themselves. These new New Englanders, as will become evident in the final sketch of this series, guided the new population of the mid Housatonic valley into a new era. It was characterized by a curious sense of valley destiny combining much embellished aspects of the past with prudently safeguarded elements of the present and the future. These villages, which have remained for almost two and one-half centuries villages of a thousand or two inhabitants with much of their physical structure intact, may well demonstrate an agreeable mcde of survival in times even more turbulent than those of the past.

CHAPTER 2

Salisbury: The Arsenal of the Revolution

In 1731 the General Assembly of the Colony of Connecticut ordered its agents to visit its still undeveloped "Western Lands" of the mid-Housatonic River valley in order to lay out the 60 square mile town, that is, township soon to be known as Salisbury. In 1738 it offered the town for sale at public auction in Hartford, any resident of the colony being eligible to bid for shares but the minimum acceptable offer being £30 for the rights to a one twenty-fifth part of all the land to be so distributed. In 1741, most of the shares having gone fast for well over £30 and some 40 families of settlers having established homesteads, the Assembly granted a petition for incorporation. The "proprietors," that is, the original shareholders and the other newly registered property owners to whom they had sold plots, were authorized to call Town Meetings. This meant that they might elect officials, decide upon town projects, levy taxes, and engage a teacher and a pastor, all in accordance with certain well understood but not always explicitly stated guidelines which signified near autonomy.

The first Town Meeting was held on November 9, 1741. There were then 46 registered property owners whose homes and farms were appraised at a total of £2,279-10-6 in value (about $7,500 at the later conversion rate of $3.33 to £1) on which were levied taxes totaling £28-13-9 ($95). These figures $7,500 and $95, which were the equivalent of $750,000 and $9,500 today, compare with the 1977 tax list of $53,000,000 and property taxes of $1,500,000 for a population of about 4,000. By 1776 the town had a population of 1,100 and a tax list of £11,576-7-6. Some of the original proprietors and their families had achieved wealth and distinction and numerous late comers had acquired quite respectable homes and farms combined ofttimes with profitable trades. Salisbury had become, in fact, the key industrial center of the insurgent Connecticut Colony with an iron furnace and foundry which made it the "arsenal of the revolution." It produced most of the cannons which gave real clout to Washington's armies and the swivel guns which supplied the sting to a mosquito fleet of privateers. For almost a century and a half thereafter Salisbury was much more important in commerce and industry, politics and culture than would seem probable from its top population figure of between 3,000 and 4,000. So too, by reason of its many prominent or once prominent residents, it remains today.

Such is not quite the full, true story of Salisbury as it should appear in even the most abbreviated history. There should also be some mention at least of Indian chiefs, Dutch squatters, English land grabbers, ore speculators, and miscellaneous more or less reputable characters who featured as founding fathers and later leaders. For town history did not begin with the town survey, nor did population numbers, property values, and economic productivity increase—and at times decline—without incident.

Long before the colonial surveyors drew their first rough maps of the region, the town was populated by Indians—never very many, never very aggressive, in fact only a few hundred living along the river bank (70 wigwams in 1741) under the aegis in the early eighteenth century of the sachem Tocconoc (hence the name Taconic applied to one Salisbury village and also to a range of mountains). The region was visited occasionally by explorers and traders. It was first settled by Dutch farmers from Livingston Manor (now Columbia and part of Dutchess County, New York), who made deals with the Indians for stretches of land defined by rather obscure reference to trees, rocks, streams, and hills for which they made payment in guns, rum, coins, and trinkets. During the period 1714-1720 some 40 persons, male and female, young and old, of the Vandeusen, Knickerbaker, Dyckman, Duyster, and Hoogenboom families, together with two black slaves and presently also William White, an Englishman married to a Dutch wife, opened up farms, mainly in the proximity of the present day village of Lime Rock. There appeared also upon the scene certain agents of Connecticut families who, by reason of special merit or influence, had received as much as half a century earlier vaguely defined grants to portions of "Western Lands" and aimed to make specific claims along the Housatonic. The Dutch, whose Indian deeds were of dubious validity, sought to fortify their claims by purchase of these slightly less questionable Connecticut grants. And at just this same time, word having trickled out that the Housatonic lands might be highly desirable, there appeared outright speculators. The rumor, presently the established fact, was that there were large deposits of especially rich and easily worked ore — 45 percent iron content, as it turned out, with minimum impurities such as sulphur and potassium. The earliest of the early birds were a trio from Woodbury — Hinman, Knowles, and Stiles, already wealthy, soon, they hoped, to become much more so. For such inducement as "80 pounds and diverse victuals and clothes" delivered to Chief Tocconoc, and for rather more substantial payment to certain of the Dutch deed and English grant holders, these shrewd operators amassed impressive sheaves of documents which they attempted in Hartford to parley into title to the entire town. In the end they had to settle for a mere sub-share of 100 acres. This denouement was so discouraging that they were willing to sell out to an apparently rash and innocent newcomer, Mr. Thomas Lamb, from Springfield, Massachusetts. Mr. Lamb, who was not even then without economic intelligence and political influence, saw to it that these 100 acres were laid out at what is now Lakeville Village where the outlet from Lake Wononscopomuc provides an unfailing source of swift flowing water suitable for powering machinery.

Mr. Thomas Lamb was the first really to entertain the radiant vision of the Salisbury future in which he quite purposefully set about creating a key role for himself, one from which he could derive maximum profit. He seems first to have appeared in the town in about the year 1731 and was alerted at once to the deposits of iron ore, the stands of timber, and the abundant water power. He realized that he could compete with the traditional English exporters of the iron, which the colonies badly needed and were only just beginning to produce for themselves under restrictive measures which the crown was soon to make almost prohibitive. He therefore negotiated with the Dutch, the English, and the Indians (whose language he spoke, whose psychology he understood), to acquire the key land and water rights which seemed to be theirs to dispose of. He made almost unerring choice of the most promising deposits of ore and of the best land bordering the most swiftly flowing streams.

Mr. Lamb presently began to play a decisive if at the same time an obscurantist role in getting the town surveyed, sold, and incorporated. In order to inhibit premature migration and to keep prices low he artfully derogated the utility of the land, scoffing at rumors about iron ore, and exaggerated the difficulties of development. When the auction was held, being a Massachusetts resident and hence ineligible to buy Connecticut land, he bankrolled the bids of proxies and patsies and gambled upon more or less licit acquisition of title later on in his own name. And when the successive parcels were opened up and individual plots assigned presumably by lot, he made quite certain that his proportionate shares covered the lands he had earlier bargained for privately and those which his later reconnoiters showed to be the most desirable. He engaged thereafter in brisk buy-sell or exchange operations and at one time or another owned a good one-fifth to one-quarter of the town. He also owned land in nearby Sharon, where he was granted one free share for having served as intermediary with the Indians, who later accused him of fraud.

Mr. Lamb's most important holdings were the Lakeville site which later became the center of the iron industry; the land along Salmon Kill (i.e., Salmon Creek) near present day Lime Rock village where, in 1735 or 1736, he built and put into operation the town's first forge, gristmill, and sawmill; the land along Fell Kill (now Riga Brook) in Salisbury village where he also built a gristmill and a sawmill; an iron mine (later called the Davis Bed) on the edge of Lakeville village; and a mine adjacent to Ore Hill. As proprietor of forge, mines, and mills and by far the largest landowner he virtually cornered Salisbury commerce and industry.

Mr. Lamb's one regret was that by reason of arriving just too late he forfeited the town's greatest single prize — Ore Hill, two miles outside Lakeville Village. Known at the time as Oar Hill or Magic Mountain, it was a 100 acre plot of almost solid ore rising several hundred feet into the sky and sinking even deeper into the earth. It is now not a hill but a water filled pit. Mr. Lamb did not fail to associate himself with the proprietors of Ore Hill and from their mine as well as from his own holdings relays of pack horses soon began to carry ore across Lakeville Town Hill, where the Hotchkiss School now stands, to his Lime Rock forge. Two blacksmiths, having caused the ore to be washed in the stream, worked it over charcoal fire into bar iron and then into nails, kettles, plows, horseshoes, sled runners, wheel rims, and other necessities for home and farm. Bar iron also served ofttimes as currency.

Ore Hill, it should be mentioned, fell to a consortium of prominent gentlemen who also appreciated the potential of Salisbury Town, chief among them Ezekiel Ashley, a wealthy proprietor of nearby Sheffield, Elisha Williams, the revered rector of Yale College, Jared Elliott, eminent pastor and physician of Killingsworth, and Philip Liviingston, *patroon* of Livingston Manor on the Hudson. These fortunate investors acquired Ore Hill thanks to the inattention of Mr. John Bissell of Windsor, heir to an imprecise land grant of the year 1674; Mr. Bissel seems to have neglected to inquire why they were willing to pay good money for a claim which he probably thought to be of little if any value and may not even have learned what they did with it. What they did was to make sure that the Connecticut General Assembly revalidated the grant and that the town surveyors fitted their 100 acres very neatly over Ore Hill, which, within only a few years, was yielding at least 1,000 tons of ore per annum valued at $5 per ton. In 1748 the Ore Hill proprietors established a forge at Lakeville, and they themselves and their successors in enterprise bought up most of Mr. Lamb's properties; meanwhile they entered into an extremely complicated series of partnerships and individual transactions which led to the establishment of forges elsewhere in Salisbury and neighboring towns (one of them in Livingston Manor), all dependent upon Salisbury ore. The suddenly flourishing iron industry put the town of Salisbury on the map as the iron capital of the American colonies.

Stockbridge Mission

Naumkeag House

Hawthorne's Little Red House (Replica)

Mr. Thomas Lamb disappeared from the scene almost as suddenly and mysteriously as he had appeared upon it, and the true story of his life and his activities is impossible to reconstruct. For a decade and a half he was by far the most prominent and important citizen of Salisbury but he seems to have inspired no affection and to have acquired no sentimental attachments. He is known to have had a wife and several children, but his family remained in Springfield. He built at least half a dozen homes in Salisbury Town and seems to have lived most of his time in quite handsome style at Lime Rock, where two black slaves, Sandy (male) and Roos (female) served him. He traveled about on a fine red roan mare which, together with his two slaves, he sold upon his departure for £250, the high price being a clue to the quality of the merchandise. In 1740 he sold a three-fourth interest in his Lime Rock operation for £700, and between 1744 and 1748 he liquidated all of his holding for prices which must have added up to several thousands of pounds when a mere one thousand represented a substantial fortune. It is impossible to do more than conjecture why he left Salisbury or how he fared thereafter, the only clue being that he went first to Dutchess County and later lived in several seaboard cities where, it seems, he engaged in marine commerce. Town historians call Mr. Lamb an adventurer, a speculator, a land-grabber, a fast operator of dubious morals and devious practices. But undoubtedly he did more than any other early resident to speed Salisbury forward.

Enter Ethan Allen. A man of daring and intellect as impressive as his physical stature (six feet four with the build of Atlas), Ethan Allen took pleasure, despite the devoted private tutelage of the town pastor, in scandalizing all Salisbury with his profanity, his drunkenness, his rowdyism, and his profession of French deism. He had an eye both for public drama and for private gain. Later to achieve fame as the leader of the Green Mountain Boys and the captor by craftiness and bravado of Fort Ticonderoga ("He could take it, but he couldn't spell it," said those who thought him an uneducated lout), Allen made himself the key figure in moving the Salisbury iron industry out of the era of blooming and puddling (primitive processing at the forge) into that of the blast furnace. In association with his brother Heman, the brothers Elisha and Samuel Forbes (village blacksmiths from Canaan), and certain other occasional partners, he raised £430 (only £50 of it his own money) to buy the Lakeville forge and adjacent property. He then both inspired and supervised the construction of a blast furnace, the first in Connecticut, the largest and best in any of the colonies.

The square stone structure, which measured 25 feet high and 40 feet square, was a marvel of technological innovation and efficiency. It was capable of handling 3½ tons of ore at its daily firing, for which were required 260 bushels of charcoal (the product of 10 cords of wood) and half a ton of lime as flux (from a Canaan limestone quarry) for output of two tons of pig iron of exceptional quality. The blast was created by leather bellows powered by the swift flowing stream. By day the furnace belched out a pall of smoke and by night the flames could be seen for miles about, a spectacle which never failed to astound incoming visitors. When the red hot iron suddenly poured out of the furnace into sand molds for shaping and cooling, spectators gasped in dismay. Ironmaster Elisha Forbes gained widespread reputation for the dramatic manner in which, at risk it would seem of his life (clumsy maneuvers were the lethal undoing of some of his rivals), he knocked out the clay plug which released the molten metal. Ethan Allen shared the glory, probably also the task.

The Lakeville blast furnace soon put a dozen scattered little forges out of business and ended the mining and working of iron as a cottage industry which certain residents had been operating on their farms. The mining of ore (at Ore Hill, on Mr. Lamb's 30 by 5-rod strip of land adjacent to the hill, and on his 3-acre plot on the edge of Lakeville village), the burning of charcoal (mainly on Mt. Riga), and the crushing of lime (at the Canaan quarry) became big scale operations providing employment for scores and scores of newcomers.

Ethan Allen eventually found Salisbury a bit too restrictive for his tastes and his abilities. He was always in trouble with the soberer citizens — once over sequestering his neighbor's foraging pigs, once for subjecting himself to smallpox inoculation which many thought spread rather than prevented plague, and many times over assault and battery. He sold out his interest in the furnace to the brothers Charles and George Caldwell and set out to seek a new career in the New Hampshire Grants (i.e., Vermont). He maintained contacts, however, with his brother Heman, who became the operator of a general store, and with his special friend, Dr. Joshua Porter, the town physician, one of his associates in the furnace project, soon to become the most prominent town patriot and a surgeon in the army of the revolution.

Ethan Allen's business transaction with the brothers Caldwell seems not to have been altogether amicable. According to the court record of rather a disgraceful scene at a farewell party in the local tavern, Ethan Allen "did strip himself even to his naked body (i.e., torso) and with force and arms, in a tumultuous and offensive manner, did assail and actually strike the person of George Caldwell of Salisbury, aforesaid, in the presence and to the disturbance of His Majesty's good subjects." Although this outrage cost him 30 shillings, Mr. Allen did yet further affront and damage to this, His Majesty's good subject, by abusing and attacking him once again on his way out of town, an indiscretion which delayed his actual departure until he had been once again charged and fined by the justice of the peace.

Under Caldwell management the Lakeville Furnace produced gratifying quantities of iron but worrisome financial losses. The Caldwells fell into debt to a Mr. Richard Smith, a wealthy Boston merchant, who repeatedly advanced them money and provided also merchandise on credit for a Caldwell-operated general store which competed with that of Heman Allen. In 1768 Mr. Smith foreclosed upon his debtors, took possession of the furnace, and operated it for the next few years in conjunction with his other interests. Hearing more and more disquieting talk, however, of impending war with England, Mr. Smith, an unreconstructable royalist, suddenly found urgent business overseas. Without delaying to make any formal disposition of his Salisbury property, he sailed for London in late 1775 and from London traveled onward to St. Petersburg and various other continental destinations, returning to America only in 1783. Upon his subsequent appearance in Hartford, he explained to Governor Trumbull that he had been unavoidably detained abroad but that his sympathies had lain all along with the revolutionary patriots. As evidence of good faith he refrained from pressing claims for compensation for the use of his properties during his absence, including the Lakeville Furnace. He volunteered, furthermore, to contribute $1,000 to the almost empty state treasury, a gesture which gave rise to malicious rumor that he had bribed the good governor. Mr. Smith's associates and acquaintances in Salisbury were not altogether convinced of his unswerving loyalty and integrity. They did remember, however, that he had once performed the public benefaction of raising £45 by subscription of 34 residents, himself being the most generous contributor, for purchase of 200 books which he had fetched personally from London as the core collection of a town library—the first in New England and the object of great pride. In any event he soon sold the furnace to Salisbury residents—Mr. William Whiting, who had leased and operated it for several years, and Whiting's father-in-law, Brigadier-General Elisha Sheldon, whose wartime record, like his pre- or post-war reputation, was not unsullied. (See below)

During Mr. Smith's prolonged absence the Lakeville Furnace operated full tilt turning out desperately needed ordnance for the continental army and navy. It did so under the aegis of Governor Trumbull, who had already made plans for just such a contingency. In 1775 he designated Ethan Allen's good friend, Dr. Joshua Parsons, to assume control and promised all possible assistance. What was most urgently required—and provided—was money for improvement of facilities of production and transportation. This meant a new foundry and a boring mill for making cannon and expedition of the movement of ox carts over mountain trails to deliver ordnance to shipment points on the Hudson or the Connecticut River. Elisha Forbes came out of retirement to serve again as ironmaster.

Technicians and laborers were introduced to cast, bore, and test the 3, 4, 6, 9, 12, and 18-pound cannon (the weight refers to the ball) which the governor wanted with all possible speed and in all possible numbers. During the last 7 months of the year 1776, when the cannon were first brought into production, the Lakeville Furnace shipped 116 tons of 9 to 18-pound cannon valued at £8,179-10-0, 40 tons of smaller cannon ("swivel guns" for the navy) valued at £3,205-1-5, 38 tons of shot and balls valued at £1,257-5-4, plus other items to a grand total of £14,542-17-10. Lakeville inns and boarding houses were packed with outside laborers who had to be gratified with special rations of meat, rum, and clothing. Forty armed guards patrolled the furnace site and maintained a round-the-clock vigil of the town in order to preclude any possibility of surprise attack by the English, who went to enormous effort to destroy small ironworks elsewhere.

Salisbury rose to the national emergency not only by producing ordnance but also by recruiting soldiers. It imposed special taxes in order to purchase uniforms, rations, and weapons, to pay bounties to recruits, and to support their families. The first overt act of defiance of the English occurred on August 22, 1774, when the voters assembled in a specially called Town Meeting in order to adopt a "Declaration of Rights" (the same basic document as approved in other towns) and to denounce the "gross outrages" which the crown was then perpetrating in Boston and elsewhere by imposition of the Stamp Act and other exploitative and repressive measures. In early 1775, when fighting broke out in Lexington, Salisbury's esteemed physician and patriot, Dr. Joshua Porter, conceived the plan of recruiting Ethan Allen, well if not always favorably known for his expertise in provocation, to recruit and lead a small band of raiders, among them Salisbury townsmen, to surprise and seize Fort Ticonderoga, as they did. It was their top secret assignment, having taken the fort, to ship the best of its ordnance, which Ethan Allen ably selected (120 large and 50 small cannon), to equip the Boston rebels with weapons more formidable than muskets for early use against the startled English enemy. Upon learning of the Declaration of Independence, which the town pastor solemnly read out from the pulpit, 234 men of Salisbury (out of a total population of 1936 whites and 44 colored) at once took the oath of allegiance to the new State of Connecticut. In the course of the next few years, a recorded total of 141 men volunteered for military service, being subjected, to be sure, to the pressure of public opinion and the inducement of town and state bounties which started at about £50 but had to be raised year by year to persuade new volunteers or re-volunteers. Thirty-three of these men were of sufficient status and education that they gained commissions as officers. Salisbury soldiers saw action in all the important campaigns of the war; twenty-six died of wounds or of disease. Others remained in Salisbury to man the ironworks, an essential service less illustrious than soldiering but much more comfortable and rewarding.

The most famous of the Salisbury soldiers was the above-mentioned Elisha Sheldon, the town's wealthiest landowner (heir to the properties of his wife's father, Samuel Bellows), who raised cavalry recruits in Salisbury and neighboring towns and was named commander of the Second Light Dragoons, commonly known as Sheldon's Horse. Sheldon's reputation at home could have done with some enhancement by battle heroics. Shortly before the war he had been suspended from church membership for having brought unsubstantiated charges of breaches of the Sabbath against a fellow parishioner who had accused him, with better reason, of "lascivious carriage." The pastor was lenient enough to reduce the charge to one of "imprudence and imperfection," to which, to his dismay, Sheldon refused to confess.

Colonel Sheldon's Horse amounted at most to a total of about 200 men, no more than half of them habitually mounted, for horses were hard to find and expensive to purchase (£100 per head) and cavalrymen, mounted or unmounted, were even more prone than were ordinary foot soldiers to vanish with all their accoutrements. The colonel himself was eager for battle, but he several times incurred Washington's extreme displeasure by failing to appear at an appointed time and place. He and his men were assigned primarily to escort and reconnaissance duties in the course of which, it seems, Sheldon and some of his officers devoted priority attention to the requisition of fine food and quarters for themselves. There was much bickering among the men, and 14 of the 18 officers drew up formal charges that Sheldon was personally to blame that "a once respected regiment was now transformed into a banditti of refugees from the justice of the country and halter." Sheldon, they said, was "indolent, ignorant, capricious, and disinterested in the welfare of his men," and he had been guilty of diverting both booty and official funds to his own purposes. Although he was formally cleared in court martial hearings, Sheldon's reputation, unfortunately, was rather more tarnished than it had been in peacetime. And upon his return from the war he made a quite imprudent and imperfect attempt to resume his former manner of living as a gentleman farmer relying upon hired hands. Life was then extremely hard for the ordinary man, many of the returning soldiers finding their lands and homes badly run down and encumbered with debts, and Sheldon's ways with reluctant and resentful low paid laborers led to rancorous accusations of exploitation. The colonel put some of his capital into industry by helping his son-in-law, John Whiting, to purchase the Lakeville Furnace. The family partnership did not prosper, neither Whiting nor Sheldon being skilled in management or indisposed to blame the other for misadventures. Their creditors took action and they were threatened with being jailed. Sheldon sold off his remaining Salisbury properties, including cattle and slaves, paid off enough of his debts to make unimpeded exit from town, and migrated to Vermont.

Other Salisbury veterans were making the same decision for other reasons. This migration to Vermont served significantly to reduce social, economic, and political pressures below the level of those in nearby Sheffield, North Barrington, and Stockbridge. In those towns numerous disaffected veterans were recruited for a sorry movement of protest which climaxed in Shays' Rebellion. Sheffield veterans who migrated to Vermont were welcomed by their former fellow townsman, Ethan Allen, who, together with his brothers Ira and Levi, had land for sale on terms which certain purchasers later called fraudulent, also by Thomas Chittendon, member of a leading Salisbury family, who migrated to Vermont in 1744, associated himself to their mutual profit with the Allens, and later became the first state governor.

During the pioneer period of immediate pre- and post-revolutionary industrialization the Salisbury social scene was advancing from beyond the pioneer stage. Salisbury, Lakeville, and Lime Rock villages became so affluent and attractive that visitors from Hartford, Boston, New York, and Philadelphia, many of whom came on business relating to the Salisbury Furnace, found almost all the amenities to which they were accustomed at home. The arbiter of manners and morals and hence of social affairs was the town pastor, the Reverend Jonathan Lee, who held office from 1744 to 1788 and became well known as one of the most popular and certainly one of the most affluent ministers in all New England. Born in 1718 in Lebanon, educated at Yale (1739-1942), trained in the ministry by the Lebanon pastor, the young Jonathan Lee was invited by the town authorities in 1743 to preach for a few months on probation. Although they had been dissatisfied with two earlier candidates, the selectmen felt no hesitation about offering Rev. Lee a formal invitation to preside over the town parish. A deliberate, prudent, indeed a carefully calculating type, the new pastor took seven months to make up his mind. He made quite certain through conversation and correspondence that there was a clear understanding: his salary would be £160 per annum with modest periodic increments; he would be supplied with a home and an adequate supply of firewood; he would assume the one twenty-fifth part of the town land which had been reserved for the first pastor, and if for any reason he resigned or was dismissed, he would retain a certain proportion of such holdings; he would officiate in accordance with the Saybrook Platform (church autonomy only mildly limited by deference to a regional council of ministers) and the Half Way Covenant (not necessarily testimony to the experience of salvation but possibly the mere promise as best one could to lead the godly life as the criterion for admission to church membership and thus to full residential and voting status in the community).

Having clarified these key conditions, 26-year-old Rev. Lee, riding horseback, with his bride, 28-year-old Elizabeth Metcalf, riding pillion and their personal belongings packed in saddle bags, made the two-day trip from Lebanon to Salisbury. The pastoral pair took up temporary residence in a small room at the back of David Allen's blacksmith shop in Lakeville. A month or two later they moved into a log cabin built for them by the parishioners on the edge of Salisbury village. Their new home was designed also to be used for Sunday services and it had two towers from which watchmen might survey the countryside in order to alert the townspeople to impending Indian raids which, in fact, never threatened. Within a year Rev. Lee and his wife had moved into a much more adequate home which they built for themselves nearby. It was a structure sufficiently spacious that they could accommodate the rapidly growing church congregation until in 1752, after several years of delay in construction while the congregation debated dimensions, location, and design, a new 40 by 30-foot two-story frame Meeting House was ready for use.

Rev. Lee was ordained on November 23, 1744, in a solemn ceremony presided over by three visiting ministers and eleven local "saints," that is, original church members of unimpeachable credentials with regard to the personal experience of salvation. The ordination was followed by a social hour which must have been well attended and much appreciated, for the parishioners supplied cakes and rum-fortified punch in quantities far more than adequate for the meager number of ministers and saints. Pastor Lee proceeded to organize and administer his parish with a firm but not too heavy a hand. He preached the standard one to two-hour long sermons each Sunday morning and afternoon. But he condoned singing, which was not yet routine, the preference of most pastors being for the "lining" out of the psalms by a reader with members of the congregation repeating the lines in anything but unison or harmony. He maintained rather erratic records of births, marriages, funerals and other events, often forgetting names and dates when he made tardy entry in the big leather bound church book which still survives. But he was vigilant with regard to absence from services, breaches of the Sabbath, profanity even on week days, drunkenness, gambling, or yet more serious breaches of mores and morals. He preferred penitence to punishment but repeated absence from his sermons, or flagrant inattention to them was likely to cost the offender ten shillings to a pound. The too sportive Seth Dean, Jr., for instance, had to pay five shillings "for assembling with others and swimming in the lake on the 11th day of June, it being Sabbath." Rev. Lee served as pastor for the marathon period of four and a half decades and performed service as army chaplain during the French and Indian wars. He always retained the esteem of his congregation and never experienced the rancorous disputes which afflicted the congregations of nearby towns.

Being as the original pastor also an original proprietor with rights to well over 1,000 acres of land, being also a man of almost as great discernment in matters financial as in affairs of the spirit, Pastor Lee figured in an extraordinarily large number of real estate deals, in none of which, it would seem, did he experience any loss. In one of the first distributions of property he acquired the title to an especially well sited stretch of land, part of the hilltop tract above Lake Wononscopomuc where Hotchkiss School was later to be built; on various of his holdings he laid out smaller plots for sale to newcomers and seems to have built houses to rent or to sell. At one point, having disposed of most of his original property to good advantage, he paid the handsome sum of £2,100 for another 545 acre estate which he proceeded to subdivide. He was easily able to finance his sons to education at Yale, and in his will he left them valuable houses and farms. One son, Chauncey, succeeded him briefly in the Salisbury pulpit, but the new fit between pastor and parish proved to be mutually distasteful, and the young Rev. Lee pursued his career elsewhere. Son Elisha became a prosperous lawyer in Sheffield; son Jonathan, Jr., became a physician in Pittsfield; sons Samuel and Milo remained in Salisbury and practiced a gentlemanly sort of farming. No descendants with the surname Lee are to be found in the town today.

The era of Thomas Lamb, Ethan Allan, and Jonathan Lee was succeeded by that of the Holley dynasty of iron magnates, a succession of Congregational (and after 18 also of Episcopalian) ministers, some of them men of stature, and an ever widening circle of town elite, of whom most were intimately associated in one way or another with the Holleys. The first of the so-called royal Holleys was Luther, grandson of one of the original proprietors of Sharon, descendant of the delebrated English astronomer, Edmung Halley. Mr. Luther Holley moved to Salisbury in the year 1774 and opened a general store which prospered so phenomenally that within the next several decades, in association with several partners, he bought out the Lakeville Furnace and built a new one on   Mt. Riga (where a forge had been established in 1781). In fact he acquired a controlling interest in the entire Salisbury iron industry which was later reorganized under the name Salisbury Iron Company (1828). His son John Milton Holley (1777-1841) continued and expanded his father's enterprises. John Milton's son, Alexander Hamilton Holley (1804-1887) launched himself into social and political activities which won him the lieutenant governorship of the State of Connecticut in 1854 and the governorship in 1857. His detractors held that he won the first nomination merely by having the fortitude to turn out in the middle of a blizzard for a party convention which chillier candidates chose to forgo, and that while he played state politics certain very dangerous rivals infiltrated Salisbury commerce and industry.

Alexander Hamilton Holley moved the family out of the production of iron into the manufacture of fine cutlery. His son, Alexander Lyman Holley (1832-1882) won national and international repute — and the resentment, or more commonly the gratitude of the local citizenry — by presiding over the transition from the age of iron to the age of steel and shifting the industry definitively westward away from Salisbury to Pittsburgh and Chicago and thus into the clutches of Andrew Carnegie. Alexander Lyman, a graduate of Brown, not Yale and not Williams (then the normal choices of a youth from Connecticut), achieved a brilliant early record as engineer (in railroading), inventor, and editor (of iron industry journals). He made frequent trips to Europe and on one of them   (1862), learning of   Sir Henry Bessemer's revolutionary new steel making process, he acquired the American rights to its application. He negotiated the rights also to a competitive American process, devised his own improvements, and proceeded to design, construct, and supervise new plants of unprecedented type and scale located not in Salisbury   but rather in Troy, Harrisburg, Pittsburgh, Gary, and Chicago. He mystified his family by neglecting, or, as the case may have been, sparing Salisbury, where the industry — by then, in any event, controlled mainly by the Holley family rivals — went into gradual decline and in 1916 became defunct.

The Holleys associated themselves with the Coffings, Captain John Coffing and his son George, who arrived in Salisbury at the time of the revolution and   involved themselves, as did virtually everyone else, in iron. The Holleys and the Coffings moved the main center of Salisbury iron working from Lakeville to Mt. Riga. There the rushing water at the outlet of South Pond could supply power for a much bigger operation, thus making it economical to haul ore, lime, and later also charcoal (when the Mt. Riga forests were denuded) all the way up rather a dreadful mountain road and iron and iron products all the way down again. The Mt. Riga furnace and forge specialized in massive 18-pound cannon, iron chains, and ships anchors which were ordered, for instance, for the *Constitution* and the *Constellation*. The Mt. Riga operation was terminated, however, in 1847, after an accident at the furnace which would have necessitated complete and expensive rebuilding at a time when supplies of charcoal had become difficult to obtain. The Lakeville furnace had already been closed down (1844). The Holleys, the Coffings, and their various partners had by then moved into other industry and commerce — general store keeping, for instance, in Lakeville and Salisbury villages, and the manufacture of cutlery at the Lakeville Furnace site. Mr. Alexander Hamilton Holley had imported skilled technicians from Sheffield, England, paying them the very attractive wage of $1.00 per day, and set them to producing a line of merchandise which almost immediately gained nationwide popularity, especially pocketknives far superior to anything which had previously appeared on the American market.

The Holleys were influential in promoting, planning, financing, and building the Housatonic valley railway, the second line of real importance to be built in the nation, which opened a stretch of track between Bridgeport and Stockbridge in 1844. Soon there was an extensive regional network with the Connecticut Western line passing through Lakeville and Salisbury villages. Railways created a larger market for iron not only for shipment to metropolitan markets but for the rails on which it was shipped, the car wheels, and the locomotives. It was not the Holleys, however, but the Holley competitors, whom the Holley family's various ventures into local enterprise had encouraged, who profited most from this bonanza. During the late Holley period several big new furnaces and foundries appeared in Salisbury — at Lime Rock, at Amesville, at Chapinsville (Taconic), but new entrepreneurs built or soon acquired control of them.

The later nineteenth century moguls of Salisbury iron were the Barnums and the Richardsons, especially Milo Barnum, his son William, and his son-in-law Leonard Richardson, who had extensive interests also in Pittsburgh and Chicago. These new entrepreneurs made Lime Rock the center of their operation. There, in about the year 1830, they took over a big furnace which had recently been built by the firm of Canfield and Robins, other competitors of the Holleys, and put up an extensive new complex of foundries, workshops, offices, and warehouses. They manufactured not only iron rails and car wheels but also, before, during, and after the Civil War, enormous quantities of ordnance for the continental armies. They built what amounted to a model company village for their employees and mansions for themselves. Like the Holleys, they too branched out into state and national politics. U.S. Senator William Barnum (d. 1889) contributing a new layer of luster to the Salisbury name by defeating Phineas T. Barnum (no relation) in his campaign for election and making Grover Cleveland his close friend. But whether gracefully or spitefully, Alexander Lyman Holley, as already noted, threw in with the Andrew Carnegie set; the Barnum and Richardson fortunes presently declined: and in 1916 the Lime Rock operation, already long since outdated and inappropriate to the requirements of the World War I period, closed down for good. Lime Rock soon deteriorated into a ghost town — destined, however, to be revived and restored in the 1950s as a gilded enclave of urban escapists.

The Civil War, like the War of Independence, brought further enrichment of the Salisbury elite but worked hardship upon many of the laboring, fighting classes. Just as some 141 Salisbury men answered the call of George Washington, so another 353 (the latter count is exact) responded, but this time less gladly and only upon being subjected to greater pressure and inducement to fill town quotas, to the summons of Abraham Lincoln. The Civil War was not a conflict in which Salisbury, where slavery had never been common and had long since been phased out, felt its own interests to be critically involved. The death of 53 Salisbury men on the battlefield or in the field hospitals, the return of many permanently   disabled, and the economic and social disruption of the immediate postwar years constituted even graver blows to town morale than did similar difficulties at the time of the revolution. World War I, in which Salisbury men saw active service and died, was to command much more popular support and to occasion less maladjustment, and so too World War II; but the Vietnam War, to bring the story precipitately up to date, was to recreate under vastly different circumstances a much intensified ambivalence.

Lime Rock, which flourished throughout the Civil War but became a ghost town during or shortly after World War I, provides a clue to the evolution of the whole of the twentieth century Salisbury Town, which has passed through comparable but not such extreme phases. When the Salisbury iron industry languished after a 150-year boom, the town found nothing to take its place. Other towns up river had industries which were good for at least a few more decades — marble, for instance, in Stockbridge, paper in Lee, textiles in Pittsfield. Towns well down river managed to maintain the old or to make transition into new industries, among them the tinsmiths of Berlin, the makers of pins, needles, and notions; the beaver and silk hats in Danbury, the specialists in hoop-skirts, corsets, straw hats and yet sturdier merchandise such as carriage springs and axles in Darby. Salisbury tried textiles but the experiment was not a success; for a few years it manufactured scythes (10,000 of them in 1830), bicycles, and various tools.

The town may have benefited rather than suffered, especially if one takes the long-range point of view as it is now being construed by the conservationists and the environmentalists. Ever since the early 1800s the Salisbury population has remained relatively stable at the 2,500 to 4,500 level and much the same in physical appearance. It had already begun to export excess population at the time of the revolution and in later decades the exodus increased, first to the new frontiers of New Hampshire and Vermont, later to the Middle West and the West, always, of course, to metropolitan Hartford, Boston, and New York. And then between World Wars I and II there began an influx which, for better or for worse, more than compensates for outflow. A new overlay population made up mainly of affluent outsiders — retirees, escapists, romantics, artists, cultists, or just ordinary people seeking security and tranquility where it can still be found, some of them backtracking from the cities to which their forebears migrated, now occupy many of the fine old homes, duly restored and embellished, or have built new ones. They engage in a social and cultural life or even in businesses or professions, sometimes in a manner self-consciously adjusted as much to old as to new New England, which gives little indication what the real and no doubt composite town of the future may be. Salisbury, in short, is a place in which to revive the pleasing memories of the past and to enjoy certain rather rarified if also agreeable aspects of the present. But among the more perceptive and sensitive the town may inspire misgivings that here both the past and the present have lessons to teach which have not yet been learned.

CHAPTER 3

Old Stockbridge: Indian Town and White Predators

The first decade of recorded Stockbridge history relates mainly to the towns (i.e., townships) of Sheffield and Great Barrington, originally known as Upper and Lower Housatonic. These were the first two towns to be laid out in Berkshire County, Massachusetts, and what is now Stockbridge was included within the upper town. The two new towns were opened in response to a petition signed by 176 residents of Hampshire County who applied to the General Court for new land upon which to resettle. On January 30, 1722, the court ruled that the surveyors should lay out two towns, each 6 miles square for allocation of homesteads to 120 carefully screened applicants. In order to cover the cost of the survey and of negotiations with the Indians, the court required each applicant to make   an advance deposit of 30 shillings for each 100 acres. The court then designated a committee of five, inclusive of John Stoddard and John Ashley (both to become very well known in town and regional affairs) to handle the arrangements with the authorities, the settlers, and the Indians.

Early in the spring the committee men traveled into the Housatonic valley to make contact with the Indians, who proved to be friendly. They invited 20 of the braves — virtually the total male adult population of a ten-mile stretch of the riverbank — to pay a visit to Westfield, where, on April 25, 1722, a contract was ceremoniously negotiated and signed. Konkapot, the sachem of Wnahktakook, or Great Meadow (now Stockbridge village) and Umpachenee, the sachem of Skatehook (on the present-day border between Sheffield and Great Barrington), and all their retinue signed away in perpetuity all rights to most of an imprecisely delineated tract of land. Approximately 4 miles wide on each side of the river, it stretched for a distance of about 12 to 15 miles north of the Massachusetts-Connecticut border. Within it the Indians reserved for themselves only the small enclaves immediately adjoining their settlements. In return for their land they gratefully accepted "460 Pounds, 3 Barrels of Sider, and 30 quarts of Rum." At the time of cession, the Indian population of the tract probably numbered no more than 10 to 20 families, the majority at Skatehook, which, half a century earlier, had been the site of the "Great Wigwam," reportedly a 60-foot long council chamber brightly painted and ornamented.

Settlement did not actually begin until between 1725 (Sheffield) and 1730 (Great Barrington) and was formally although not actually suspended between 1731 and 1733 while Massachusetts worked out a tentative agreement with New York concerning the priority and validity of obscure but conflicting claims. A score or so of Dutch settlers from Kinderhook, New York, who either preceded or immediately followed the English into the region, proved to be embarrassingly self-assertive. Most objectionable among them was Jehoiakim van Valkenburg, to whom Chief

Konkapot had granted some 20 acres of river valley land at Great Meadow and another 200 acres or more in the nearby hills. Van Valkenburg, who did a lucrative business trading rum for furs, played a curiously ambivalent role in the subsequent English-Indian exchanges. He served at times as interpreter, at other times as provocateur, plying the Indians with rum and both the Indians and the English with rumors. Van Valkenburg and other obstinately obstructive Dutchmen instituted action in New York courts against the English settlers, one of whom was arrested and jailed in Albany from whence he made his exit only by posting and forfeiting bail. They bribed or otherwise subverted surveyors; they incited the Indians with allegations that the English intended not only to deny them their rum but also their freedom; and they panicked timid white newcomers with gory details about Indian massacres. Eventually the English either confirmed the Dutch in their holdings or else bought them out, van Valkenburg being the last to accept a settlement and then only because a brief-lived temperance movement on the part of the Indians confronted him with the specter of penury.

The new Sheffield Town was incorporated in 1733 with a total of some 50 registered property owners, many of them Dutch. The most important of the settlers were the brothers John, Aaron, and Ezekiel Ashley, members of a family already prominent in Massachusetts, themselves very soon to take their place among the valley gentry known as "The River Gods." John Stoddard, associate of John Ashley in negotiating for the towns, acquired no property in Sheffield but made up for this oversight in other towns, and he too joined the riverine deities. As two distinct centers of settlement emerged, one called Sheffield and the other Great Barrington; the latter was designated as a separate parish (1740), then as a separate town (1761), having meantime been pruned in 1736 of some 9,200 acres (6 ½ square miles) which became the nucleus of the new town of Stockbridge, incorporated as such in 1739. Early Sheffield was an unremarkable little village, but early Great Barrington earned the reputation of being populated by rather an unruly lot of settlers who drank, cursed, and caroused in truly scandalous fashion. Rev. Samuel Hopkins, who assumed office as the first pastor at a time when the town had only 30 families and among them exactly five "saints" (i.e., full-fledged church members), had reason to despair of his charges, but perhaps they too of him. He departed the parish many years later amid exchange of allegations that the church failed to pay him his £100 per year salary and that even by the standards of the times his two-hour long sermons were much too dense and dreary.

The first two decades of Sheffield-Great Barrington town history were marked, as noted above, by acrimonious disputes with the Dutch, but the Indians at least gave the new settlers no trouble. The Housatonic Indians, soon to be known as the Stockbridge Indians, came to be regarded in fact as singularly tractable representatives of their race. Chief Konkapot in particular was said to be "strictly temperate, very just and upright in his dealings, a man of prudence and industry, and inclined to embrace the Christian religion." This report rejoiced certain Christian gentlemen who had argued, without much supporting evidence to date, that Indians could and should be converted, civilized, and saved. Early experiments on the part of a few missionaries working at army posts with rum, loot, and scalp-happy Indian hangers-on had led to the conclusion that the proper place to preach repentence and salvation was the remote Indian village.

The above mentioned Rev. Samuel Hopkins of Springfield lighted and brandished the missionary torch. He took counsel with Colonel John Stoddard, famous as a fighter both against and with the Indians and as an authority on the various tribes.When Stoddard gave the Housatonic Indians an exceptionally good character, Rev. Hopkins approached Rev. Stephen Williams, one of the "redeemed survivors" of the Deerfield massacre whose prolonged captivity in the forest had taught him to admire his captors. He also got in touch with William Williams of Hatfield, another of the very numerous and influential Williams clan. These three, in turn, appealed to the top clergy and officials (among them Governor Jonathan Belcher) who were the Boston Commissioners for the London-based Society for the Propagation of the Gospels in Foreign Parts. These gentlemen at once offered moral support and what was yet more useful, they raised funds. In May of 1734 Rev. Hopkins and Rev. Stephen Williams traveled to the Housatonic, ostensibly to congratulate Chief Konkapot and Chief Umpachenee upon the fact that in reward for unspecified services of the past or the future, the Governor had decided to designate them Captain and Lieutenant respectively in the colonial militia. The reverend gentlemen's real objective was to elicit a request for the assignment of a missionary. Konkapot was cordial, Umpachenee was cool, and the two together asked for time in which to confer with their tribespeople. The visitors then took temporary leave, and when Rev. Williams returned in July, he received assurances from both chiefs that the tribes would welcome a resident missionary.

The Boston Commissioners lost no time in recruiting their representative — Mr. John Sergeant of Newark, New Jersey, a gentle, studious, very popular tutor at Yale College. Mr. Sergeant had already made known to his friends that he felt the call of the forests, the Indians, and his maker and that he would cheerfuly forgo the pleasures and comforts of Yale for the rigors of service on the frontier. He tentatively accepted the offer of appointment at £100 per annum as missionary-pastor of a new Indian parish to be organized on the Housatonic. In October, prior to making a firm decision, he journeyed into the valley and preached a trial sermon to an audience of 20 Indians, among them Chief Konkapot and his family. He also made his first convert, an army-trained, English-speaking Indian named Poopoonah who was serving as his interpreter. Poopoonah, a befuddled and bedazzled youth whom Sergeant baptized as Ebenezer, made a well rehearsed public speech in which he declared with greater eloquence than comprehension, "I therefore freely and heartily forsake *heathenish* darkness and embrace the *light* of the Gospel and the way of holiness...." Mr. Sergeant was invited to remain in the region through the winter and found board and lodging with an English family in Great Barrington. The Indians built him a primitive church-school midway between Wnahktakook and Skatehook; there he preached every Sunday, and although he used the cynical van Valkenburg rather than the convert Ebenezer as his interpreter, the results were most gratifying. With the aid of an assistant also recruited and paid by the Boston Commissioners — Mr. Timothy Woodbridge, member of a prominent Massachusetts family — he also began to operate a school in which about a dozen Indian children turned up more or less regularly.

For both leaders and followers the pathway to education and salvation was beset with thorns. The leaders at times wearied, the followers wavered, and the wicked example of Dutch and English settlers was difficult to reconcile with promises of beatitude. John Sergeant succeeded nevertheless in winning the confidence of both Konkapot and Umpachenee, each of whom entrusted his eldest son (ages nine and eight respectively) to his custody and tutelage when he returned temporarily to Yale in December, leaving Mr. Woodbridge in charge of the mission.

Very soon after Sergeant's departure the rumor spread through the region that the Indians of the Hudson valley were so enraged with the Housatonic Indians for their compact with the white men that they were plotting to poison both Konkapot and Umpachenee and to disperse the tribe. Rev. Hopkins, Rev. Stephen Williams, and Mr. John Ashley hurried back to Housatonic to discredit the report and promise protection. Preaching before an audience of some 150 Indians—a figure which would indicate the probable presence of outsiders—Rev. Williams managed to dispel their fears and gain reconfirmation of their approval of the mission. It was an occasion which clearly called for celebration by feasting, drinking, and dancing. The next day two of the celebrants fell ill and died, and there were mutterings about the red man's or perhaps the white man's witchcraft. The visitors managed to convince the survivors that it was not the evil eye which had done the deceased in but their overindulgence in meat and spirits. In the spring Captain Konkapot, Lieutenant Umpachenee, and Ebenezer Poopoonah visited John Sergeant in New Haven, where they were properly paraded and feted. Mr. Sergeant returned with them briefly to the valley and there preached to a congregation which was tearfully happy to see and hear him, the most copious of the tears being shed by Chief Konkapot and by Chief Umpachenee's wife, both of whom seemed on the verge of conversion.

The time was at hand for Mr. Sergeant's formal ordination, and Governor Belcher, who maintained an active interest in the mission experiment, decided to make it a most memorable occasion. The Governor had already scheduled an important meeting in Deerfield with chiefs of the powerful Mohawk tribe and other members of the Six Nations. He decided that Mr. Sergeant's ordination would provide an appropriate climax to the ceremonies, one which would signify the new era of tranquility and brotherhood which, he hoped, was about to set in. The governor appeared in person for the ceremonies together with a retinue of high civil and military officials, all in resplendent costume. A hundred Indian chiefs turned out in feathers, beads, paint, and deerskin. Three leading clergymen, dressed in sober black and white, lent an air of solemnity. At the climax of the ceremonies, the members of a delegation of Stockbridge Indians, rather overwhelmed by all this grandeur, were asked to signify their consent to Mr. Sergeant's ministrations and did so by rising and gesticulating with great dignity.

In October Mr. Sergeant took up his duties as duly ordained pastor. His tenure began most theatrically with the conversion and baptism of Chief Konkapot and his wife, known thereafter as John and Mary, the marriage of Saint (full-fledged church member) Ebenezer Poopoonah to a pretty young convert, and most satisfying of all, since he had been hard to win, the conversion and baptism also of Chief Umpachenee (Aaron) and his wife (Hannah). In succeeding weeks the flock multiplied and Indians of other regions began to join the Housatonic tribe on the fringes of the church-school. First came Unnuquanut, a Susquehanna brave of evil repute as a vicious, drunken brute, whose life, after conversion, was so exemplary that this change could only be attributed to divine grace. Within a year there were 40 children in the school and 50 to 100 converts. The lure of the new life of virtue was so dazzling that the community solemnly foreswore the demon rum. It was a pledge which most of the Indians kept throughout the duration of at least one festival and later sought bravely if vainly to fortify by imposition of a £40 fine upon anyone who put temptation in their way.

Reports of the success of the Stockbridge mission delighted the sponsors in Boston and London and led to the implementation of phase two of the project. This was the scheme to gather together into one settlement the people from widely scattered wigwams on the Housatonic and elsewhere with special effort to entice the ofttimes belligerent Mohawks. In this new style village the Indians were to be educated and converted; they were to live in houses, to cultivate farms, to keep poultry and livestock, to plant orchards, to learn crafts such as weaving and carpentry. In short, they were to lead settled, regulated, soberly productive lives instead of merely roaming, hunting, gathering, fighting, and debauching themselves, as was their usual practice. To this end it was decided to set aside a new six-mile square town in which the Indians, under the guidance of Mr. Sergeant, with four families of white settlers as models, would engage in New England village style social, economic, political, and religious activities.Such civilized Indians, it was cogently argued, would prove reliably loyal to their patrons and protectors and would exercise an altogether salutary influence upon the still benighted heathen whose capability for trouble-making they would serve to offset. Colonel Stoddard masterminded the subsequent maneuvers. This entailed the passage of an act by the General Court (1735), persuasion of the Indians to relinquish their Skatehook enclave, arrangement for all to congregate at Great Meadows, later Stockbridge, and compensation in cash or kind for the white settlers who had already acquired rights within what was to be the new Indian town. It was agreed that one-sixtieth part of the town lands (approximately 480 acres) would be allotted to John Sergeant (whose salary was raised to £200 and later to £300), another sixtieth share to Timothy Woodbridge, and appropriate parts (it proved to be 150 acres each) to the four white families whom Colonel Stoddard was to select. The Indians were to hold their land in common with right to farm individual or joint plots as they so chose.

The new town was duly laid out to cover previously unsurveyed and unsettled land just north of the original Housatonics plus the northern third of what had earlier been allotted to Great Barrington. The original white settlers were resettled elsewhere, and in 1736 Captain Konkapot and Lieutenant Umpachenee led their tribe into the promised land. After taking possession of a greater Great Meadow, the Indian braves marched onward to Boston, there to pay homage to the governor, who graciously presented them with guns and blankets and promised them funds for building a Meeting House, i.e., a combined town hall, church, and school. In rather an excessive display of not unsuggested reciprocity, the Indians thereupon deeded to the whites a 2-mile wide strip of land reaching 25 miles along the as yet rather dimly marked trail leading from Stockbridge eastward, i.e., 52 square miles in return for 36 which were theirs to begin with. After no more than normal bureaucratic delay for delivery of funds, and with the Indians providing most of the materials and labor, the Governor's gift Meeting House went up on the new village green, and along what is now the Stockbridge Main Street the Indians began converting wigwams into frame houses. The church people of Boston sent them a big

South Seas conch shell upon which Jehoiacin Metoxin, a brave gifted with extraordinarily powerful lungs, blew the call to school, church, and meetings. Dr. Francis Ayscough, chaplain to the Prince of Wales, sent the new congregation a Bible — two folio volumes handsomely printed, gilded, engraved, and bound. At the first Town Meeting, held in 1739 immediately after the receipt of a charter of incorporation, the villagers elected Mr. Ephraim Williams, the first white settler, as Moderator, John Konkapot and Aaron Umpachenee as selectmen, and Josiah Jones, the second white settler (and Ephraim Williams' brother-in-law), as clerk-constable. The Stockbridge Indian Town was auspiciously launched, and for the first decade of its history (1739-1749) its prospects seemed reasonably bright.

Between 1739 and 1749 the Indian population grew from 120 to 218 (53 families); of these 182 had been baptized but only 42 had as yet been admitted to full church membership; 40 children were enrolled in school learning the 3 R's, the catechism, the English language, and the practice of singing, in the latter of which they greatly excelled. Twenty of the 53 families lived in English style houses, that is, log cabins or simple frame structures with furnishings which were probably meager even by early settler standards. The women were learning housewifery and men were learning systematic farming. It would be erroneous, however, to state that the general Indian outlook was as yet very profoundly changed.

Chief Konkapot, unhappily, soon died (1745). Chief Umpachenee, even more unhappily, lapsed into drunkenness and licentiousness. Chief Hendrik, a famous Mohawk warrior, presently joined the community, however and brought with him 70 families of Mohawks and Oneidas. King Ben and King Solomon succeeded Konkapot and Umpachenee in authority over the Housatonics, but their prestige could not compare with that of Chief Hendrik, who never made a permanent commitment to the community and eventually withdrew, along with most of his followers. Attendance at church fluctuated alarmingly, as did attendance at school, and John Sergeant was loath to become a stern disciplinarian even with regard to the consumption of rum, which he called the Indians' "beloved Destruction." Worst of all, the English settlers — not just 4 families, as originally agreed upon, but 6 by 1740 and 18 by 1750 — set almost exactly the example which John Sergeant and Timothy Woodbridge most deplored. John Sergeant, who married the very stylish and frivolous daughter of the leading settler, Ephraim Williams, averted his eyes from the spectacle of the whites, immersing himself in study of the Indian language, preparation of his weekly sermons (two for the Indians, two more for the whites), visitations to nearby tribes, and guidance of his charges in the ways of industry and rectitude. He left it to his assistant, Timothy Woodbridge, to assuage the increasingly numerous and rancorous Indian grievances. Then on July 17 , at the age of 39, after 20 days serious illness with "nervous fever and canker of the throat," John Sergeant died. The Indian town of Salisbury lost forever the sense of purpose which he had rather flickeringly inspired.

Ephraim Williams of Hatfield, Mass., John Stoddard's choice as the ideal white settler, was educated, affluent, bigoted, and pompous. He was a scion of the important Williams clan, which, along with the Stoddards and the Ashleys, fitted into the constellation of River Gods whom the ordinary settlers did not always by any means revere but seldom dared to cross. Being both avaricious and cunning, Ephraim Williams deliberately set about making Stockbridge a white man's town and himself its richest, most powerful resident. He built himself a pretentious two-story home on the ridge overlooking the Indian village. It was so stoutly constructed with massive oak beams and three-inch oak planks and so amply equipped and stocked as to seem more like a fort than a home and to become known as the Williams Castle. Later white settlers, naturally, emulated the Williams example, so from the outset there were two villages, not one. In the Indian village in the valley John Sergeant caused the Indians to build him a modest home adjacent to school and church, and in the English village on the hill, several years after his marriage and by going deeply into debt, he built an especially handsome mansion to his wife's discriminating specifications. Although John still spent most of his time working with or for the Indians and had 12 little Indian boys living in his new home for a year and a half as his pupils, it was clear that his vivacious wife Abigail regarded his Indian charges, young and old, as ungrateful, treacherous savages.

Ephraim Williams, Abigail's father, who was originally allotted 150 acres of land, eventually ran his holdings up to well over 3,000. He achieved his first big coup by persuading certain of the Massachusetts clergy to buy out the vexatious van Valkenburg and to present the Dutchman's 250 acres or more to the Indians. He then persuaded the Indians to reciprocate by presenting some 4,000 acres of as yet undistributed land in what is now the town of Lee for the use of the whites, thus expanding the Indians' earlier gift of land to the governor. In return for his skillful intermediation, Ephraim took title to the 900 prime acres surrounding Laurel Lake. Some of his later maneuvers were no less complicated and no more ethical. He staked Indians to clear and plant land which he then pre-empted as his own. And he lent money to Indians to purchase rum and other niceties of civilization in the general store which he established with government subsidy. Being predictably unable to repay even a modest loan, the Indians in effect mortgaged their land and waited for Ephraim, Senior, or presently his son, Elijah, to foreclose.

In the early years, as noted above, the Indians owned their land in common. They allocated and developed it on the basis of chance or of need, never actually utilizing more than a small fraction of the 25,000 acres which were available. More or less voluntarily they encumbered some of the land informally and formally with debts and permitted the whites to make use of it. The Williams clan and other whites soon pressured the General Court to regularize the much confused situation regarding ownership and proprietorship. In 1750 the court took the misguided action of commissioning a detailed survey to delineate plots actually occupied by the Indians, stipulating that a total of up to 100 acres each was then to be designated as individually owned, the registered owner, being forbidden, however, to transfer title to a white man. In 1765 the court took cognizance of the status quo by legalizing outright sale even post facto by Indians to whites in discharge of debts. Meanwhile Elijah Williams, who became head of the family upon the death both of Ephraim, Sr., (1754) and Ephraim, Jr., (1755), granted numerous petitions such as the following:

"Please to Let Me have Som money for which I desire that you take 50 Eacors of Land for Which I will Give Good deed I am allmost dad for Want of Provetion and I Prey Let Me have fore Pounds of Money Out of my Land My Brother Jacob has already said something to you about it and Let My Brother Jacob Aukenock have 4 Pounds out of my Land for Me. -- No more at Present & but Remain yr Humble Servent Abram Aukenock."

Elijah was perhaps overly generous in advancing a few pounds here and there to needy, thirsty Indians such as Abram Aukenock in full expectation, of course, of acquiring legal title to more and more Indian lands just as soon and as fast as legal procedures could be devised. In the case of one Robert Mungkouwat, for instance, having already in 1763 negotiated a 499 year lease upon a tract of 140 acres of land for payment of precisely one peppercorn per year, Elijah found it quite simple later on to satisfy the most exacting legal nicety merely by working out a quick, cheap quit claim to acquire a freehold title.

By procedures such as these Elijah Williams made himself the proprietor of Indian lands within the originally settled parts of Stockbridge Town and even more extensive holdings in the twilight zone just to the west, where no one yet knew whether Connecticut, New York, or Indian claims would prove to be more valid. In this area, where the new town of West Stockbridge was to be surveyed and incorporated in 1774, Elijah Williams became the founding father of a village called Queensboro (now West Stockbridge). There he built and occupied a fine home, brought an iron furnace and a gristmill into operation, engaged in trade in local produce which involved, for instance, export of iron and potash to Boston and overseas. He also established a general store, and dealt promiscuously in land for which incoming white settlers were willing to pay good prices. Either in competition or in association with Elijah, some 40 families of settlers populated West Stockbridge well before it received legal recognition in 1774. Elijah Williams' close colleague in this pioneering venture was a canny young lawyer by name Jaheel Woodbridge, son of Timothy Woodbridge, one time *bete noir* of old Ephraim Williams.

The Indians, being so rapidly squeezed off the lands which, to be sure, they had very indifferently developed, enjoyed a brief reprieve from tedium and despair by reason of the outbreak of the war of the revolution. Many of the Stockbridge braves quite bravely and loyally served as Washington's scouts, taking their families with them, as was their ancient custom, to live in lttle wigwam villages close to the zone of combat. But upon their return to Stockbridge at the end of the war they found themselves in what was clearly a white man's reserve, one in which they felt acutely uneasy and unwelcome.

The sad Stockbridge Indian saga related not just to land but also to church and school. In 1743, when he already perceived certain grave flaws in his Utopia, John Sergeant drew up a proposal for a yet more perfectionistic scheme for the uplift of what he described in altogether melancholy vein as "a Miserable and Degenerate Part of our Race," "a People *difficult* to reform from their own foolish, barbarous, and wicked Customs." He appealed to churchmen in Boston and London for funds to establish a boarding school in which the most promising boys and girls between the ages of 10 and 20 would live, study, and work under the strict supervision of two English masters. As "recreation" after their studies the girls would practice the domestic arts and the boys would plant crops and herd cattle on a 200-acre farm. Being largely detached from their still primitive community, these chosen young people would be inspired to become the leaders of a new movement of modernization grounded in frugality, diligence, industry, discipline, and other civilized and Calvinist virtues.

The plan attracted enthusiastic and generous support both at home and abroad. The Governor made a grant of £500 per annum in the hope of taming the ferocious

Mohawks, who, it was conjectured, might provide a major part of the school's clientele, and Mohawk Chief Hendrik was in fact induced to settle tentatively in the town along with some 90 of his tribespeople. The Prince of Wales subscribed 20 guineas, as did his brother, the Duke of Cumberland. Rev. Isaac Hollis, a Baptist minister of ample means and eccentric (some thought demented) practices, a nephew of Thomas Hollis, benefactor of Harvard, sent remittances from London of £25 per annum for each of 12—later 24—boys, rejecting, however, all intimations that girls too might benefit from his benefactions. Numerous other persons made contributions—or promises.

The school proved difficult to launch and yet more difficult to operate. Fresh outbreaks of hostilities between the English and the French served mainly to dampen but occasionally to excite the interest of potential patrons. Ephraim Williams and certain of the other white settlers suddenly contributed £115 and sought to take over control of the school. They aimed to make quite certain that the guiding purpose was to convert the Indians into military allies. Under pressure to get the school started in troubled times, John Sergeant consigned the first batch of 12 Hollis scholarship boys to a certain Captain Martin Kellogg in Newington, Conn., for interim instruction. A retired army officer highly recommended as an expert in Indian languages and psychology, Kellogg proved to be illiterate, drunken, dishonest, licentious, incolent, and conniving. Although he failed to provide the boys with instruction and exploited their labor on his farm, he ingratiated himself with the Williams clan and won their support for appointment as headmaster. When the school was ready for occup a sturdy   ell-built two-story structure very well equipped with furnishings, tools, and books—the Boston Commissioners named Martin Kellogg as first master, and Gideon Hawley, a timid but earnest little man, as second master, while theoretically retaining Timothy Woodbridge in overall charge of educational programs. The Williams candidate thus emerged as the man in control of John Sergeant's dream school, where the parents of the 50 resident Indian boys, mainly Mohawks and Omeigas, began at once to complain of neglect and disorder. Gideon Hawley, whom Timothy Woodbridge backed, was relegated to running an adjacent school in which the Stockbridge (i.e., Housatonic) Indians studied. Hawley's school mysteriously caught fire; Kellogg's school was boycotted by irate Mohawk parents, most of whom abandoned the village altogether.

In 1756, at a time when French and Indian attack upon Stockbridge seemed imminent, the boarding school pupils were evacuated to a distant town, but the project was revived several years later as a dual institution. One part was represented as a boys' "Charity School" under the control of the Williams clique and the direction of Timothy Dwight, stepson of John Sergeant's widow, Abigail, recently remarried to General Joseph Dwight. The other was to be a girls' boarding school under the direction of Abigail herself, who was to draw £100 per annum for no very specific services and to profit also from sale of land—John's land, which by then had considerable value—for the new school site. By that time Timothy Woodbridge was involved in open clash with the Williams clique over many, many abuses of the Indians and he had won the support of the celebrated Jonathan Edwards, John Sergeant's successor as pastor. The Boston Commissioners, who received and studied detailed catalogues of charges and countercharges drawn up by the Williams and the Edwards factions, quashed the Williams scheme. But they also in effect wrote finis to the John Srgeant fantasy of a New England village inhabited by educated, converted, Anglicized Indians.

The Jonathan Edwards pastorate in Stockbridge was brief (1751-17   ) and for the Indians unproductive. One of the most profound and most obscure of the grimly Calvinistic divines of the country, Edwards was already far past his prime. He was more mellow than in the days when he terrified his congregation with lurid previews of hell and damnation, being now more disposed to dwell upon divine grace rather than vengeance. But Edwards, who was indisposed to master a primitive language or to minister to unsophisticated people, was no pastor-teacher for an Indian church and school. He devoted himself to the white congregation and to the authorship of formidably learned tracts and treatises. He delegated responsibility for the Indians to Timothy Woodbridge and after the latter's death in 1774 to John Sergeant, Jr., who, unhappily, lacked his father's drive, vision, and personality.

When Edwards was originally mentioned for the Stockbridge pastorate the Williams clan vigorously opposed his appointment, alleging that he was already both senile and futile. They presently bethought themselves, however, that the well-known Edwards name would enhance the value of the Williams's Stockbridge real estate and therefore withdrew their objections. They had reason to regret their change of mind, for Edwards, once sufficiently aroused, was still a fighter, and Timothy Woodbridge convinced him that the Williams schemes were evil and must be blocked. So eventually, on behalf of the Indians, to whom he had previously paid very little attention, Jonathan Edwards boldly confronted the whole of the Williams clan — Elijah, who succeeded old Ephraim as the head, Abigail, who always played the role of the great lady, General Joseph Dwight, a distinguished soldier and polished gentleman, whom Abigail married 18 months after John Sergeant's death, and the very numerous relatives and associates who shared old Ephraim's views on Stockbridge as the white man's town.

Old Ephraim Williams became enraged and some thought crazed when the Boston Commissioners withheld their support from the schools. They favored Jonathan Edwards instead, mainly, it would seem, because Edwards pointed out that the Mohawk Indians were departing en mass and the Housatonic Indians, alleging betrayal, were demanding the return of all their original lands. Ephraim made a whirlwind round among the other white settlers, some of whom were on the Edwards-Woodbridge side of the dispute, seeking to buy up their property for spot cash. It was his intent, apparently, to make himself virtually the sole proprietor of the town and then to punish and expel his enemies. His attempt miscarried and very shortly thereafter he transferred his holdings to his sons, Ephraim, Jr. (who died very soon afterward), Elijah (a worthy successor), and Josiah (who was always frail and inactive). General Dwight and his wife, Abigail Williams Sergeant Dwight, very soon moved to Great Barrington, where Abigail caused her new husband to build her a new mansion even more splendid than the one John Sergeant left her, to which, however, she returned after the general's death (1765). It is some clue to the Williams' family fortune at the time that old Ephraim transferred to his sons his Stockbridge "castle" and 1,505 acres of land for token payment of £1,000, a sum which everybody regarded as a risible fraction of the true value.

Ephraim Williams, Jr. (1715-1755), eldest son of old Ephraim, made himself popular with many of the townspeople, even the Indians. He first appeared in Stockbridge in the year 1745 after a decade of study and travel in Europe. He was welcomed by the Stockbridgeans as a gentleman of learning and sophistication, and he made friends also of influential Bostonians. Being fat, jolly, and convivial, he put people at their ease, as other Williamses did not. When French and Indian troubles broke out, he was a natural choice for commission in the militia. He was given the rank of captain and placed in command of a chain of small forts which Colonel John Stoddard was constructing between the Connecticut and the Hudson Rivers with Fort Massachusetts (near present day Williamstown) as the key position. Captain Williams rode the circuit of the forts, and during an interval of relaxation of tensions he genially allowed numerous men of the bored and sickly garrisons to return to their homes on leave while he sought out personal diversion in Boston. Fort Massachusetts, being then manned by a mere dozen or so unalert and indeed scarcely ambulatory soldiers, proved to be an irresistible invitation to the French and the Indians, who overwhelmed the position and took the survivors to Canada as captives. By his promptness in building new defenses, where, in 1748 the garrison withstood a strong French and Indian attack, Captain Williams ingeniously contrived to convert debacle into accolade.

Captain Williams divided his time between Stockbridge and Boston during the next few years and was not again in the limelight until 1755, when new troubles broke out and Stockbridge seemed to Stockbridgeans at least to be especially threatened. Matters came to a crisis when two of the town's white men clashed with two Indians of the Schaghticooke tribe over the ownership of two horses. The white men shot one of the Indians dead, and all Indians near and far were outraged. The whites were brought to trial in Springfield, where one was acquitted and the other was punished only by imposition of a light fine for manslaughter. The Indians being then yet more outraged and the whites badly frightened about reprisals, the authorities tried to appease the Schaghticokes by a payment of a £20 indemnity, which, naturally, was deemed insulting.

One Sunday morning in late summer, just as Jonathan Edwards was getting well into his two-hour long sermon, a man burst into the church in great agitation to announce that he had just seen an Indian tomahawking a white child outside the Chamberlain home; upon entering the house he had found a second child dead in its cradle, a negro servant dead on the floor, and Mr. Chamberlain and his two other children (who should, of course, have been in church) huddled in fright under a bed. Stockbridge braced itself for attack and lived during the next few weeks under imaginary state of near siege. A detachment of militia moved in to take up quarters with Jonathan Edwards, whose home was converted into a fort. The soldiers performed no useful function, and as Jonathan Edwards presently reported, they cost him "800 meals of Victuals, Pasturing for 150 Horses, and 7 gal. of good West Indian Rum." Various Stockbridgeans took flight, among them General and Mrs. Dwight, who entrusted their three-year-old daughter, Pamela, to a negro servant London, who, being distraught, dropped the child in a raspberry patch and went his way. The child was soon discovered, fortunately, by an indentured Irish servant, Larry Lunch, who was fetching the family silver and added Pamela to his burden.

Captain Ephraim Williams boldly remained in the   town from whence many had fled. He was raised to rank of Colonel and put in command of a Berkshire Regiment which was ordered to serve with General William Johnson, a landed Irish gentleman of the Hudson valley, as a contingent of the huge new military force then being assembled by English General Braddock to put an end for all time to the French and Indian menace. Colonel Williams recruited numerous men in Stockbridge and nearby Berkshire towns and had assigned to himself as an aide the well-known Mohawk Chief Hendrik (brother of General Patterson's Indian mistress), a sometimes member of the Stockbridge Indian community, who brought with him some of his Indian scouts.

General Johnson's personal contribution to the campaign was nil save for his great influence with the Indians, who had made him an honorary chief and followed him gladly, but he was rewarded for his services by being knighted. General Braddock, as every reader of American history must know, bungled his way into catastrophic defeat. Colonel Williams, as may have escaped the attention of the less indefatigable scholars, marched his men into an ambush which his friend and companion, Chief Hendrik sensed just too late. The night before the encounter, to be sure, Hendrik had shrewdly observed of Williams' men, "If they are to be killed, too many; if they are to fight, too few." The force of 1,000 men was saved from massacre only by the opportune arrival of unexpected reinforcements. But Colonel Williams and Chief Hendrik were killed by the first enemy volley. By the colonel's will, as noted above, most of his fortune (in fact mainly the fortune of his father, who had died just the year before) went for the establishment of a Free School (now Williams College) in a new village of which, according to his stipulations, the name had to be Williamstown. Thus did a good part of the Stockbridge Indian patrimony pass from the Williams family to Williams College.

The outbreak of the war of the revolution was more divisive for Stockbridgeans than for any of the neighboring townspeople, for the Williams clique was royalist by instinct and the more recent settlers almost automatically anti-Tory, pro-Whig, and hence ardent patriots. Nevertheless, upon receipt of reports concerning troubles in Boston, the Stockbridgeans called a congress in the ballroom of the Red Lion Inn to which came representatives from a dozen nearby towns and villages. The congress drew up a manifesto, later referred to as the First Declaration of Independence, in which the signers proclaimed an embargo upon all business dealings with the British and their own determination to achieve self-sufficiency in necessities such as woolen cloth. The Stockbridge signers were aghast, however, when the common people seemed to prefer action to rhetoric. Fifteen hundred strong from villages near and far, they rallied in Great Barrington to demonstrate against the King's court of justice. The crowds abused the officials, including local dignitaries, stalled the court, and applied kangaroo court justice (tar and feather) to at least one "particularly obnoxious Tory." Amid anomalies like these Committes of Correspondence began to exchange exhortations to unity and Minute Men began to drill on the village green. The most conspicuous of the latter in Stockbridge were numerous Indian braves recruited by Jehoiakin Metoxin, the conch shell virtuoso.

Stockbridge Minute Men, including Indians, reported themselves in Lexington and Boston at the time of the early skirmishes with the English and were integrated into the two Berkshire regiments which constituted an important part of the early continental forces. Stockbridge whites saw service in all the major campaigns of the war, and Stockbridge Indians performed highly prized services in reconnaissance and guerrilla fighting. The Indians proved to be difficult to command or to discipline and vulnerable in pitched battle such as that at White Plains, where four were killed. Again and again the Stockbridge townspeople assessed heavy taxes for purchase of food, rations, weapons, and uniforms to send to their soldiers in the field. Few such supplies, however, reached the cold, hungry, thirsty Indians. Whites and Indians alike celebrated the end of the war, the Indians the more flamboyantly. By personal order of General Washington the Indians were treated to a barbecued ox and generous portions of rum. At the climax of the subsequent revels, they hanged Benedict Arnold in effigy, tomahawked the dangling dummy, burned the remains, and buried the hatchet.

The residue of 40 years of white man's influence deterred the Indians from taking up the hatchet again when peacetime life in the new white man's town proved to be intolerable. Indians still held token offices as selectmen and deacons but Indian self-esteem was irreparably shattered in the new tribal role as indigent, drunken, mendicant derelicts in a rapidly growing white man's community. Between 1783 and 1785 the great majority of the residual Indian population, a total of some 200 persons, migrated to the Oneida Reservation in New York, there to create a New Stockbridge village, where John Sergeant, Jr., presently joined them. Jehoiakin Metoxin took with him his precious South Seas conch, the deacons took with them their velum-bound Bible, and in New Stockbridge they reopened the school and the church. John Sergeant taught and preached. His daughter organized a Female Society for Promoting Good Morals, Industry, and Manufactures, which held weekly meetings and monthly concerts. New Stockbridge never had even the promise of the old Stockbridge experiment from which, at the very least, a few Indian boys did emerge, equipped with knowledge of English language and the Bible, to continue their studies at Dartmouth College and occasionally to startle some church or civic body with their eloquent espousal of some worthy cause. Most fell victim to rum and other evils as they moved forward, that is, backward, into the yet more distant reaches of what had once been their continent in their forlorn hegira toward their already forfeited racial identity and destiny.

Before, during, and after the revolution, while the Stockbridge Indians were experiencing humiliations, so too, although of a different order and with different results, was their familiar nemesis, Elijah Williams. Elijah, unlike his brother Ephraim, was never popular. He made a spectacle of himself by his overbearing conduct and by addiction to haberdashery of a type regarded as overly foppish even at the time and certainly at the place. One of his outfits, according to the tailor's bill, called for "scarlet cloth, shalloon, gold velum lace, fustian, two pairs of pockets and lining for breeches, velvet for the collar and two gold straps" at cost of £12/3/9. It may well have been this costume which he wore in his wooing of a Mistress Mary Wilson upon whom he bestowed an eighteen-carat golden bauble crafted by Paul Revere. Mistress Mary presently took Master Elijah to court to demand and get support for her illegitimate child, the court case almost coinciding with Elijah's marriage to a wealthy widow. The piously Calvinistic townspeople were given thereafter to mocking at the pompous Elijah, this treatment being, as they knew, much more excruciating than excommunication. And from the moment of the outbreak of the war of the revolution they branded him a Tory. By exercise of his potent political influence, Elijah obtained an official certification of his loyalty to the revolutionary cause but all the same he twice went to jail, not in Stockbridge but in Northhampton and again in Boston, where his business took him and enemies dogged him.

Timothy Edwards, son of Jonathan Edwards, who returned to Stockbridge in 1772 to open a general store which competed with Elijah Williams' store in West Stockbridge, also ran into trouble with the Whig Vigilantes. Timothy made the patriotic gesture of converting £1,000 worth of gold coins into continental paper currency and of selling goods on credit to soldiers' families. Yet certain unidentified ruffians waylaid him one night and gave him the violent treatment then being meted out to numerous Tories, some of whom were driven to take shelter for months at a time in caves in the mountains. Young Jaheel Woodbridge was also suspected of disloyalty but he seems to have been spared any drastic reprisals, possibly because he was known to be quite adroit at resorting to the law.

At the end of the war the friction between the Whiggish rabble and the Toryish gentry became yet more dangerously combustible. Too many of the returning heroes found themselves all but ruined, their houses and their farms badly deteriorated by reason of neglect, their families in want, themselves unable to earn a decent living either at farming or at day labor and badly harassed by wealthy creditors who readily advanced them money in expectation of foreclosing upon their properties. The direct consequence was Shays' Rebellion, which spread throughout much of Massachusetts and found especially numerous and desperate adherents in the mid-river valley. It was a semi-valiant, semi-farcical attempt on the part of the populist underdogs to overthrow not only the aristocratic "River Gods" but the whole still insecure apparatus of the new state government.

Daniel Shays, the personable, plausible, but demagogic and opportunistic leader of the rebellion, staged a series of mob confrontations of the courts in the endeavor to halt the legal processes of confiscation. In order to arm the masses he also tried to seize the Springfield Armory; when that attempt failed, he fled to Vermont, leaving his deputies in command of an already shattered movement. Ex-Captain Perez Hamlin of Lenox rallied the Berkshire remnants of Shays' forces and threatened to seize control of the entire region. West Stockbridge, where the closure of Elijah Williams' iron furnace deprived at least 100 men of paid employment, was one of Shays' strongholds. The Shays' rebels swaggered about the village wearing sprigs of green hemlock in their hats to provoke the law abiding citizenry, who wore white cockades as counterprovocation. The state militia, most of whose members were ex-soldiers recently discharged from the revolutionary army and paid off in virtually worthless continental currency, seemed either impotent or indifferent. But as incidents multiplied in West Stockbridge and other villages, Great Barrington's redoubtable Judge Theodore Sedgwick (lately an army general) marched into West Stockbridge at the head of 27 infantry men and 7 cavalry to seek a showdown. When the troops and the rebels were virtually eyeball to eyeball—and those on both sides knew one another well—Judge Sedgwick addressed certain of the rebels by name, demanding in his most stentorian courtroom voice that they lay down their arms, as some of them at once did while most of the others took to flight. But other encounters at Lee, for instance, demonstrated that the Shays could still cause real trouble.

During the bitterly cold nights of February 26-27, 1787, and the following day, a party of 100 Shays' men made their last stand, or, more precisely their last lurch, in the region of Stockbridge, Great Barrington, and Egremont. The caper began in Stockbridge when a party of raiders slipped into the village by sleigh, moving so stealthily that they surprised most of the townspeople in their beds. Masked men suddenly materialized in bedrooms, inviting the drowsy occupants to lead them to their cash and their treasure, also, since the callers were cold, hungry, and thirsty, to their larders and their caches of spirits. They sought, for instance, thus to honor Judge Theodore Sedgwick, who was not at home, but whose loyal and quick-witted black servant, Mum Bett, entertained them, to so speak. When the raiders proposed to inspect a chest which contained the Sedgwick family silver, Mum Bett threw them off balance by shouting, "You'd open a poor nigger's trunk, would you, you who consider yourselves so fine?" After a few more of Mum Bett's taunts and without much loot, the raiders adjourned to the nearby home of Deacon Ingersoll. While the deacon prayed, his wife opened bottles of brandy and thus buoyed the visitors on their way toward the premises of Jaheel Woodbridge and Timothy Edwards. In Timothy Edward's store they quickly located and tapped his casks of rum and whiskey. Most of the party presently rendezvoused at the Widow Bingham's (The Red Lion Tavern). After prudently concealing the   visiting sheriff in a closet, Mistress Bingham served her unexpected callers with complimentary cocktails. Having by then grown a bit unsteady on their feet, the raiders took again to their sleighs, and herding numerous "silk stocking" hostages in front of them, they headed southward. In Great Barrington they visited the jail, there to liberate all prisoners, and then adjourned to the adjacent tavern, where the hostess, the wife of the jailer, was invited to be hospitable. The proprietress cheerfully obliged, and while measuring out numerous libations to liberation, she serenaded her clients by singing them her favorite hymn, "Ye living men, come view the ground where you must shortly lie."

By this time it was morning and those of the raiders who were still coherent discovered that they had urgent business across the state line in New York. The militia, such as it was, had meanwhile been mobilized in Sheffield, where Colonel John Ashley succeeded in inspiring obedience and action by threatening to execute on the spot any man who did not volunteer. Some 80 sleigh-mounted militiamen proceeded under Colonel Ashley's command to execut a well-timed flanking maneuver which enabled them to take up battle formation across the Great Barrington-Egremont road to block the movement New Yorkwards of the raiders and their hostages. Upon sighting the militia, the raiders resorted to the simple tactics of taking shelter behind their hostages, one of whom, the Stockbridge schoolmaster, was killed in the first exchange of shots, his own rash decision suddenly to take to his heels having perhaps provoked the shooting which neither side wanted to start. In the brief engagement which followed, two of the militiamen and two of the raiders were killed and almost a hundred rebels were captured. Since the Shays' cause in fact elicited widespread public sympathy, and the danger of serious disorders was obviously past, most of the prisoners were almost at once released. Fourteen were placed on trial and sentenced to death, but 13 were soon pardoned, and sentence of the fourteenth was commuted to 7 years at hard labor. Certain prisoners taken elsewhere were not so leniently treated. In Pittsfield two of Shays' men were publicly hanged. Thousands of persons turned out in holiday mood to witness the spectacle. A fife and drum corps escorted the condemned men to the gallows. Dr. Stephen West of Stockbridge preached a moving sermon (later published), presumably reconciling the victims, who were so obviously on the preordained Calvinist roster of the irrevocably damned, to the fate which, after two hours of sermonizing, they may well have been ready to accept, if not exactly in the interest, as the pastor put it, of "the Glory of God."

Dr. Stephen West, who preached the memorable Pittsfield sermon on the beatitude of execution, was the successor to John Sergeant and Jonathan Edwards as Stockbridge pastor and a town figure of major importance in the post-Elijah Williams era. Dr. West was a saintly little man who seemed at times almost transfixed by religious fervor and at other times all but desiccated by theological erudition. While serving in Stockbridge he went through the profound emotional and spiritual experience of re-salvation when he became convinced that in seeking to make salvation relatively effortless for his charges he had in fact placed his own immortal soul in jeopardy. After tormented self-examination and self-criticism, he reverted from a liberal position which he had come to regard as heretical to the preaching of something like orthodox Calvinism. He tended to evade the harshest of the Calvinist doctrines and to dwell instead upon divine love and grace, thus offering sinners some slight hope of dodging predestination, but he went through intellectual agonies in reconciling such teachings with those of his colleagues. He devoted much time to the composition of erudite treatises which shaded Calvinist tenets a bit more than some of his colleagues condoned, and in the pulpit he delivered abstrust theological treatises which tended more to mesmerize than to enlighten his congregation. But he excelled in reading the Scriptures aloud and commenting extemporaneously upon them, being able, given the time available (two hours each Sunday morning and again each Sunday afternoon) to work his way through much of the Bible in the course of each year. His growing reputation for both profundity and eloquence attracted young students of divinity, some 10 to 20 of whom were generally enrolled in the "School for Prophets" which he conducted in his home. These earnest young men were encouraged not only to perfect their theology by day but also to participte in the evenings in a debating society in which the analysis of moral dilemmas was treated as a form of recreation. Every ten years Rev. West scheduled a series of religious revivals which attracted great crowds of enthusiastic churchmen and penitent sinners and made Stockbridge the center of a little Great Awakening of the sort induced by the great evangelists of the past.

Dr. West was methodical in his personal habits and courtly in his manner. His daily routine was inflexible; he timed his entrances and his exits, his meals and his devotions, his hours of reading, writing, and reflection to absolute exactitude. His clothing, which consisted of identical sets of sober clerical garb, was always immaculate. He measured out and consumed each day precisely the same amount of bread, meat, tobacco, and wine. His daily ration of wine, however, may have been somewhat self indulgent. In his late seventies, when his conduct sometimes seemed a bit confused, the town was swept by allegations, made by a malicious new pastoral assistant, Rev. Seth Swift, that Dr. West and his equally saintly and aged wife, were confirmed alcoholics. No one quite dared openly to accuse Dr. West, but formal charges were lodged against his trembly little wife, who was humiliated by having formally to request forgiveness of the church committee of inquiry for ever having "given anyone" cause to suspect that "she made too free use of strong drink." The testimony of her character witnesses and her own deportment satisfied all but the most teetotalitarian zealots that she had never, or at least seldom, exceeded the limits of ordinary prudence in seeking stimulants in times of failing health.

The earlier case of the frolicksome but less easily intimated Widow Lavinia Dean occasioned even more protracted gossip and investigation. Schoolmaster John Fisk was a roomer-boarder in Lavinia's home, and the two decided, possibly none too soon, to marry. Dr. West's congregation arose in protest: Mr. Fiske, they said, was profane, immoral, and atheistic; Mistress Lavinia would be dooming her own immortal soul and those of her two innocent young children if she were to marry him. Lavinia persisted in her folly, married Mr. Fiske (Dr. West reluctantly performing the ceremony), and was promptly excommunicated. Mr. Fiske demanded an inquiry into the actual state of his beliefs and morals. A committee of churchmen, declining, perhaps out of a sense of delicacy, to state their evidence, pronounced him "openly immoral and profane." Several eminent divines, one of them Dr. West, were inspired to publish religious tracts debating the issue of confirmation in state of grace as a condition of legal or happy matrimony. While Dr. West's prophets and men of more mortal stature were still bemused by such ecclesiastical disputation, Jonn and Lavinia migrated to Vermont, where, at least by Vermont standards, they seem to have led a life altogether blameless and unexciting.

By the time of Dr. West's death, the town of Stockbridge was already so much transformed and expanded that a new generation of Stockbridgeans had almost forgotten its origins and history. They were all aware, of course, of the Indian Mission, John Sergeant, Abigail Williams Sergeant Dwight, and the splendid Sergeant mansion, the so-called Mission House, still standing on the hilltop. But the curious impression had come to prevail. an impression which persists today, that an early English town of Salisbury had been the site of a mission station experiment which quickly flickered out by reason of the Indians' innate inability to adjust to civilization. People conveniently forgot that the original town was in fact an Indian town into which the white settlers were invited as exemplary models. There was as little in the English as in the Indian record of early decades to provide the stuff of which heroes of history are made. The gentle unworldly John Sergeant qualifies for hagiography, but the stylish Abigail Williams Sergeant Dwight presides still in spirit over the town's most important monument, the elegant Mission House, so totally unsuggestive of dedication to the uplift of the original Indian population.

CHAPTER 4

Litchfield: An Inland Connecticut Boston

In May of 1715 Mr. John Marsh of Hartford undertook a five-day horseback journey through what is now Litchfield Town in order to determine its suitability for settlement. The Hartford Town Clerk paid him the sum of £2, half as honorarium, half for expenses, and received in return what seems to have been a glowing report about the beauty and fertility of the region and the paucity and amiability of its Pootatuck Indians. Several subsequent encounters occurred between representatives of the whites and the redskins, and on March 2, 1716, 11 Indians (among them 2, named Corkscrew and Suckqunnockqueen) sold to 6 Hartford men (among them John Marsh) for total consideration of £15 cash in hand the vaguely defined area then known by its Indian name as Bantam. The purchasers conveyed the Indian deed to Hartford Town, which, in turn, in 1718 offered for sale at public auction 57 shares of a 7-mile square segment of Bantam land, reserving an additional 3 shares for the first pastor, the church, and the school. Would-be settlers (among them Mr. Marsh) bid a total of 250.14.0 for approximately 42,560 acres of land, i.e., a penny and a half per acre. Deeds of conveyance were issued on April 27, 1719, and settlement began early in 1720, the first lot to be assigned to each shareholder being within what is now Litchfield village.

Within the next 4 to 5 years some 40 settlers built crude log cabins and cleared and planted small plots of land. Complaints were lodged almost at once about non-settling shareholders who intended, apparently, to avoid the labors and taxes of the pioneer but later to enjoy the profits of the land speculator. An even greater cause of disquiet and conjecture was the attitude of the Indians. This was a period of renewal of Indian troubles in regions not far distant (mainly in Massachusetts), and the Litchfield settlers rather easily convinced themselves that the local Indians, who meant them no harm, were bent upon looting and massacre. There did occur exactly two real or alleged Indian outrages. The first was the kidnapping in 1722 of Captain Jacob Griswould, who escaped his abductors with such ease and promptitude that he could scarcely even make a good anecdote of his experience. The second was the shooting and scalping in 1723 of Joseph Harris, who may have given provocation. Against this Indian menace, mainly imaginary, the Litchfield settlers tried to protect themselves by building palisades—one in the center of the village, four at outlying points. Each palisade had quarters for guards and refugees and a mound on which to station sentinels.

These five positions, as gradually converted into forts, called for a bigger garrison than the village could provide, so the General Assembly sent in militiamen as reinforcements. The settlers soon found, to their dismay, that they were neglecting their homes and their farms in order to build their defenses and maintain a constant state of alert; and what was more, they had hungry, quarrelsome militiamen billeted at their expense within the very palisade which their own families wished to occupy in case of trouble. They petitioned the General Assembly for redress and were allowed five shillings sixpence per week per militiaman's billet and board,plus eighteen pence to three shillings per day for militia duty which they themselves performed. Friendly Indians, incidentally, were engaged at 10 to 18 pence per day for scout and patrol duty; the scalps of unfriendly Indians fetched £ 1 in bounty. It may not have been easy to distinguish between the scalps of and unfriendly Indians, but some of the visiting if not also the local militiamen claimed such payment. On balance, it would seem, the Litchfield settlers enjoyed excitement, security, and not ungenerous subsidy while continuing to clear and plant more fields and to build finer homes. It was a better deal than that of the visiting militiamen, who claimed that they served no useful purpose and were neglecting urgent business at home.

Life in early Litchfield was not really very eventful by the standards of the times, nor was life in the Litchfield of subsequent centuries. The town was known from the very first mainly for its beauty and serenity. An essential element of its lasting charm was that very little actually happened to arrest the attention of any observer who demanded dramatic events. It is not that Litchfield lacked distinctive character or characters, just that for all its obvious importance as the county seat of northwest Connecticut, what most people knew or now know about it is its splendid colonial and federal architecture and the well advertised scenic "Lure of the Litchfield Hills." The true town character is perhaps easiest to describe by literary reference. Litchfield is a Jane Austen sort of village in which the minutiae of gracious living among highly civilized people must suffice as the basic stuff for the chronicler. Although nearby Sharon and Egremont would dispute the claim, Litchfield is the nearest extant approximation of a late eighteenth century New England village arrested at its physical and intellectual prime and still preserved and populated by people who prize former values. The town's great characters were such individuals as Oliver Wolcott, Sr. and Jr., Benjamin Tallmadge, Sally Pierce, Tapping Reeves, and Lyman Beecher, each an extremely powerful personality but today, for the outsider, perhaps only the name Beecher stirs even faint recognition.

It seems permissible then to leave to the town's numerous avocational historians the systematic account of the manner in which the early settlers and their successors developed just the same sort of agricultural, commercial, and industrial enterprises which were to be found also in nearby towns; how the established church (Congregational) and its pastors dominated village life and only gradually relaxed the enforcement of Calvinist regulations; how the townspeople participated in the

First Congregational Church, Litchfield

Tapping Reeve House & Law School

French and Indian Wars, the War of the Revolution, and the Civil War; how within the past century the town has found a new role in providing a pleasant retreat for summer visitors and a point of refuge, ofttimes in retirement, for persons who crave exactly what it has to offer. What Litchfield offers is calm and culture and the dignity of not being trampled in the mass migrations of bewildered moderns toward new modes of maladjustment. It would therefore suffice to establish one important dimension, perhaps the key dimension of town history, to introduce a few of the inhabitants and institutions of the Litchfield past.

Litchfield's big men of the revolutionary and early national period were Oliver Wolcott, Sr. (1726-1797) and Oliver Wolcott, Jr. (1760-1833), members of a family which had been prominent in New England ever since the arrival in 1630 of Henry Wolcott, their ancestor. Oliver Wolcott, Sr., settled in Litchfield in about the year 1751 as owner of a property confiscated from an original proprietor who had failed to fulfill his obligation to develop it. By profession a physician, with experience as an army surgeon during the French and Indian Wars, Oliver Sr. engaged very actively in Litchfield public affairs. He served successively as High Sheriff, Judge of Probate, Judge of Common Pleas, and became recognized as one of the town's leading citizens. He was a sponsor and in all probability one of the main drafters of two important historical documents. The first was the Litchfield Declaration of February 24, 1766, rejecting the Stamp Act and all other such oppressive measures of the English King as "utterly irreconcilable with every just Idea of Freedom." The second was the Litchfield "Declaration of Independence" of August 17, 1774 (shortly after the Boston Tea Party), denouncing the "heretofore unknown and un- heard of Exertions of Parliamentary Power...in such a manner as cannot fail of striking every unprejudiced mind with Horror and Amazement, as being subversive of all those inherent, essential, and constitutional Rights, Liberties, and Privileges which the good people of this Colony have ever held sacred and even dearer than Life itself." The Litchfieldians promised "their unhappy distressed brethren of... Boston all reasonable Aid and Support," maintaining "their inflexible attachment to those inestimable Privileges which We and every honest American glory in es- teeming our inalienable Birthright and Inheritance."

Oliver Wolcott, Sr., naturally, was named Litchfield representative in the Conti- nental Congress, and in due course he signed the Declaration of Independence. By spending about half of his time in Philadelphia and half in Litchfield, he per- formed miscellaneous services for the new nation. Commissioned a brigadier- general in the Continental Army, he saw some service in the field, leading three to four hundred Litchfield volunteers, for instance, in the campaign against General

Burgoyne and being charged with overall responsibility for the defense of the Connecticut coast. But for the most part he devoted himself to examination and certification of candidates for appointment as surgeons in the army medical corps and to coordination of the Litchfield war effort with the national authorities. He served as moderator, for instance, at various town meetings which determined policy on raising volunteers and voted taxes for payment of bounties and procurement of uniforms and equipment. He also supervised the Litchfield supply depot, a major point of collection and distribution of foodstuffs and munitions. On at least one occasion he played breakfast or dinner host to George Washington in his Litchfield home and he routinely received other visiting dignitaries such as General Lafayette and Count Rochambeau. He was frequently assigned as special commissioner for Indian affairs,and after the revolutionary war he served successively as Lieutenant Governor and Governor of the State of Connecticut.

Oliver Wolcott, Sr., is best remembered for his role in a Litchfield historical episode which makes a very popular act in commemorative pageants. He was present and assumed custody of the remains when a mob of patriots in New York City pulled down a gilded lead statue of King George III. He caused this presumed work of art (minus the head, which loyalists rescued) to be transported by ox cart to the apple orchard behind his house in Litchfield. There he vigorously wielded an axe to dismember the carcass and engaged his children in what one of them described as the "frolic" of melting down the metal and casting it into bullets. With the aid of three ladies of the neighborhood, daughters Laura (age 15) and Mariann (age 11) and son Frederick (age 9) manufactured a total of 42,088 rounds (Laura 8,378, Mariann 10,790, Frederick 936) which the General duly turned over to the almost empty military supply depot, "melted majesty," people said, to be poured right back into the king's men.

Oliver Wolcott, Jr., surpassed even his father in distinctions. During the first several years of the revolutionary war he was still a student at Yale or at Tapping Reeve's law school in Litchfield; but he several times interrupted his studies to go on wartime missions with other volunteers, as, for instance, when Litchfield men marched to Danbury to harass the British troops then beating strategic withdrawal to their ships after burning most of the town. For the most part he served later as aide to his father, turning down a commission as ensign at his father's behest, and taking over responsibilities, for instance, for the Litchfield supply depot. In the bitter winter of 1780, when Washington's army was in great distress near Morristown, Oliver, Jr., responded to emergency appeal for provisions by organizing a train of ox-carts to deliver 200 barrels of flour, 100 barrels of beef, and 100 barrels of pork to the hungry soldiers. "If the Lord could make windows in heaven, might this thing be," wrote George Washington upon learning that the effort was being made. The Wolcott family responsibility extended also to general supervision of the Litchfield jail, in which were lodged not only numerous prisoners of war but also certain distinguished loyalists, among them William Franklin (son of Ben), one-time Governor of New Jersey, and David Matthews, one-time mayor of New York. It was not to the Wolcotts, however, but to the Seymours, actual custodians of the jail, that Mr. Matthews made grateful acknowledgment of what seems to have been most lenient treatment of rather a worrisome   charge. According to an early town historian, when Mr. Matthews "walked abroad one day for the benefit of the air, he neglected to return, very much to the satisfaction of all concerned in his detention," having first, however, entrusted his personal carriage to the permanent safekeeping of the jailer's wife. Mrs. Seymour rejoiced thereafter in the use of the first and finest such vehicle to be seen in eighteenth century Litchfield, quite ignoring the invidious remarks, prompted no doubt by sheer jealousy, of certain of her neighbors.

Oliver Wolcott, Jr., went on after the war to become the close friend and colleague of Alexander Hamilton, who regarded him a man of "rare merit," as did George Washington, who appointed him Secretary of the Treasury (1791) and considered him very seriously for the post as Secretary of State. But Wolcott became embroiled in the internecine intrigue of the capital city and very injudiciously collaborated with Hamilton in a virtually libelous attack upon John Quincy Adams, thus making himself a target of the extremely powerful anti-Hamiltonian faction. He was publicly accused of various "defalcations" and "peculations," even of having inspired efforts at arson within the Departments of War and of Treasury in the effort to destroy the evidence.   Although he was   formally cleared of any culpability and commended for his services, his career in the capitol was ruined. He went on to new careers in commerce and industry and later in state politics, serving repeated terms as Governor of the State of Connecticut and playing a key role in drafting the new state constitution. In commerce he very shrewdly associated himself with four prominent New York City partners, who provided the capital ($60,000) to set up a commission agency called Oliver Wolcott and Company to engage in the very lucrative China trade. The company went through various transformations, later becoming the Litchfield China Trading Company in which Benjamin Tallmadge and Josiah Deming were partners with the ship *Trident* making regular runs between New York City and Canton. The *Trident*'s cargoes of silks, teas, porcelains, lacquers, and other exotic products laid the basis of the new Wolcott, Tallmadge, and Deming family fortunes. Wolcott invested part of his profits, in partnership with his brother Frederick, in the establishment of woolen mills in nearby Torrington (then known as Wolcottville) which were among the largest and most profitable in all of New England.

Frederick Wolcott (1767-1837) was content with life in Litchfield, Torrington, and Hartford. He was active in community religious and educational affairs and served almost constantly in public office as Clerk of Courts, Judge of Probate, State Representative and other capacities. Brothers Frederick and Oliver, Jr., together were responsible for one special community benefaction for which posterity has always been grateful. Wolcott, Jr., began it, when in about the year

1780 he decided to do something about the bleak appearance of the all but treeless village. He then set out 13 sycamores, one for each state of the new union, but only one (that dedicated to Connecticut) survived for long (and still stands today). In about the year 1790 brothers Oliver and Frederick together started planting elms, a practice which other villagers emulated. The soon to be famous John Calhoun, then a law student in Litchfield, also planted a few elms and in 1825 the towns-people began systematically setting them out along the main streets. In 1835 the citizens subscribed $600 to grade, plant, fence, and otherwise beautify the town green. Other villagers followed the Litchfield example, and by the end of the century majestic trees shading much sanitized streets had become the pride of many a town. It was commonly assumed by later generations that the founding fathers themselves must have spared at least certain of the more ornamental trees, as was rarely the case.

A much more dazzling figure at the time than either of the Wolcotts was Benjamin Tallmadge, a singularly handsome and daring cavalry officer then in his twenties. Tallmadge and his men, who rode sleek dapple gray horses, wore gold braided uniforms, carried shining swords, and seemed bent upon combat, adventure, and romance, attracted admiring attention wherever they went. Major Tallmadge recruited four companies of dragoons in Litchfield to join the cavalry regiment known as "Sheldon's Horse," which was commanded by his friend, Colonel Elisha Sheldon, son of a prosperous Litchfield inn keeper but himself a gentleman farmer of Salisbury. Colonel Sheldon and the main body of his troops fell into disrepute by reason of the men's proclivity toward despoilation and desertion and their commanding officer's alleged incompetence, indolence, ignorance, dishonesty, and malfeasance, charges of which he was formally cleared in court martial although many of his colleagues remained unconvinced. Major Tallmadge emerged from the war with his reputation unsullied; in fact, being commonly deployed with his men on special missions of reconnaissance and intelligence in regions remote from the regimental headquarters, he achieved certain personal and company feats which much endeared him to George Washington.

It was Major Tallmadge, for instance, who discovered, starting with observation of his military bearing, that an innocent seeming British civilian by name John Anderson was in fact Major John Andre, British Adjutant-General, to whom the American traitor, Benedict Arnold, reported. Tallmadge was Andre's custodian throughout his detention and acquired such esteem and affection for him that, as he later wrote, "When I saw him swinging under the gibbet, it seemed for a time as if I could not support it." Tallmadge also distinguished himself by planning and exercising certain critical maneuvers. In September 1779, he led 120 of his men in a surprise attack upon the 500-man garrison of a British fort at Lloyd's Neck, Long Island. At loss of only one man, he destroyed most of the installations and took hundreds of prisoners. In autumn 1780, having discovered on a dangerous mission of reconnaissance the details of the British defenses at Smith's Manor, Long Island, he ferried 100 dismounted dragoons across the sound, and again with loss of only one man, he seized the fort, and destroyed an immense quantity of British stores. He captured one British lieutenant-colonel, one surgeon, and 50 ordinary soldiers, the latter of whom he loaded down with very valuable captured equipment and caused to be marched off to Fairfield. With ten picked men he himself deviated to Coram to destroy yet another fortified position and take still more prisoners and booty. For these and other signal services to the revolutionary cause, Tallmadge received the commendation of the Continental Congress and the public, thanks of General George Washington.

When the war was over Tallmadge returned to Litchfield, where he went into commerce and built up great wealth. He operated a general store, of which he established branches in other towns (perhaps the first chain store operation in the states). Later he became part owner of the *Trident*, a vessel which made several Litchfield fortunes (one of them the Wolcotts') in the China trade. Tallmadge lived in one of the village's most luxurious mansions; his wife was widely acclaimed as the most beautiful and charming of the Litchfield ladies; she bore him five sons and two daughters, all of whom did him credit. His was a success story in which even the most persistent researcher can detect no flaws.

Of all the great New England families, the Beechers—Litchfieldians only by adoption—were perhaps the most extravagantly gifted and provocative. The progenitor of the line was David Beecher, "the learned blacksmith" of New Haven, whose smithy and home were the sites of literary, philosophical, religious, and political soirees patronized by statesmen and professors. The nationally celebrated Beechers were David's son Lyman, and his very numerous offspring (seven sons and four daughters, by three wives). The then still multiplying family spent only 15 years in Litchfield (1810-1826), where Lyman was pastor of the First Congregational Church (salary $800 per year, plus a mountain of firewood, the parsonage, which he bought at price of $1,350, being his own responsibility). The years were seminal ones for both family and town, and the reciprocal impact virtually fused the Beecher-Litchfield names in subsequent memory.

Rev. Lyman Beecher had both the build and the mind of his blacksmith father, and although he suffered periodic attacks of depression and dyspepsia, he passed on to his offspring the physical and intellectual ruggedness which help account for the New England character. Lyman Beecher was also, naturally, like almost all Beechers and New Englanders, something of an eccentric. He had to be constantly reminded, for instance, where he was, where he had been, and where he was going, and by his own admission, "he spent half of his life hunting for his hat." He also searched periodically for his teeth, which, since they gave him discomfort, he often removed and secreted, sometimes in a coat pocket, not infrequently under the seat of a stagecoach. His coat pockets, upon inspection, also yielded fish; on one occasion, being summoned belatedly from a trout stream to evening prayers, the still live fish flopped out of his pocket to bemuse the congregation; on another occasion, putrified fish created a crisis in the family wardrobe.

Rev. Lyman Beecher discovered very early in his career that orthodox Calvinist dogma collided with reason and emotion. After endeavoring manfully to reconcile the doctrine of predestination with that of free will, he all but admitted failure. In his subsequent endeavors to humanize the arid Calvinist theology he came so dangerously close to heresy that he was in fact put on trial by his peers and only most reluctantly cleared. It was their father's influence which led all of his children openly to reject Calvinism; what he bequeathed to them in its place was the social conscience. For Lyman Beecher gained regional, national, and international fame not only by reason of his heresy trial but also for the sermons, widely distributed in print at home and abroad, in which he attacked dueling, drinking, and slavery. His "Six Sermons on Temperance," most celebrated of all his works, launched the W.C.T.U. on its mission of prohibition. He was convinced against his will of the evils of strong drink, for he had worked his way through Yale by dealing in spirits, and like most of his parishioners he fortified himself against the New England climate by reaching for whatever grog was handy. Once self-convinced, he sobered his thirsty Litchfield parishioners, temporarily at least, by the temperance sermons which he later made yet more agonizing on the lyceum circuit. He left it to his daughter Harriet really to sound the tocsin on slavery. But he offered shelter in his Litchfield home to his wife's sister, Mary Foote Hubbard, who had married a West Indian planter but deserted his bed and board upon discovery that he had a slave mistress and a family of mulatto children. Thus he exposed his innocent little daughter to shocking accounts of the degradation worked by the institution of slavery upon both servant and master and planted in her soul the seed of Uncle Tom's Cabin.

The year 1852, a quarter of a century after Rev. Lyman Beecher moved to Boston, was the Year of the Beechers and by reflection also the Year of Litchfield, which was electrified by each new Beecher event and claimed credit for having nurtured the Beecher genius. In 1852 Rev. Lyman Beecher published his *Views on Theology*, the summation of all his works, doing so just in time to catch the attention of a public about to tire of clerical discourses as recreational reading. Almost simultaneously, his son Rev. Edward Beecher published his *Conflict of the Ages*, an ecclesiastical manifesto which carried his father's implicit heresy over into open revolt against conventional dogmas. Edward's sensational work earned nationwide applause and condemnation, his father neatly combining both in his remark: "Edward, you've destroyed the Calvinistic barns, but I hope you don't delude yourself that the animals are going into your little theological hencoop."

Daughter Catherine that same year organized her American Woman's Educational Association which opened new vistas not only for women's education but for education in general; it also created even wider audiences for her madly popular magazine articles, pamphlets, and books on housewifery, cookery, women's and children's rights, mental and physical health, and similarly edifying topics. Son Henry Ward Beecher meanwhile made himself the nation's most famous preacher, packing the Plymouth Church in Brooklyn with audiences which worshipped almost as much this God-like mortal as they did his Maker, mesmerized by his passionate eloquence, overwhelmed by his magnificent presence. He was preparing them for the ultimate in churchmanly showmanship which was very soon to come, when, for instance, he introduced into the pulpit a lovely mulatto slave girl and bid his hearers buy her free. They did so with gold and jewels and banknotes almost equivalent to her weight and a comparably generous outpouring of tears and sobs, Hallelujahs and Amens. And Harriet Beecher Stowe, also in 1852, propelled Uncle Tom, Topsy, and Simon Legree surely and swiftly toward immortality and the nation toward military conflict.

From these and other Beechers there were many more startling events yet to come. Harriet alone was responsible for a dozen subsequent publications which created furors; not the least of these was her account, based upon personal confidences, of her friend Lady Byron's break with Lord Byron after his confession to her of having committed incest with his sister. It was reserved for Henry Ward Beecher to create the greatest sensation of all when he attracted prolonged worldwide publicity by what was at best his maladroit handling of private and public accusations and a subsequent law suit concerning his allegedly improper relations with pretty little Elizabeth Tilton. A Sunday School teacher in Beecher's church, a singer in his choir, a volunteer worker in church projects of community welfare, an adulatory admirer of her personable and affectionate pastor, Elizabeth was also a compulsive maker and retractor of confessions and accusations, perhaps not a deliberate accomplice in a scheme to blackmail the nation's most venerated and vulnerable clergyman. Elizabeth was the wife, unfortunately, of Beecher's editorial assistant and professional protegé, the dashing young Theodore Tilton, who proved to be an apostle of free love; Tilton promoted his cult in articles in Beecher's theological journal,and upon being reproved,he argued that Beecher too was a practitioner, Elizabeth being just one of many corespondents. At cost of well over $100,000 in lawyers' fees, paid by his loyal congregation, Beecher was formally cleared of guilt, but even his own brothers and sisters felt that,to say the least,he had been imprudent.

Besides the fame of Henry Ward and Harriet that of the other Beechers seemed dim at the time and most if not all of them have since been forgotten. There was Catherine, for instance, desolated by the death at sea of her fiancee,who was doomed, she feared, forever to burn in hell, because he had never experienced salvation; Catherine's now disregarded sublimative labors have already been noted. There was also Isabella, one of the most active and articulate of the early suffragettes, a co-agitator with Susan B. Anthony. Isabella is now forgotten by the fickle feminists. Thomas, who overcame many doubts, established fame as a preacher in Elmyra, which, had Elmyra not been Elmyra, might have rivaled Henry's fame in Brooklyn, for Thomas was a pioneer in focusing church services upon community welfare. James, who knew he was predestined for theology, ran away to sea for a few years to escape his fate and sailed as deck hand or later as officer on some of the fleetest of the China clippers. Having at last exposed himself to the seminary, he served as head of the Seamen's Bethel Mission in Hong Kong and then accepted a commission as chaplain in the Union Army. Rather than comforting the dying, however, James preferred to inspire the living, so he applied for and obtained the command of a regiment of black volunteers whose record, previously dismal, at once became heroic. But James died young and in obscurity, and even Charles's fame did not last. His *Conflict of the Ages* died the early death of most theological tracts,and nobody ever advertised his contribution of key characters and episodes to Harriet's *Uncle Tom's Cabin.*

Miss Sarah Pierce (1767-1852) and Mr. Tapping Reeve (1744-1833) were the two early Litchfieldians other than the Wolcotts and Major Tallmadge whose names were known far beyond the town and the state, Miss Pierce for her pioneer female academy, Mr. Reeve for his pioneer law school. Sarah's father Colonel John Pierce, an Army paymaster and a friend of Washington's, decided that his daughter should be a teacher and what was more,that she would first learn all the arts of gentility. He therefore sent her to New York City to move in refined society.

to acquire all the   proper female accomplishments and social graces. Beginning in 1792 Miss Pierce began accepting girls into her home for private tutoring, and so delighted were the town fathers with what they saw and heard that in 1798 twenty-six of them subscribed a total of $385 to build her an Academy. Between 1792 and 1827 — when the school was much enlarged and Miss Pierce retired — the Litchfield Female Academy evolved an educational program which greatly enhanced not only charm but also intellect. Miss Pierce taught drawing, embroidery, singing, dancing, and housewifery, to be sure, but she held that girls, like boys, should be exposed to geography and philosophy (the latter a comprehensive discipline including ethics and natural science), also, botany, astronomy, and chemistry. The very best families of Western Connecticut and Massachusetts sent their daughters to study under the stern but affectionate Miss Pierce and to room and board with vigilant neighboring housewives, as did families from points as distant as Hartford, Boston, New York, Philadelphia, and Albany. Discipline inside and outside the classroom was rigorously enforced, and each of the 150 or so young ladies whom the school normally enrolled had to be able to repeat with evidences of conviction the 23 rules of ladylike deportment, among them the followng: "You must suppress all emotions of anger, fretfulness, and discontent"; "No young lady is allowed to attend any public ball or sleigh party till they are more than 16 years old"; "It is expected that you will attend public worship every Sabbath." Opportunity was provided, however, for seemly recreation, of which one famous aspect was the Sunday morning parade to and from church and the daily promenade for exercise and pleasure. The young ladies, dressed just within the permissible limits of finery, bearing themselves in their most fetching manner, marched demurely through the village to the accompaniment of the music of a flute and a flageolet, exquisitely aware of the favorable attention which they attracted.

The habitual and at times deplorably forward spectators were the 50 or so fine young gentlemen normally enrolled in the closely adjacent law school, conducted by Mr. Tapping Reeve. The Pierce and Reeve enterprises maintained in fact a symbiotic relationship of romance which helped to sustain the enrollment in both. Mr. Reeve attracted students from the North, East, and South, many of them the scions of important and affluent families. Few of them lacked the time or the inclination to ogle the Pierce parade, to participate in the balls and the sleigh rides which made the Litchfield social season, or to engage in the spring nighttime serenades, not to mention also brawls, which scandalized sober citizens more interested in sleep than in music or violence.

Mr. Tapping Reeve determined the content and the methodology of legal education in America and trained at least 1,000 lawyers who almost automatically achieved distinction. Prior to his time education in law meant apprenticeship for a year or two to a practicing lawyer, and licenses were issued on the recommendation of an influential patron. Professional education in theology and medicine was on the same ad hoc basis of ofttimes casual trial and error; but incompetence in the law was more readily demonstrable, hence the realization of a need for standards such as Mr. Reeve came more or less accidentally to set. Finding himself deluged with applicants as apprentices, for he had the reputation of really grounding his young men in correct theory and practice, Mr. Reeve announced the formal opening of a school, which functioned continuously between 1764 and 1833,

Julius Demming
1793
Oliver Wolcott, Sr. 1753

Ethan Allen's
Birthplace? 1736

Benjamin Tallmadge 1775

Sheldon's Tavern 1760

closing only after his retirement and death and the beginning of vigorous competition by Harvard (1817) and Yale (1824).

Mr. Reeve commanded enormous admiration and affection on the part of his students. A gentle little man who seemed positively irradiated by wisdom and kindness, he was brilliant in his exposition of the law and inspirational in his insistence that the right meant fundamentally the rights of men, not just males but females as well, and not just adults but also children. His impassioned introduction of women's and children's welfare into the domain of chilly legal disputation lent his school a cachet which appealed especially to those of his students who were Southern gentlemen. He risked offending their sensibilities, however, in the historic "Mumbet Case," when he represented a runaway female slave and persuaded the court of her inalienable right to freedom. Mr. Reeve charged his students $100 for tuition for the first year, plus $60 if they chose to remain for the two to four additional months which were required to complete the full cycle of lectures. Room and board in the homes of neighbors cost them about $4.00 per week, plus extra for laundry, firewood, and special supplies or services, such as upkeep for a horse. The daily program consisted of two hours of lectures, plus an additional four or five hours devoted to transcription of lecture notes into folio size ledgers, which served the students later as references, and to reading in Mr. Reeve's private library. Teachers and students participated each Friday evening in a model court, and each Saturday afternoon there were examinations over the week's work.

Mr. Reeve and his son-in-law, Mr. John Gould, were the two main teachers, and a more sharply contrasting pair could scarcely have been found. Mr. Reeve, who suffered from throat trouble, never raised his voice above a hoarse whisper; his thoughts ran so far ahead of his words that he seemed at times almost incoherent and incomprehensible; his piercing blue eyes seemed to dwell as much upon eternal truth as upon the classroom scene. Yet his students idolized him, memorized his dictums, once they had them deciphered, and entertained one another endlessly with tales of his unworldliness. He was known, for instance, to walk down the street holding a bridle in his hand, then to attach the bridle to a hitching post and enter a building, all the while under the impression that he had been riding a horse.

Mr. Gould was organized, concise, and eloquent; his diction was impeccable; he was absolutely precise in his statement and analysis of legal cases; he spoke deliberately, repeating each sentence, and expected his students to take their notes verbatim. The students thus filled four or five big ledgers with notes from Mr. Gould and perhaps no more than one with notes from Mr. Reeve, but it was Mr. Reeve who fired them with enthusiasm. As one of his most famous students put it, Mr. Reeve "found the law a skeleton and clothed it with life, color, and complexion." The overall report card on distinguished alumni reads as follows: 1 Vice President (Aaron Burr), 5 Cabinet Members, 17 United States Senators, 53 Members of Congress, 5 Diplomats, 3 Associate Justices of the United States Supreme Court, 4 Justices of the United States District Courts, 7 Chief Justices of State Courts, 27 Associate Judges of Supreme Courts, 15 State Judges, 10 Governors of States, 7 Lieutenant Governors, 2 State Secretaries, 3 State

Attorneys, 3 State Chancellors, 4 Speakers of State Houses of Representatives, 3 College Presidents. One should make mention also of Horace Mann, the educator, George Catlin, the painter of Indian life, Julius Smith, the sponsor of the first Trans-Atlantic steamship, and three presidents of important railways.

Morris Academy, founded at South Farms in 1790 by Captain James Morris, prominent farmer and revolutionary wartime officer, merchant, and churchman, was a pioneer co-educational institution which for a time scandalized the community. (Mr. Morris was accused of walking home late at night with some of his young ladies.) Eventually it was rated with Miss Pierce's seminary and Mr. Reeve's Law School as a great town asset. Captain Morris was influential also in the new missions movement. He helped to found the Litchfield Foreign Missions Society (1811) which joined other such societies in establishing the American Board of Foreign Missions to send missionaries to Hawaii, China, Africa, and the Middle East. In 1813 he accepted into his South Farms school the young Hawaiian student Obookiah and several other youths from "heathen lands", and in 1816 he organized there the famous Mission School which in 1817 transferred to Cornwall. Rev. Lyman Beecher was also a sponsor of the Missions Society and the Missions School and delivered a famous sermon in Cornwall at the time of the death (1818) and burial of Obookiah.

Late eighteenth and early nineteenth century Litchfield seemed to many to give promise of becoming one of the major urban centers of New England. In 1810 it was the fourth town of Connecticut in point of population, then ranking not far behind New Haven, Hartford, and Middletown. It had numerous industrial establishments of impressive size, many of them exploiting the water power of Bantam River. It had, to be exact, 4 forges, 1 slitting mill, 1 nail factory, 1 cotton mill, 1 oil mill, 1 paper mill, 2 cording machines, 6 fulling mills, 5 grain mills, 18 sawmills, 5 tanneries, 2 comb factories, 2 hatter's shops, 2 carriage makers, and 5 saddlers. It was also famous for certain arts and crafts — cabinet making (superb examples still in use, one of them in the one-time home of Tapping Reeve, who purchased it for $100); clock and watchmaking (the steeple clock of the Old Dutch Church in New York City, for instance, a self-winding marvel with windmill attachment), and the now rare and costly grandfather clocks and pocket watches; gold and silver work (competitive with Paul Revere's). Litchfield boots and shoes were famous for craftsmanship, durability, and comfort, featuring right-left foot distinctions which were long uncommon among other makers. The town had a daily newspaper, the *Monitor and American Advertiser*, first published in 1784 (with advertisements in the first issue by William Russell, stocking weaver; Zalmon Bedient, barber offering "cash for human hair," and Cornelius Thayer, brazier, jeweler, and silversmith). It had two very famous schools, as noted above, also the later established Morris Academy. It was a busy county seat and a communications and transportation center of the Housatonic valley with frequent stagecoach service north, east, south, and west, and half a dozen inns and taverns catering to travelers and townspeople. There was every reason to believe that Litchfield would grow and grow and grow. Somehow this did not happen.

Commercial and industrial Litchfield assumed relatively less rather than more importance as the decades passed. The case of a Phineas T. Barnum, the future circus impressario, was symbolic. In 1848 Barnum invested $10,000 in a Litchfield farm and attempted to parley it into a Litchfield iron rush comparable to the California Gold Rush. Litchfield had had little iron furnaces and foundries ever since revolutionary times, their operation being dependent upon ore from other towns. Barnum entertained the vision of making Litchfield a bigger, better Salisbury, and he spared no ballyhoo. He mined no iron, but he recouped his original investment from suckers who poured at least $1,500,000 into swindles advertised by his successors in proprietorship as latter day versions of "Aladdin and his wonderful lamp." For gold, not iron, was reported, very, very confidentially, to be the metal all but visibly present. The slender basis of this mirage was the record of the Roxbury Mine not far distant, where a specially imported German metallurgist, Herr Feucher, more an alchemist, obliged his employers by finding traces of precious metals. Upon being sacked at last for incompetence, Herr Feucher contrived to have his trunk full of personal belongings break open within view of a bedazzled black slave who reported that it contained gold bars, thus creating excited speculation whether the mine had been seeded or pilfered. Within a decade the Litchfield mining bubble was pricked, and nobody placed much credence thereafter in the town's industrial or even commercial future, partly, perhaps, because the town never got on an important rail line. Litchfield had in fact already become a backwater community, but one of the most agreeab   and affluent of its kind.

What interested Litchfieldians—and an ever increasing number of summer visitors and urban retirees—was the quiet life of people of quality. Many of them were landowners whose farms produced very comfortable incomes; others held investments so prudently managed that one never "touched capital." Almost nobody scrambled for wealth or power, for it was sufficient just to maintain self-assured status. The status-holders put themselves publicly on view at Sunday church services (with Methodists, Baptists, Episcopalians, and Catholics becoming almost if not quite as respectable as Congregationalists), at the casino (a social and literary club, not a gambling resort), at the library and historical society (both pioneer institutions), at village fairs and fetes, and at very genteel home entertainments perhaps in private ballrooms. To be sure there were dinners of gargantuan proportions and dances of a gaiety which would have appalled good Calvinists who were already sufficiently shocked in 1748 at the extravagance and sinfulness of the town's first recorded public dance. A score or two of the more emancipated youth had then laid out a total of one dollar each to serve refreshments and to pay a fiddler.

The leisurely Litchfield routine speeded up a bit in the late afternoon when the town's leading citizens turned out for a parade of health and fashion. The younger set might be mounted on horseback, but the most sedate—or the more exhibitionistic—rode in stately carriages or sporty little vehicles such as buckboards and pony trapsalmost everybody casting an appraising eye upon horse and other flesh and all the trappings. The procession wound around and about through town and off into the countryside with frequent pauses to exchange greetings and admire views. The cult of the horse and the horse-drawn vehicle involved also frequent hunts, races, shows, and fairs. The attention to building, equipping, and stocking a stable compared with that bestowed upon a house, and the pride that was taken in a spirited animal, a stylish vehicle, a handsomely liveried groom and coachman was second only to that taken in family itself. Citations from the *Litch-*

field Enquirer reveal something of the connoisseur's interest which the competition created:

"The Lindens" — Mrs. Perkins' health does not permit her often to avail of the facilities which the stables at this place possess, but her daughter Miss Edity, thoroughly enjoys driving her pair of brown cobs, "Derby" and "Ascot," which she handles with perfect skill, before her Brewster cart. We noticed a brown roadster "Barney," in one of the commodious stalls. Livery, dark blue, drab and silver. The stables at this place are most conveniently arranged, being finished in Georgia pine and black walnut. Peter Matthews has charge of the establishment. A straw mat made by the dexterous fingers of Peter, with a border representing the national colors stretches across the stable immediately in the rear of the iron latticed stalls, the turned locust posts being finished with "pelicans" in Old Country style.

President Union Pacific Road, "Vaill Cottage" — Mr. Dillon of late years has become so attached to Litchfield that he gives a large portion of his summer to it. He is fond of a good horse, and we notice likes to drive a different pair each day. Sometimes it is his large team of dapple grays, with their fine knee action; again he will be seen with his coal black paid, with their splendid flowing tails, the animals alike as two peas, and not infrequently with his light stepping cross match, a black and bay. Livery, dark blue and silver.

New York, "Fernwood" — This stable, the building itself of granite and a model of convenience, contains a large number and variety of fine carriages and horses, perhaps the most stylish turnout among them being Mr. Goddard's dog cart, hung very high, to which he drives his tandem team, "Paris" with "Vim" in the lead, and trained to work there, with which he easily rattles off eight miles an hour over the hills. Mourning livery.

New York, "Belair" — Park phaeton, mahogany bays. Miss Wheeler drives a pony (rumble) phaeton, drawn by a handsome sorrel pony. Mourning livery.

Thus it was that Litchfield cantered rather than galloped into the twentieth century in the course of which, much as life has been transformed by modern science, it is no mere quaint illusion that the life of the villagers, native and simulated, retains something of the genuine quality of the past. Litchfield is especially fortunate, in fact, in that in certain significant respects it has actually improved upon its beginnings. The village has been much beautified by urban disdevelopment and reaforestation; much of the countryside has been converted into a protected green belt which precludes urban sprawl and induces environmental conservation. This unpaved Litchfield parkway is 5,000 acres of land along Bantam River and Bantam Lake which has been replanted with 750,000 trees and now provides both wild life sanctuary and public recreation grounds. The gift in 1913 of Mr. and Mrs. John Jay White, who bought up exhausted lands and ramshackle buildings to let nature redeem itself, this White Memorial Foundation Park has become a town, state, and national treasure. The Bantam which John Marsh bought from the Indians has at last reverted in part at least to even better than its pristine state, being now all but free of "pizin serpants," "varmints," and certain other pests and both readily and pleasantly accessible. All in all, Litchfield has much to teach those futurists whose prime concern is the preservation of natural and human values.

CHAPTER 5

Later Stockbridge and Lenox: Parnassus and the Gilded Age

The long tenure of the saintly if perhaps somewhat tipsy Rev. Dr. West as Stockbridge pastor bridged the transition of Stockbridge and other towns of the mid-Housatonic valley from the postrevolutionary into the precontemporary period. Town history has since then so blended with regional and national history that chronological recital of events becomes superfluous. What has characterized the Housatonic towns have been not individual developments, as before, but distinctive personalities. Of all the personages of the valley it was the Sedgwicks who did the most to set the new pace and tone. The autocratic revolutionary patriot, Judge Theodore Sedgwick, who lived and practiced successively in Cornwall, Sheffield, Great Barrington, and Stockbridge was the family patriarch. His blue-stocking daughter, Catherine, of Stockbridge and Lenox, was the family celebrity. It was Catherine who created and popularized a new outlook upon the New Englanders as the repositories of much that was genuine and valuable in the American people, an indefinable characteristic which, like later writers, she defined, rather ambiguously merely as character.

Judge Theodore Sedgwick was the son of General John Sedgwick I, Cornwall's most distinguished soldier of the War of the Revolution. He was the uncle of General John Sedgwick II, the hero of the bloody Civil War battle of Antietam who should, many people thought, have been made Commander-in-Chief of the Union armies. Judge Sedgwick achieved fame shortly before the Revolution by presiding over an historic court case in which a runaway black slave was declared "inalienably free" of her abusive mistress, the wife of Sheffield's revered Colonel John Ashley. This ex-slave, Mum Bett, became a loyal Sedgwick family retainer, as did yet another ex-slave, Agrippa Hall, onetime servant of Count Kosciuszko, the Polish general who championed the American cause. Both Mum Bett and Agrippa regularly regaled Sedgwick family guests with their somewhat fanciful life histories. During the War of the Revolution Judge Sedgwick was a Colonel in the Continental Army he was a member of the First Continental Congress and served numerous terms in the national congress and the state Supreme Court. Always a federalist and a Hamiltonian, who referred to the proletariat as the *sans culottes* or as Jacobins, he deferred nevertheless to the irresistible surge of Jeffersonian democracy. Although he played a vigorous military role in the suppression of the Shays' Rebellion, he refused to prosecute the defeated remnants. In his later years he moved from his Greek Revival mansion (still standing) in Sheffield to a newer mansion (later much Victorianized) in Stockbridge. There, with the aid of his wife, Pamela, the daughter of Abigail Williams Sergeant Dwight, he played lavish host to an incessant procession of regional and national dignitaries. He also played stern but affectionate father to a family of three sons and one daughter. The latter's achievements dimmed those of the brothers in whose lives she tried for years to immerse her own.

Two of the three Sedgwick brothers, Theodore Jr. and Henry Dwight, achieved national prominence as lawyers. Theodore, who sought not just to practice law but also to enlighten the common man with regard to its intricacies and the problems also of agriculture and industry, wrote and published popular tracts entitled *Hints to My Countrymen, Public and Private Economy*, etc. Robert, the most brilliant of the three, wrote a famous pamphlet, *The English Practice*, in which he pronounced the hand-me-down English law code "incompatible" with the conditions in America and urged its complete reformulation. But Robert suffered a series of nervous break-downs and died before fulfilling his bright promise. Charles, the youngest, despairing perhaps of competition with his seniors, settled for the life of the country squire. He supplemented his inheritance by serving for 35 years as Town Clerk in Lenox. There he helped to finance the young ladies seminary which his wife very profitably conducted, an institution which achieved éclat matching that of Miss Pierce's school in Litchfield. His one literary effort was a deservedly little known history of the town of Sharon. But he created a happy home for his sister Catherine, who brought him reflected fame.

Catherine Sedgwick, whom William Cullen Bryant-described as "the perfection of high breeding" and Nathaniel Hawthorne, only somewhat objectionably, as "our most truthful novelist," became at age 22, to her own studiously modest surprise, a much acclaimed literary prodigy. A pious spinster who had refused, or perhaps repelled, numerous suitors for whom the Sedgwick name alone was a considerable lure, Catherine's first attempt, *A New England Tale, or Sketches of New England Character and Manners*, began as an anti-Calvinist, pro-Unitarian tract but turned into a "novella." It was an uplifting little homily which related the stages whereby Jane Elton, a morally and intellectually chaste young lady, was emancipated from Calvinism through love for Erskine Lloyd, a sober middle-aged gentleman of lofty unitarian principles. By way of sub-plot, the novellaiste portrayed how self-righteous Aunt Eilson, convinced of her own salvation and the damnation of her neighbors, worked her personal perdition in this world and the next. The tale is stilted, contrived, and by present day standards, unreadable, but the New England scene, characters, and yes also character, ring true. The author therefore rates as an important innovator within the American literary and intellectual scene, one of the very first of the even mildly realistic local colorists.

In her next novel, *Redwood*, Catherine muted her proselytizing, amplified her characterizations (especially that of a New England spinster of compelling integrity and idiosyncracy) and added the gothically sentimental and melodramatic touches which befitted her overwrought prose and the tastes of her audience. Catherine lived to write many, many more books of various genres, and her fans loyally perused even such effusions as *The Poor Rich Man and the Rich Poor Man, Live and Let Live, Means and Ends*. She did draw some flack, however, for *Clarence*, which idealized the modest working girl in contrast to the strident new careerists and feminists. Whatever the literary blemishes of her voluminous output, Catherine did carry conviction in her underlying but unstated thesis that there was something uniquely valuable about New England life. She implied, in fact, that there was a special Berkshire legacy which could enrich the national future.

Catherine Sedgwick's home in Stockbridge and her later home (in fact that of her brother Charles) in Lenox became the mecca for national and international literary pilgrims and other intelligentsia seeking the heartland and the soul of New England. In Stockbridge this "American Jane Austen" presided graciously over literary soirees and matinees held in season on her garden terrace overlooking the Housatonic with roses in bloom and fresh strawberries in cream on the table, and in Lenox her salon was equally elegant and memorable. Catherine was sought out, for instance, by Harriet Martineau, English feminist, abolitionist, and indefatigable reformer of almost everything which was or was not in need of being so tampered with. Not normally a cheerful companion, Miss Martineau turned positively radiant when little Stockbridge children, perhaps not unrehearsed, pelted her with flowers and sang and danced for her as she walked arm in arm with Catherine discussing profundities which even Catherine sometimes found tedious. While seeking to compile materials for his study of American democracy, the French philosopher Count Alexis de Tocqueville contrived reasons to linger in the Sedgwick home and in Catherine's absence found her precocious young nephew, Theodore III, an amiable substitute. The caustic English traveloguist, Mrs. Trollope, reported that the Berkshires were benighted and bigoted even beyond the American norm, but she did discern some merit in Stockbridge and would probably have discovered still more had not Catherine, yet once again, been absent on one of her frequent visits to New York City or Europe. One visitor who became an habitue was the English actress, Fanny Kemble, daughter of the proprietor of the Covent Garden Theater, niece of Sarah Giddons, wife of Pierce Butler, a wealthy slave-owning Southern gentleman of meager intellectual resources whom she presently divorced. Fanny Kemble bought and occupied a house (The Perch) in Lenox, joined the intimate little inner Sedgwick clique, and set about accommodating herself rather too patronizingly to the community. Lenox was not yet quite ready, it seemed, for Fanny Kemble. She greatly scandalized the entire literary circle when, in response to numerous requests not to do so, she fulfilled her promise to read in public some of the bawdier passages from *The Merry Wives of Windsor*. The region entertained no misgivings whatever about yet another of Catherine's devotees, George Payne Rainsford James, English author of 91 massive but now unremembered historical novels, most of them in two or three volumes, some of them written in Stockbridge. Mr. James, who was served by a multidexterous quadrilingual (English, French, German, Italian) butler-secretary-valet, the brother of an unknown Irish baronet, delighted the locals with his cosmopolitan urbanity.

The Stockbridge-Lenox cultural scene of the mid-century, which soon extended itself into Pittsfield, was ornamented by native New England writers whose impact upon literature was much more lastingly significant than that of Catherine Sedgwick, the doyenne of the set to whom all paid homage. The most noteworthy among them were William Cullen Bryant, Herman Melville, Nathaniel Hawthorne, Henry Wadsworth Longfellow, and Oliver Wendell Holmes.

William Cullen Bryant practiced as a reluctant and not very successful lawyer in Great Barrington while achieving the fame as a poet which enabled him to move on to the literary Elysium of New York City as a professional writer and editor. In his poetry he celebrated not the Berkshire life and people, which and whom, in general, he abominated, but the inspiring grandeur of nature and the beauty of all its creatures save only man. He first won fame by his majestic threnody *Thanatopsis* but later permitted himself to dwell upon thinner themes, as in "To a Waterfowl," "Autumn Woods," and "Summer Wind." Possibly his greatest work was his "Monument Mountain," his celebration in stately verse of the effect upon man's mind and spirit of a visit to this Berkshire landmark, where

> ...thy expanding heart
> Shall feel a kindred with that loftier world
> To which thou art translated, and partake
> The enlargement of thy vision....

It was a visit to Monument Mountain which occasioned the most celebrated personal encounter among Berkshire men of letters. David Dudley Field, New York lawyer, member of the famous Field family of Stockbridge, arranged at the behest of a new acquaintance, Evert Duyckinck, a leading New York editor, to entertain in his Stockbridge home a party of guests inclusive of Bryant, Holmes, Melville, and Hawthorne (no male chauvinism here, for Catherine was away). After consuming roast beef and turkey, strawberries and champagne at the Sedgwick table in Laurel Cottage, the party traveled by carriage to Monument Mountain with intent to climb to the peak, picnic there upon more turkey and champagne, and hear Bryant recite his famous ode. Half way up the mountain the climbers were overtaken by a sudden storm, but having sought out somewhat leaky shelter and fortified themselves with champagne against the chill, they continued the climb when the storm passed. Melville created diversion by leaping from crag to crag poetically defying the elements. Holmes complained mock-plaintively of vertigo induced as though by ipecac. Bryant eventually gave his reading, and there ensued a group inquiry into the values of life and of letters in the course of which Melville and Hawthorne discovered a bond of elective affinity.

Melville, who occupied his brother's farmhouse, Arrowhead, just outside Pittsfield, and Hawthorne, then living in the "Little Red House" close to what is now the back gate of Tanglewood, entered into a relationship of mutual admiration and stimulation. Melville, recently back from the South Seas and already something of a sensation and scandal for his daring accounts of life among the uninhibited Polynesians, was at work on *Moby Dick*, which, upon publication (1851), he dedicated to Hawthorne. Hawthorne, having already shocked New England with *The Scarlet Letter*, was at work on *The House of Seven Gables*, but under inspiration of the Berkshires, was diverting himself with the infinitely more cheerful *Twice Told Tales* and *A Wonderbook for Boys and Girls*. Professing, Rousseau-like, to be cultivating his small garden and observing the bucolic scene — in fact a superb view of lake and mountain, Hawthorne was deeply stirred by his Berkshire experience. Even though he hated the winters, longed for the seacoast, and experienced fits of depression, he let the Berkshires illuminate his spirit and his works. Melville, whose *Moby Dick* reflects no influence whatever of the Berkshires, remained there for years after Hawthorne's departure, gradually becoming sensitized to the place and the people. He was later to write about the Berkshires in a light-hearted mood, but eventually he fell into deep melancholy and impenetrable mysticism.

Hawthorne's acclaim of *Moby Dick* and Melville's acclaim of Hawthorne's work helped to condition the public to the acceptance of both as major literary figures. It quite escaped Melville's attention, perhaps, that Hawthorne's story, *Ethan Brand*, seems to have been modeled upon his own life history. In *Ethan Brand*, a Melville-like figure seeks fiercely in far places for the unforgivable sin, returning eventually to New England to find it within his own soul in arrogance of intellect.

Henry Wadsworth Longfellow spent two long summers in the Berkshires, working or trying to work on *Kavanagh*, which created within him as also within its few readers a sense of *deja vu* and *ennui*, the hero being an insipid moralist and the setting a pale shadow of the Berkshires. To Longfellow the region long represented failed inspiration and public rejection but he returned again and again on brief visits and eventually found in the Berkshires a stimulus to genuine creativity.

Dr. Oliver Wendell Holmes (1809-1894) summered regularly in the Berkshires on the family farm where he presently built Holmesdale, his year round home. After having been the "Autocrat of the Breakfast Table" in New York City, he found a yet more congenial literary calling as a folksy country gentleman and Berkshire poet laureate. "The best tonic," he said, possibly a bit too often, "is the Housatonic," which he bottled into commemorative verse for country fairs and the great Berkshire Centennial celebration of 1844. On this latter occasion others of the Sedgwick set made widely-acclaimed platform appearances which constituted a choral swan song. Among them they fabricated an enduring Berkshire mystique. Compounded in part of pride in Berkshire traditionalism, in part of self-hypnosis, it was a vision of a glorified new Berkshire provincialism as insulation against the hazards of the rapidly changing world. Oliver Wendell Holmes, like Catherine Sedgwick, labored to slay the dragon of Calvinism which so long terrorized the region. His "Deacon's Masterpiece," the wonderful one-hoss shay which disintegrated on its centennial day was a transparent parable, as was his *Elsie Venner*, which added fictional venom to poetic wit. But neither Oliver Wendell Holmes in his commemorative ode, nor Mark Hopkins, in his commemorative sermon, nor various other dignitaries in their quite extended remarks made it clear how the genuine Berkshire legacy was to be interpreted. It is a riddle which has defied subsequent reading but not for lack of erudite essays.

The mid-century Berkshire literati were matched by a parallel intelligentsia of lawyers, teachers, preachers, scientists and other persons of achievement among whom must be mentioned at once the brothers Hopkins and Fields. Rev. Samuel Hopkins, the first pastor in Great Barrington, a stern Calvinist in the pulpit but an indulgent parent at home (known to his offspring as "Old Benevolence"), was the progenitor of the Berkshire Hopkins line of which Mark Hopkins the teacher and Mark Hopkins the railroader were the most celebrated scions. Mark the teacher, having been trained in the three professions of law, medicine, and theology, achieved fame as professor of moral philosophy and rhetoric and long-time president of Williams College (1836-1872). Although he was much too solemn ever even to have thought of sitting on one end of a log with a student on the other, he did begin the liberalization of the college curriculum by interspersing formal classroom lectures with scraps of Socratic style teacher-student dialogue. Mark Hopkins excelled, however, not so much in the classroom as on the lyceum platform, where only Ralph Waldo Emerson and Henry Ward Beecher were more eloquent or popular. Mark's brother Albert, a morose, reticent type, became famous at Williams College as professor of mathematics, natural philosophy, and astronomy, a trinity of disciplines which almost outweighed even divinity on the scales of learning. Another brother, Henry, seems to have opted out of the competition. Having squandered his patrimony in New York City by financing implausible inventors and inventions, he returned to the Berkshires to earn great affection but not much esteem as a dilettante writer and painter.

The famous Mark Hopkins of the next generation, a distant cousin of Mark the teacher, migrated from Stockbridge to San Francisco. By applying the brilliant Hopkins intellect to railroads and real estate, he amassed a fortune rivaling those of his partners and rivals, Huntington and Stanford. When this Mark Hopkins died intestate, his much younger wife, a one-time belle of Great Barrington, left it to other would-be heirs to squabble over the great bulk of the estate which eventually enriched mainly the lawyers. With what was not exactly a widow's mite she returned to Great Barrington in company with a certain Edward Francis Searles, her adviser on interior decorating, her inseparable companion, and presently her second husband. In Great Barrington Mr. Searles caused to be built for her and at her expense an enormous pseudo-chateau, which, a few years later, he himself inherited to pass on in turn to his own male companion and secretary.

The brothers Field were yet more numerous and more prominent than the brothers Hopkins. They were the sons of Rev. David Dudley Field, the successor to Rev. West as pastor of the Stockbridge church, the inspiration and the editor of the famous *History of Berkshire County* (1829), which set a new fashion for the compilation of local annals. David Dudley Field, the eldest son, became the most famous New York City lawyer of his day. A brilliant performer in the state courts and the United States Supreme Court, he was the author (inspired by Robert Sedgwick, his one-time partner) of the state's revised civil and criminal code. David Dudley, however, was not altogether discreet in his personal and professional conduct. He was perhaps a bit too close to Jay Gould, Jim Fiske, and Boss Tweed, and it was alleged but never proved that he performed certain services for them which were not in keeping with the highest ethical standards. Another brother, Jonathan Edwards Field, a lawyer-politician-teacher, was three times elected to the United States Senate. Matthew Dickinson Field was a civil engineer who built some of the nation's earliest great suspension bridges. Timothy Beal Field, reputedly the most talented of the lot, became a naval officer, but while still a very young man he was mysteriously lost at sea. It was Cyrus West Field, Stephen Jonathan Field, and Henry Martyn Field who attracted the greatest attention on the part of the general public.

Henry Martyn, the youngest of the brothers, entered Williams College at age 12 and by age 14 was already lecturing in public on the topic of temperance. After qualifying as a Presbyterian minister but before accepting a church, he elected to see the world. He traveled throughout Europe and settled lengthily in Paris, and there he had his most memorable experiences. Paris was rocked just then by the sensational murder of the Duchess de Praslin and the subsequent trial of the pretty young family governess, Laure Desportes, on charges of having made away with the Duchess in order to marry the Duke. Young Henry Martyn attended the trial and later, after her not altogether unequivocal exoneration, befriended her. He stayed on in Paris to watch the Revolution of 1848 and then returned to New York, whither Laure Desportes presently migrated and, having renewed her acquaintance with Henry Martyn, became his wife. Henry and Laure bought and renovated old Ephraim Williams' Stockbridge "castle," converting it into a mansard-roofed Victorian mansion. There they deported themselves so regally that even the other Fields, who were not especially fond of Henry Martyn and rather dismayed at his choice of a bride, were much impressed with the couple's sophistication.

Stephen Jonathan Field began his career at the age of 15, when he went to the Levant with his brother-in-law and sister, Rev. and Mrs. Josiah Brewer, then on assignment as pioneer American missionaries in Smyrna. For the next few years he spent his time mainly in Athens studying language, history, and culture and becoming proficient in modern Greek. Upon his return to America he entered law school and upon his graduation joined his brothers' practice in New York, only very soon to join the gold rush to California. Rather than prospecting personally for gold, he speculated in creation of a gold miners' town over which he presided most profitably as mayor, landlord, general storekeeper, sheriff, and judge. His not altogether contented townspeople presently caused him to be disbarred and jailed. Although threatened with total ruin, he quickly repaired his fortunes and went on to become a member of the state legislature and a judge of the state supreme court, also a man of wealth and fashion. His *Reminiscences of Early* Days in California (1877) appealed to old-timers and newcomers alike, and in his later years, Stephen Jonathan enjoyed a widespread reputation as an historical curiosity and engaging raconteur.

Cyrus West Field, as almost everyone still remembers, laid the first Atlantic cable. Cyrus began his career as an errand boy in New York City, working for A.T. Steward, dealer in dry goods, at wages of $1.00 per week, depending upon his brothers for an additional $1.00 per week just to cover room and board. Somehow he soon launched out into business on his own, prospered, went bankrupt, conceived a great idea and convinced certain speculators to back him. The project was the Atlantic cable. On his first attempt an Atlantic storm forced him to cut the cable free and let it sink irretrievably into the ocean depths. On the second attempt the cable broke and vanished, as it did on the third, the fourth, and the fifth. The sixth try climaxed in firm attachment of the cable to stations on both sides of the Atlantic and the transmission of state messages which sparked joyous celebrations. While the press was still congratulating him, the cable went dead. Cyrus raised more money, chartered the *Great Eastern*, the world's largest ship, and persevered through many more setbacks until at last the cable was firmly in place and flawlessly functioning. Throughout this period a little building on the main intersection in Stockbridge was rigged with a telegraph line to serve intermittently as command and control post.

When Rev. Dudley Field and his wife celebrated their golden wedding anniversary in Stockbridge in 1853, they were honored by a total of 7 children and 28 grandchildren present on the spot. Among the company was one member of the next generation who was to achieve fame comparable to that of his father and his uncles. It was young David Dudley, son of Stephan Jonathan; after installing the first successful long distance telephone line in California (60 miles, 24 stations), David Dudley settled in Stockbridge, apparently just to putter about in his garden, barn, and home. One summer afternoon in the year 1880 he invited his neighbors to view and to test a curious electrical contrivance—ten feet long, four feet high, an amusing toy on rails. The guests scooted about the garden on this miniature trolley, nobody taking it very seriously. But at the Chicago Railway Exposition of 1882 the inventor exhibited the full scale model which was soon to revolutionize urban and interurban transportation. In 1898 he was engaged by the Swiss government to build a 150-mile electric railway along Lake Leman which ushered in a new era in long distance transportation.

The Berkshires sheltered other technicians, inventors, scientists, and miscellaneous innovators, among them George Westinghouse, who made of his summer home outside Lenox an incubation chamber for many new ideas. A young Westinghouse protégé, William Stanley, living in apparently premature retirement in Great Barrington, quietly perfected the electrical transformer which made it feasible to deliver alternating household current far from the generator. On March 20, 1886, he threw the switch which resulted in the dazzling illumination of 25 buildings in the center of the town and thus introduced modern urban lighting. Stanley emerged from his quasi-retirement to establish and operate the Stanley Plant in Pittsfield, the precurser of the enormous General Electric operation which has been the key factor in the city's industrialization.

In Sharon the Hotchkiss family displayed comparable ingenuity and prescience. Originally the proprietors of a small ironworks which turned out kettles and plows, they eventually became the proprietors of one of the world's great armaments operations, with factories in New York and Hartford and branches, agents, and clients all over Europe and Asia. The family's inventive genius, a semiparalytic son, Anthony Hotchkiss, patented the key devices which led to the production of the repeater rifles and machine guns with which later nineteenth century wars were fought. It led also to the accumulation of the fortune which endowed Hotchkiss School, where the offspring of twentieth century barons of commerce and industry, among them the Fords of Detroit, are gently introduced to culture.

One Berkshire figure who might have become famous but died in obscurity was Anson Clark, a cooper by trade with his shop in West Stockbridge. In his spare time he built a hand operated electrical dynamo which seems to have predated the patented model. He also contribed improved musical instruments including melodeons and parlor organs. His prime achievement was work with the daguerreotype, which, it seems, he developed well beyond the technical level of the original by grinding and polishing his own lenses and devising new plates. In 1838, together with his son Edwin, he opened a photographic studio in which he offered to take portraits which would be "forever fixed, engraved as it were by sunbeams," capturing "expression... too fleeting to be caught by the painter." He also offered to provide instruction and equipment for aspirant practitioners of "one of the most extraordinary discoveries of the ages."

Despite its early entrepreneurs and inventors and its industrial installations, the mid-Housatonic valley was not fated to become a center of large scale modern industrial enterprise. Many, many factories which seemed enormous in their time—iron mills, textile works, paper factories, and the like—were built and operated in the mid-valley towns during the first part of the nineteenth century. Beginning in the 1840s, the builders of railways linked the mid-valley towns with New York, Boston, and Albany, and it seemed for a time as though the region might become a miniature industrialized Rhineland. Yet only Pittsfield was doomed to truly massive industrialization of the late nineteenth and early twentieth century order. In the other towns—Lenox, Stockbridge, Great Barrington, Sheffield, Salisbury, Canaan, Cornwall—industry after industry closed down, and both employers and employees went elsewhere. Nobody can very convincingly explain just why this happened, but the pretty little Housatonic valley villages became even prettier than before and no less prosperous. Agricultural operations sufficed to maintain what was already a richly endowed region. It was not large scale agriculture and in fact the total area under cultivation was very greatly reduced as relatively unproductive land was allowed to revert to forest. It was small scale farming, especially dairy farming, which supplied the urban markets with fine, fresh Berkshire produce shipped over a network of rail lines which provided good, fast, cheap service even for the smaller villages.

The mid-Housatonic valley towns, in short, made what seems to have been the indeliberate choice of stressing cultural rather than material values and providentially maintained both. They did so, perhaps, in keeping with the new Berkshire mystique of a New England individualism so rugged as to triumph even over Calvinism. The true New Englander retained nevertheless the unshatterable conviction that while others might be damned, the chosen few would win salvation, which, in modern terms, means perhaps just an extraordinarily agreeable life in the world of the present well removed from noise, smoke, hustle, and hassle.

Thanks perhaps to the Sedgwick set and the repute which they brought it, the Berkshires became widely known as a surpassingly pleasant region in which to live—one endowed with all the scenic and cultural advantages and afflicted with no serious drawbacks except for the severe winters. The Berkshires became a region of summertime retreat or full-time retirement on the part of persons discriminating or wealthy enough to choose life in or near a beautiful, tranquil New England village not too far from the great Eastern cities. The move began in mid-nineteenth century, when the Sedgwick clique flourished and their visitors caught the Berkshire contagion. It gathered momentum after the Civil War when the nouveaux riches found that within a few hours easy train ride from noisy, filthy, congested New York City they could rusticate in luxury. The symbol of the new era in the Berkshires was the millionaire "cottage," typically a monstrous pile of masonry built in imitation of a Loire valley chateau, a Rhineland castle, an English manor, a Florentine villa, a Spanish hacienda. Or it might be a mongrelized composite of several motifs furnished and decorated with pilfered antiques and staffed by imported butlers, cooks, chambermaids, carriage-men, grooms, and gardeners. These latter day proprietors sought to outdo one another in ostentatious display of wealth and power—also, it often seemed, in self-indulgence in the most extravagant eccentricities. None of this, to be sure, was without regional precedent.

From the very earliest days the settlers of the mid-Housatonic valley had exhibited a predilection for fine homes and stylish mode of living not always in accordance with the standards of good taste generally associated with colonial architecture and deportment. One of the most famous mansions and menages was that of Colonel William Williams of Pittsfield, a blustering hero of the French and Indian Wars, a land speculator who could and did calculate to the pound, shilling, and pence his own and his rivals fortunes a lawyer and judge who intimidated both clients and culprits more by arrogance than by learning. In about the year 1750, when Pittsfield was still a small clearing in the forest, Colonel Williams built his much envied "Long House." It was a two-story structure 80 feet long with gambreled roof, double doors of massive oak, wide central reception hall and other rooms of overpoweringly elaborate decor and furnishings. It cost exactly £1,373 17s and 6d to build, a princely sum at the time. The colonel's notes showed that he laid out £41/6 for lumber, £19 for nails, £15 for glass, also £26.16.6 in pay for carpenters and £6 for their board. In his garden he planted imported fruit trees, berry bushes, vegetables, herbs, and flowers of astonishing variety. For maintenance he relied upon a corps of liveried black slaves.

In 1785 Colonel Williams took his leave forever of all this magnificence, bequeathing it to his third wife, Hannah, age 55, a widow not long overcome by grief. A vigorous young farmer, Joseph Shearer, 25 years her junior, soon made Hannah his bride. Hannah eventually had reason to become suspicious of his motives; she hailed him into court on charges that he had booby trapped the well, into which she tumbled, had enticed her to mount an unbroken colt, which threw her, and had given other indications of malevolence. The judge dismissed the case and the couple were reconciled. Mistress Hannah proved durable enough to survive to the age of 91; her spouse, who lingered yet another 17 years to enjoy her fortune, deployed part of the Williams patrimony in prudent philanthropies which tended to dispel ancient scandals.

The Pittsfield-Lenox region, where memory of the "Long House" and its tenants persisted long after the site was swallowed up into the later village and city, was the focus of much of the early settlement by millionaire urban escapists. In Lenox in the course of the several decades the value of good building sites escalated from $5 per acre to $50 and even $500. Little Lenox village, situated amid the most idyllic and majestic of the Berkshire hills, suddenly became very, very fashionable. It was already graced with a town hall, a church, and a collection of inns and homes of singular perfection; and it was populated both by amusing Yankee rustics and witty sophisticates. It was provided with a library, an athaneum, a girls' finishing school, and other cultural institutions. In the 1880s and 1890s the Lenox landscape began sprouting millionaire mansions set in spacious grounds. By the turn of the century there were at least one hundred great estates and a thousand restored or newly built homes of more modest but by no means meager dimensions. The Lenox extravagance lasted until the adoption of the income tax and the disappearance of servants exposed the futility of trying to live like European aristocracy within a democratic society. While it lasted, the spectacle was one of banquets, balls, garden parties, fox hunts, tallyho rides, croquet, tennis, golf, fetes, and carnivals enough for the sturdiest social climber. Ladies and gentlemen of fashion, it seemed, led lives of limitless leisure and pleasure within a charming and charmed setting. It was just what Marie Antoinette would have prescribed had she cited her Petit Trianon not in late eighteenth century Versailles but late nineteenth century Lenox.

Anson Phelps Stokes, international banker and industrialist, tried to set the ultimate unsurpassable standard when he lavished half a million 1892 dollars upon Shadowbrooke. It was a grandiose folly of one hundred rooms covering an acre of floor space behind a pastiche facade of incongruously jumbled genres. Set in formal gardens of vast expanse, it commanded a superb view over lake and mountain. The house passed successively to Mrs. Cornelius Vanderbilt, Andrew Carnegie, and the Jesuit Order. In 19   it burned to the ground, and out of the ruins sprang a theological seminary of repellent modern design which makes the original Stokes taste seem almost commendable by comparison.

It cost   a certain Géraud Foster two million 1898 dollars to build Bellefontaine, modestly modeled not upon Le Grand but merely Le Petit Trianon, now transformed, after ruinous fire and subsequent sale for $50,000, into a Roman Catholic girls school. For those who preferred the convenience and economy of a public house, there was the Aspenwall Hotel, a $1 million, 5-floor, 400-room mountain top monument with ballroom accommodations for 500, and 447 acres of grounds. John D. Rockefeller frequently found sanctuary here, as did Theodore and Franklin D. Roosevelt. Aspen Hall vanished one spring night of 1931, consumed in a conflagration of sensationally distant visibility.

The Berkshires, like Newport, seemed to breed idiosyncracies. While George Westinghouse built his palatial summer home Erskine Park not far from Lenox, Mrs. Westinghouse, who preferred it to any of her other mansions, decreed that here she would live precisely as she chose. For decor, interior and exterior, and insofar as possible, human, animal, vegetable, and mineral, she chose white, beginning with white marble. She herself dressed exclusively in white and as jewelry spurned everything except diamonds and pearls. In her white drawing room a stuffed white terrier crouched beneath a glass bell on a white enameled table on a white rug amid white upholstered furniture and white silk draperies. Among the white flowers of her garden paraded white peacocks. The servants wore white liveries, and although guests were not actually obliged to present themselves in white, they were the more cordially greeted if they did so.

Mrs. Westinghouse's social rival, Mrs. Charles Lanier was partial to no particular color but to rather a peculiar pet, a purebred bull which she rode daily to the post-office, rather to the dismay of the apprehensive postmaster and assembled on-lookers. Mrs. Edwards Spenser fancied a little pig which went everywhere that Mrs. Spenser went; once, after being misidentified and humiliated as a mere pig-pen pig while trotting through a neighbor's garden party, the pet was escorted home by limousine by an apologetic chauffeur.

The summer cottagers, many of whom, sooner or later, became year-round residents, included personages of greater intellectual attainment than the Lenox society ladies and their ofttimes much cowed husbands. But Mr. Joseph Hodges Choate, prominent New York lawyer, one-time Ambassador to the Court of St. James, was a gentleman of urbane tastes and wit. He engaged Stamford White, America's leading architect, to design his Norman manor style mansion, Naumkeg, with its Chinese garden built on the ridge above town overlooking the Housatonic River and Monument Mountain close to the site of old Ephraim Williams' "castle." Mr. Choate fueled Stockbridge small talk with his spontaneous bons mots. He was the originator, for instance, of the remark that the Pilgrim mothers had to bear not only with frontier hardships but also with the Pilgrim fathers, and upon asking who he would rather be if not himself, he at once replied "Mrs. Choate's second husband." When a judge once accused him of trying to show contempt for the court, he gently responded that he was trying rather to conceal it. When asked to subscribe for the construction of a wall around the graveyard, he declined on the basis that no one who was in wanted to get out and no one who was out wanted to get in. He castigated his own caste by pointing out that whereas the normal man had only five senses, one of his friends had "a sixth, very keen and powerful—a sense of property." The remark, as he well knew, could apply equally well to himself, for he had earned the undying gratitude of his class by arguing successfully before the Supreme Court for the repeal of the first graduated income tax law.

Along with the migration into the valley of the wealthy and the important came also the aspirant and the gifted and all other types caught up in a faddish movement. The emphasis upon ostentation was accompanied and eventually surpassed by a patronage of art and culture. This signified both veneration for Old New England, including its arts, crafts, and antiques, and the creation of a whole new cultural complex with institutions dedicated to symphonic music (Tanglewood), chamber music (Magic Mountain), dance (Jacob's Pillow), and the proliferation of resort communities on mountains and lakes. Cultural renaissance signaled, inevitably, the invasion also of the counterculture. Stockbridge, the site of early effort at conversion and civilization of the Indians, was the scene of the most widely applauded and deplored episodes prior to Woodstock in the celebration of a new sort of liberation. The names Alice Brock and Arlo Guthrie must take their place alongside those of Chief Taconic, John Sergeant, and Catherine Sedgwick on the roster of Berkshire notables whom history may remember.

It started in the Stockbridge High School where a young rebel named Ray Brock was teaching arts, crafts, and alienation, his wife Alice was librarian and joint liberator, and a collection of advantaged and sometimes accomplished youth, among them Arlo Guthrie, son of Woodie Guthrie, were ripe for rebellion. Roy and Alice set up a commune in a long abandoned church in Van Deusenville where their adolescent acolytes congregated to eat, drink, smoke, sing, dance, play the guitar, and deport themselves as blissfully emancipated hedonists. Arlo and a friend named Rick deposited the commune's Thanksgiving Day trash and garbage in a restricted dump. Arrested by Police Chief William J. Obanhein, they each paid a $25 fine and then proceeded to immortalize their experience—including Arlo's subsequent rejection for military service on grounds of his past "criminal record"—by singing about it to the accompaniment of electric guitars. Alice meanwhile opened a health food restaurant. Arlo's song "Alice's Restaurant" and the moving picture based upon it entranced the nation's more unstable youth. Stockbridge was overrun by hippies, flower children, and hustlers questing after the fountain of eternal innocence and excitement.

Stockbridge has bounced back from the Alice-Arlo era, and the center of village attraction today is the Norman Rockwell Museum, packed with paintings representative of an America and a New England which may or may not be more genuine than the version of the Calvinists or the guitarists. The whole mid-valley of the Housatonic has been metamorphosed—some say glorified, some say debased—into a natural and human preserve in which many mid-twentieth century Americans seek to rediscover the life of the not altogether vanished and increasingly appealing past. The illusion, if such it is, is threatened by the now alarming degree of pollution of the lakes as well as the river and by the erosion or defilement of facades by reason of heavy traffic of tourists. Yet more and more tens of thousands of modern cultural fugitives or conservationists continue to find here what all too many of them describe as the most self-fulfilling alternate life style, be it that of the drop-outs of one ilk or another, or that of the real estate developer, or something in between. What people unanimously seek is the better life, which was, after all, the target also of the original settlers. Both old and new New England are here permanently on display. One may wonder just what to make of them.

CHAPTER 6

Ancram: The *Patroons* and the Tin Horn Indians

The early story of Ancram village and town (i.e., the 42 square township) and of nearby areas of eastern Columbia and northern Dutchess County, New York, constitutes a revealing chapter in the little known history of Livingston Manor, a 250 square mile estate of the Hudson River valley close to the domains of the great Dutch *patroons*, the Rhinebecks, the van Rensselaers, the Schuylers, and the Beekmans. Robert Livingston (1654-1728), the founder of the manor and the family dynasty, was an English born adventurer who climbed from precarious status as religious refugee in Holland to occupy simultaneously under the new English administration of what had recently been New Holland the highly advantageous positions as town clerk in Albany, collector of customs, commissioner of excise, and secretary of Indian affairs. Having occasion to take a wife, he very prudently chose the multiply well-endowed Adelia, widow of Nicolas van Rensselaer, daughter of Philip Schuyler, kinswoman of almost every *patroon* in the valley.

In his calculated rise to riches and power, Livingston did inevitably make certain blunders. He aroused animosity among his wife's kinfolk, for instance, by the too crafty devices whereby he acquired title to extensive properties which stretched the dimensions of his own holdings to the detriment sometimes of theirs to some 500,000 acres (800 square miles). He invited opprobrium also by sponsoring in London a certain Captain Kidd to head an expedition of privateers to prey upon the French nation and at the same time to exterminate pirates, whom the muddled captain, having taken no French prizes, presently joined. But by adroit manipulation of the law and by dispatching official agents to negotiate with the Indians on his private behalf, Livingston built up a truly princely domain. The key element was the aforementioned Livingston Manor, a 170,000 acre property which stretched for 12 miles along both banks of the Hudson and projected fan-wise eastward to the as yet undrawn borders with Massachusetts and Connecticut. In 1686 King James II of England was pleased to confer upon Robert Livingston and his heirs and assigns forever "The Lordship of the Manor of Livingston," which, to be sure, the said Robert by then already ruled, the grant signifying uncontestable title to "all waists, estrays, wrecks, deodars, goods of vandals...." plus "rights of avowsen."

It was a private fiefdom covering most of what is now Columbia County and part of Dutchess County, plus slices of Berkshire County (Massachusetts) and Litchfield County (Connecticut). The Lord of the Manor exercised virtually sovereign powers over the land and its occupants, whom he recruited and introduced as laborers and tenants. The only recourse of the settler against the *patroon* was to address a petition to the inattentive state capital in Albany, where the relatives and the friends of the Livingstons occupied most of the key positions and complaints were heard, if at all, only in the Dutch language and were dealt with in accordance with Dutch colonial practices.

The modus operandi on the manor was quite simple and to the *patroon* quite gratifying. Livingston undertook originally to recruit settlers on four year contracts for payment of about $75 per annum to clear and plant the land (wheat and corn being the main crops); to establish industries (timber camps, sawmills, gristmills, mines, etc.) and to build roads, bridges, and other essential installations. His agents provided them with free tools, equipment, seeds, livestock, and basic rations, other necessities being made available by the manor's storekeepers. At the end of the original contract period, the settlers might apply for leases on the lands which they had developed, the homes which they had built, and certain facilities such as smithies and tanneries which they had created. Any suggestion of outright purchase, however, was categorically rejected, and any reminder that promise of freehold title had been part of the original understanding was categorically repudiated.

Livingston, who had paid on the average about four cents per acre to other *patroons* or to the Indians, assumed a market price of $3.00 per acre and therefore set the annual leasehold fee at a modest 6.66 percent on value, i.e., approximately $20 per 100 acres payable in prime winter wheat (approximately 20 bushels). The return took on a somewhat different aspect, of course, if calculated as 500 percent per annum on initial invested capital. The leasehold, furthermore, proved to be highly conditional. The *patroon* reserved the right to renew or under certain circumstances not to renew, to approve or veto transmission by inheritance, and always the privilege of "quarter-sale," that is, the claim to 25 percent of the proceeds if the lease were sold to a third party. What was more, he stipulated that all stands of timber and mineral deposits were his to exploit and he prohibited tenants from engaging in the highly lucrative trade in furs. The ultimate humiliation, from the tenant's point of view, was that he was obliged to perform free labor on public works (theoretically only one day each year, actually much more) and to present himself regularly at one of the numerous Livingston mansions as a humble servitor with medieval-style tribute of four fat fowls for the already amply laden manorial table.

The villages of Livingston Manor, some of which were founded decades earlier than those of adjacent Berkshire County, Massachusetts, and Litchfield County, Connecticut, were thus very much retarded in development of the normal democratic system of colonial America. Robert Livingston and his numerous heirs ruled in autocratic magnificence from a dozen stately mansions along the Hudson and county seats scattered throughout their holdings. They exercised their authority largely through *schepen*, who combined the functions of supervisor, rent collector, policeman, magistrate, and informer. These *schepen*, relatives or sycophants of the Livingstons, earned special privilege and might even on occasion acquire freehold properties by performing loyal or at least unscrupulous service. They were dignified by authorization to carry silver plated rapiers and to wear big plumed hats as they made their appointed rounds of inspection and coercion. But as the population grew, even the Livingstons had to recognize the existence of certain distinct village entities in which the people assumed routine functions such as voting taxes for new bridges and roads (taxes which the tenants, not the owners, had to pay), building schools and churches (also out of taxes and on land leased from the manor). What was more, they voted in state and national elections for candidates who eventually had to take a stand on the issues of leases and rents. In the 1820s and 1830s some of the villages were at last incorporated, and villagers began to challenge the sheriffs (the successors to the *schepen*) and their posses whom the Livingstons at times dispatched, even the state militia which the Governor eventually felt obliged to introduce in order to uphold manorial pretensions. But that is the story to be told in due sequence of the "anti-renters," the "Tin Horn and Calico Indians," and the end of the manorial epoch.

The first settlers in Livingston Manor were some of the 2,700 German refugees who congregated forlornly in England when the Catholic soldiers of King Louis XIV of France in 1674 overran and ravaged the petty Rhineland state of the Protestant Elector of the Upper Palatinate. Taking calculated pity upon these hardy peasants, among whom the English traditionally recruited mercenary soldiers, good Queen Anne caused them to be transported to the Hudson valley, where their labors were urgently needed. Robert Livingston graciously accepted onto his estate as many of them as he could lure with prospects of good land in return for congenial labor—a total of several hundred families. To their great consternation, the simple-minded newcomers—better off perhaps than certain Dutchmen who had been lured by invitation of a free Sunday boat ride in Amsterdam harbor only to find themselves landed weeks later at Nieuw Amsterdam—found themselves consigned to primitive timber camps to render pitch out of pine trees. Little or no provision had been made for shelter or other amenities save for a meager ration of bread and beer. Those who stuck it out eventually got land—leasehold, not freehold—and some of their descendants prospered. But many defected to seek out land on better terms from other *patroons*, some of them being among the first settlers on the Nine Partners Patent just to the south.

Later comers to the manor were engaged to operate the iron furnace which the Livingstons established in Ancram in 1740, their gristmill near Gallatin (1742), their iron mines at Copake (1776) and other enterprises such as sawmills, tanneries, fulleries, cobbler shops, smithies, harness-making works, and the like. Such workmen or their offspring presently acquired land leases and many of them turned to farming as their primary occupations.

Relations between the Livingstons and their tenants were always tense, as were their relations with Connecticut and Massachusetts settlers nearby, whose freedom and prosperity constituted a rebuke to the autocratic *patroons*. In the early 1700s some men from Livingston Manor drifted across the still vague Connecticut-Massachusetts border to settle on plots of land which they bought from the Indians, and to engage in illicit traffic in furs, for which, much to the outrage of Massachusetts and Connecticut as well as New York authorities, they paid in rum and guns.   Men from Connecticut and Massachusetts, in turn, infiltrated Livingston Manor, at times quite flagrantly staging raids. In 1755 and again in 1766, for instance, the infiltrators seized and for a short time held the Ancram iron furnace and made use of hostages to avert reprisals. The Livingstons had grounds for their suspicion that the raids were not uninvited by the villagers nor the hostages unwilling, the operations being widely regarded as preliminaries to liberation.

The Ancram iron furnace and its subsidiary operations—forges, foundries, smithies, iron mining—constituted the primary focus of early enterprise in eastern Columbia County, but the Gallatin gristmill nearby ran it a close second. Philip Livingston, eldest son and heir of Robert and a gentleman of comparably opportunistic enterprise, bought into the iron industry of adjacent Salisbury Town, Connecticut, at a very early stage. He established his own furnace on Rudolf Jansen Kill at Ancram village in order to rival the more celebrated but not much more massive Salisbury furnace. At first he imported his ore from the famous Ore Hill mine in Salisbury but later (1776),he discovered and worked deposits within his own domain at nearby Copake. During the War of the Revolution the Ancram furnace and associated foundries and workshops turned out cannons, swivel guns, cannon balls, and other munitions which greatly supplemented the Salisbury output. The two operations together accounted for a major part of Washington's heavy armament, the most numerous and the best of the remainder being what was acquired in time of peace or seized in time of war from the English. The Ancram Furnace, like the Lakeville Furnace in Salisbury, was so important to the war effort that a detachment of militia mounted round-the-clock guard to preclude any possibility of surprise attack or seizure.

The "Defiance" gristmill at Scotchtown was at times as important to Washington's commissary as was the furnace to his military logistics. It employed several score laborers who ground and transported many thousands of tons of flour (an indication of the scale at the time of the region's agricultural enterprise) for shipment down the Hudson to the ravenous, at times in fact the starving continental soldiers. It too was patrolled day and night by a detachment of military. The mill on Punch Brook survives in abandoned but reasonably well preserved state today; the Ancram furnace on Rudolf Jansen Kill has been replaced by a big modern plant which produces paper and cigar wrappers. Punch Brook, it should be interpolated, was so named in commemoration of the doleful misadventure of a wagoner who crashed his vehicle against rocks while fording the stream and watched in agony as a shattered whiskey cask yielded a watery punch which could not be jugged.

Roeliff Jansen Kill, which flows north-south through Ancram Town is named for an early Swedish settler who once, when traveling by boat between Albany and New York, was caught by the winter freeze and marooned on shore for a week or so at approximately the spot where an important stream joins the Hudson, a stream which presumably took his name because he explored it. Roeliff Jansen's life story warrants an aside as a revealing episode in the history of the region and the state. Born and brought up on the Swedish island of Marstrand, Jansen emigrated to Amsterdam in search of advancement, then onward to America (1630). He was accompanied by his wife, Anneke, his two daughters, and Anneke's mother, Tryn, by profession a midwife, a calling much in demand. In America he settled in what is now New York State, rising from status as tenant farmer to *schepens* (sheriff) on the manor of Killian Van Rensselaer, and becoming a prominent figure at Fort Orange (Albany). Falling out eventually with the Van Rensselaers, he transferred himself and his family to Nieuw Amsterdam and entered the service of the Dutch West India Company on its Manhattan Island farmlands. There he acquired title to much of Lower Manhattan, which, upon his death, he left to his widow, Anneke, who later married Dominie Everhard Bogardus, pastor of the Dutch church, and leader in the community, by whom she had several children. Upon the dominie's death by drowning when his ship foundered off the English coast, Anneke inherited his considerable properties to add to her Jansen holdings. Not long after Anneke's own death in 1663, her children by her two marriages sold her property to Francis Lovelace, new English Governor of New York, who, in turn, transferred it to the Duke of York in settlement of certain large debts. The property passed presently to the British Crown, which, in 1704, bestowed it upon Trinity Church. By that time property in Lower Manhattan had increased enormously in value and in mid century (1750, to be exact) the by then rather remote and numerous descendants of Anneke Jansen-Bogardus, duly advised by their lawyers, discovered a flaw in the Bill of Sale which had been signed in the 1660s. It seems that the signature of one of the heirs had been omitted. The subsequent case tied up the New York courts for 150 years, but in the end Trinity Church retained the land. The Jansen-Bogardus litigation broke all American legal records for duration.

Upon the outbreak of the War of the Revolution, the Livingstons and the other Hudson valley *patroons* sagaciously chose the cause of the rebels,   Robert himself being a signatory of the Declaration of Independence. Incongruously, had it not been for the factor of anti-Livingston sentiment, many of the tenants sympathized with the Tories. Nevertheless the farmers and workers answered the call for volunteers for the Continental Army and at least 16 men from Ancram village, for instance, lost their lives in their country's service. At the end of the war, hundreds of discharged, unemployed, landless veterans from various states were bedazzled by the dim old vision of plentiful good land on easy terms within the domain of paternalistic *patroons* who, having signed the Declaration of Independence, were presumed to be sincere believers in liberty, equality, and fraternity. But the Livingstons, like the other *patroons*, exerted every effort to keep the manorial clocks stalled on Amsterdam time of the seventeenth century. As the population of the manor rapidly increased, new agricultural and industrial enterprise made the family even more wealthy and powerful than before. For the astonishing period of three quarters of a century the Livingston tenants continued to endure what they themselves came to describe as the shameless exploitation of victimized serfs within the land of fraudulent freedom.

During the 1776-1850 period the center of Ancram Town enterprise shifted from Ancram village to nearby Ancramdale, best known then as Hot Land, for rich lead deposits were found there in 1808 and, as everyone realized, such minerals heated the terrain. The Livingstons, naturally, exploited the mines to enormous advantage, and when the Ancram furnace was destroyed by flood, Ancramdale superseded Ancram village in importance. The center of the Columbia County iron industry, meanwhile, shifted to Copake, where a big new blast furnace was built in 1845 immediately adjacent to important deposits of ore. The Copake ironworks rivaled the more famous Barnum and Richardson operation of Lime Rock (Salisbury Town) in production of rails and car wheels for the railroads which penetrated the region in the 1840s and 1850s; it was also important for output of munitions during the Civil War.The new railways—with three different but interconnecting lines crossing Ancram Town—allowed for fast, efficient freight and passenger service to New York, Albany, Hartford, Boston, Pittsfield, and Bridgeport. As economic activities multiplied, the irrepressible conflict between the oligarchic landlords and the populist tenants at last surfaced.

The end of the manorial era was signaled in 1789 by the death of Stephen van Rensselaer III, the "good *patroon*." Stephen the Good left to his numerous heirs an estate worth some $20 million and an injunction to his eldest son, Stephen IV, vigorously to undertake the collection of $400,000 in overdue rents. Stephen the Good's benevolence, it seems, had its roots in lethargy, a failing which "Stephen the Bad," i.e., Stephen IV, did not share. Stephen IV put the sheriffs on the road with writs to serve upon delinquent tenants and cranked up the courts to confiscate the properties of the recalcitrant. The van Rensselaer tenants, whom the Livingston tenants next door promptly emulated, devised a singularly effective method of obstructing the law. Masquerading as Indians, masked, painted, befeathered, draped in calico cloaks of exotic print and cut, wielding tomahawks, clubs, saber, and pistols, emitting blood-curdling war whoops, blowing upon shrill tin horns to sound the tocsin and create panic, the "anti-renters" rallied by the scores, the hundreds, and eventually the thousands. Derisively referred to by the *patroons* as the "Ancram Screechers," they trailed, taunted, terrorized, and immobilized the sheriffs who were sent to collect rents and to auction off the livestock and household possessions of those who refused to pay. They demanded and frequently got the legal documents which the sheriffs carried and as they stoked these papers into festive bonfires they applied tar and feather to the bearers. The wheels of injustice were all but stalled. The *patroons,*by exertion of their formidable political influence in Albany,persuaded the authorities to send in big posses of armed men, but the "Tin Horn Indians" easily routed these reluctant law-enforcers whom the press promptly lampooned as bumbling poltroons. Such demonstrations resulted, as was inevitable, in deaths by violence, and just as the *patroons* hoped, official and public reaction set in against the antics of the anti-renters. But by then the incontrovertible point had already been established—the tenants had already paid for their land many times over in labor, rent and tribute, and condemnation to perpetual leasehold status was immoral if not actually illegal. The politicians and the courts were at last compelled to take cognizance of a dilemma which, to be sure, they never formally resolved but one which, once given widespread publicity, dissolved itself.

Ancram village became one of the key centers of the anti-rent movement. A certain John A. Rockefeller (no kin of John D.), Ancram storekeeper, postmaster, leasor of the Punch Brook gristmill, an impassioned convert from the Democratic to the new Republican Party, elected himself as a gadfly of the pro-patroonists. He achieved such fame as an agitator that his village earned the name Black Rock—black for its Black Republicans, rock for its leading citizen. But Black Rock did not provide either the venue nor the top cast for any of the truly dramatic episodes of the anti-rent movement, several of which occurred, however, just a few miles beyond the town boundaries.

The Tom Paine of the Anti-Renters was Thomas Ainge Devyr from Donegal, Ireland, a celebrated pamphleteer against English oppression in his homeland. After spending several years as a jailbird convicted of sedition, Devyr took advantage of a brief reprieve from prison to sail secretly for the United States. In the New World he found his new calling as editor first of the radical *Williamsburg Democrat* and then of the Albany *Freeholder*, a new daily dedicated to the Anti-Rent movement. The Abraham Lincoln of the Anti-Renters was Dr. Smith A. Boughton of Alps (Rensselaer County), about 10 miles north of Ancram, a kindly physician of French Huguenot extraction who set an arm or leg at $.50 per bone, practiced dentistry at $.25 per tooth, and midwifery at $3.00 per child. Dr. Boughton waived his fees for patients who could not afford to pay, a category into which, as it seemed to him, most of the Livingston tenants fitted. The good doctor converting his rounds of medical visits into occasions for spreading the anti-rent message was soon devoting most of his time to speech making and demonstrations. Widely advertised under his own name as the heroic spokesman of the oppressed, he chose generally to appear in public in the disguise of Chief Big Thunder and defied the Livingston spies to prove his real identity.

Three of the most stirring incidents of the movement occurred in quick succession on December 11, 17, and 18—two of them involving Dr. Boughton in the immediate vicinity of Ancram. On December 11, Sheriff Henry Miller rode boldly into Copake village with warrants to sell off the possessions of two rent delinquent Livingston tenants. On the edge of the village he was confronted by Chief Big Thunder, Chief Little Thunder (Mortimer C. Belden), certain lesser chiefs, five hundred tin horn and calico Indians, and 1,000 undisguised farmers and workers. Chief Big Thunder escorted Sheriff Miller to Sweet's Tavern and there, behind closed doors, the Sheriff professing himself to be at heart an anti-renter, they worked out the day's agenda. Chief Big Thunder, the Sheriff, the Indians, and the townspeople paraded from Sweet's Tavern to Abraham Vosburg's farm about a mile and a half from town, where Sheriff Miller went through the pantomime of putting the farmer's personal possessions up for auction while Big Thunder and the Indians threatened to do violence to any bidder. Sheriff Miller then suspended the sale. The procession moved to the farm of Abraham Vosburgh, where the pageant was re-enacted. Repairing to the tavern, the Indians relieved the sheriff of his legal documents and consigned them to a bonfire in which they also burned an effigy of Patroon Livingston. These ceremonies being duly consummated, the crowds dispersed and the chiefs invited the sheriff to dinner. Over beakers of cider brandy everyone toasted everyone else's good health and the success of the anti-rent movement.

Not all encounters began or ended so auspiciously. On December 18, at Smoky Hollow (now Churchville), just as Dr. Boughton, then dressed in mufti, stepped forward to address a crowd of 3,000 anti-renters from both Livingston and van Rensselaer Manor, a pistol shot was heard above the war whoops of the Indians and William Rifenburg, a young farm hand, dropped dead at the doctor's feet. The subsequent meeting was much subdued, and it was not until days later that a well founded rumor began to circulate. The pistol shot, it was said, had been fired not by a trigger-happy Indian but by one of the sheriff's men with intent to provoke an incident which would lead to dispatch of the state militia. Such an incident had in fact already occurred just the previous day. On the Rensselaer's Manor at Grafton, one of the *patroon's* agents, Elijah Smith, had attempted over protest of the Indians to cut and haul a load of timber. A pistol shot rang out. Elijah Smith dropped dying beside his ox-cart. The anti-renters and the authorities blamed one another, but the *patroons* won their point—the anti-rent movement was taking on the dimensions of a revolution which had to be put down regardless of legal niceties.

Dr. Boughton was arrested, tried for subversion, jailed, reprieved, re-arrested, re-tried, re-jailed, condemned to life-long imprisonment but after two and one-half years released. Scores of other anti-renters were similarly treated and if the Livingstons had had their way, it would have been hundreds if not thousands. General Jacob Livingston, last of the Lords of the Manor, played a key role in building up an anti-anti-rent countermovement. He did so, of course, in order to preserve his property, but also to restore his personal dignity. The General was smarting from an especially humiliating experience to which the Tin Horn Indians had subjected him. Upon riding out one summer day in his fine four-horse carriage from his mansion at Hudson to demonstrate in person to his agents how easy it was to overawe those whom his supporters called "ignorant, big-britcheted Dutchmen" and to collect their overdue rents, General Livingston was rudely surprised. He found himself being pursued by a band of 50 mounted Indians who tooted their horns derisively, shouted abuse, brandished tomahawks, and panicked his horses and his driver. The general fired off his pistol at his tormentors, thus provoking them to yet more disrespectful conduct. He then bolted his wildly swaying carriage to take sanctuary in the providentially adjacent home of his friend, Judge Frederick M. Mattice, to which the Indians laid noisy seige. That night the judge's son slipped past the Indian pickets to summon aid in Hudson, and the next morning the general was safely escorted back to his manor house. General Jacob Livingston, who did not forget or forgive this outrage, was the last of the direct family line. His numerous heirs squandered the family's by then much diminished fortune. A dozen family mansions, now owned and occupied by others than the Livingstons, constitute the surviving evidence that Livingston Manor was once a princely state comparable to a European Duchy.

In 1850 the anti-rent cause was all but vindicated when the Supreme Court of the State of New York ruled in a test case that the quarter rent clause in the manorial leases was invalid and that rents were uncollectible. The legal issues, unhappily, were enormously confused when the decision of 1850 was rescinded and new rulings were introduced which not even the most astute lawyers could convincingly interpret as conclusively favorable either to the tenants or to the *patroons*. After the 1850 court case, however, the *patroons* panicked; they sold off their leases for what they could get from speculators—as little in some cases as five cents per acre. The most prominent of the speculators was one Walter Church, a landowner from western New York, a scion in fact of the Schuylers. Church acquired technical title to scores of thousands of acres and made an avocation of converting antique documents into spot cash. With the aid of bribed officials he harassed and intimidated Livingston tenants, whose knowledge of or confidence in the law as the courts so obscurely interpreted it ofttimes made them prefer payoff to perennial threat of eviction. But the proceeds of blackmail eventually proved to be incommensurate with the costs of bribery; Church died a virtual bankrupt in 1890 and he had no successor in his chosen career. Nevertheless, even in recent decades a few lessees have paid minute rents or tributes in cash (no wheat, no fowls) to the holders of heirloom leases. In occasional instances the clearance of a land title may still involve some token settlement with a lease-holder who cannot realistically expect any court to uphold his claims. Thus, two centuries after the achievement of national independence, the legal basis of the old Dutch colonial system of land tenure, by then already antiquated in Holland, has not been definitively settled. The question has long since become academic, but up through the period of the Civil War it remained at least a mildly significant subsidiary issue, closely related to the much more widely supported antislavery and free soil movements.

The post-Livingston era in Columbia County was inaugurated, unfortunately, by an incident which achieved nationwide notoriety and made the name Ancram almost as infamous among the enlightened citizenry as it had been among the pro-patroonists in the time of the Tin Horn Indians. The incident occurred not in Ancram village or even actually within Ancram Town proper but close to little Boston Corner, a village in the extreme northeast corner of the township. Boston Corner and its immediate environs warrant a vintage village vignette, which is in fact to be found, flawed perhaps by excessively melodramatic and romantic embroidery, in the novel *Hells Acres* by Clay Perry and John L.E. Pell (New York, 19   ). The village is built on the edge of the famous "Oblong," a strip of land 51 miles long and 1¾ miles wide which was ceded by Connecticut to New York in 1731 in rectification of errors made in surveying the long disputed state boundaries. It commands the notorious "Tri-State Triangle," a tract of 1,000 acres which, through inadvertence or ignorance, was left to Massachusetts, from which it is isolated by rugged mountains. The triangle came to constitute a scrap of pariah real estate. Massachusetts couldn't police it; New York didn't want it; Connecticut tried to ignore it. It was a welcome sanctuary, however, for horse thieves, counterfeiters, fugitives from justice, ruffians and riffraff and roustabouts whose most urgent business was to vanish from their more accustomed haunts. The accessible portion of the acres, a valley of deceptively idyllic aspect, was farmed by five or six respectable families. These sober citizens repeatedly petitioned Massachusetts to cede the land to New York and New York to accept it and appealed to anyone who would listen for the establishment of law and order. For many years formal cession seemed to be in immediate prospect—but the immediacy was that of two state bureaucracies which, being under pressure from a mere handful of virtually stateless persons, felt little urgency to get on with the paperwork.

In 1853 the anomaly and scandal of the Boston Corner-Hell's Acres enclave suddenly hit the national headlines. The development of the regional railway system had just made Boston Corner the junction for lines serving the metropolitan areas, the completion of the Harlem Line in particular bringing this minute village within a few hours of New York City. Big time prize fight promoters, finding that the law interdicted the more brutal and popular practice of their manly sport, devised a truly brilliant scheme for introducing this aspect of urban culture into the retarded but accessible hinterland. They scheduled a fight for a $2,000 stake between world champion Yankee (James) Sullivan and his new challenger, John Morrisey, and announced that this elevating spectacle would occur on Wednesday afternoon, October 12, in a sylvan glade at Boston Corner. They scheduled special trains to transport connoisseurs of mayhem from the depths of the Bronx to this bucolic bivouac. Some 4,000-5,000 sports lovers packed themselves aboard the trains and ate, drank, sang, danced, gambled, caroused, and brawled their way to the Boston Corner depot. There they were joined, or to be more precise, confronted by another 4,000-5,000 bloodthirsty pilgrims, who arrived by train or stagecoach, in carriages, on horseback, or by foot from other points north, east, west, and south. That afternoon, that night, and the following morning there were preliminary unscheduled bouts over provisions (requisitioned farm products) and shelter (barns), cards and dice, liquor (whiskey preferred but cider brandy acceptable), and ladies (one of the most stylish was Helen of Troy, New York).

The fight, which came off on schedule in a by then no longer pristine Hell's Acres meadow about a mile from the Boston Corner station, disappointed no one's most ghoulish expectations. Sullivan, whose build and stance were suggestive of a redwood stump, was the bettors' favorite and seemed at first like a sure winner. But Morrisey, an ex-river boatman of more flexible musculature and agile tactics, presently began to seem, if not actually more indestructible at least less subject to near term pulverization. It was 37 rounds and 55 minutes of blood and gore—no gloves, no rules, no deference to the Marquis of Queensbury. It was a tossup who was the worse bruised, mauled, bloodied, maimed, and stunned. But the referees, alleging that Sullivan had left the ring, as seemed improbable, so nearly blinded, mashed, swollen, and immobilized had he by then become, declared Morrisey the winner. The seconds, naturally, thereupon locked one another in mortal combat; belligerent bettors pounded into the ring to reason with the referees; the ensuing battle lasted longer than the prize fight and it was difficult to distinguish between winners and losers. Once the pandemonium began to die down, the survivors pellmelled to the railway depot, where they commandeered each passing train to carry them onward, if only as far as a nearby town in which, presumably, provisions and accommodations were to be found. There ensued in various villages something like what is still vividly remembered as "The Sack of Millertown." The principal pugilists, upon being revived, vanished from the valley with unexpected fleetness.

They turned up mysteriously, in search perhaps of protection, in the custody of the Massachusetts police in Pittsfield. Both posted $1,500 bail to gain release from jail. Sullivan jumped his bail and returned to New York to fight again. Morrisey, a man of sharper vision, remained long enough in Pittsfield to get a refund on his bond by paying a $1,200 fine and then migrated to Saratoga, the center of the yet more gentlemanly and certainly more gentle sport of horse racing. At less hazard and far greater profit, he dedicated himself for years to the turf, but eventually he found yet ampler range for his talents by becoming a state congressman and a crony of the Tammany clique.

Hells Acres was annexed to New York State in 1857 and since then it has been sedate. The whole town of Ancram and neighboring towns as well went through a period of long delayed accommodation to the realities of the late nineteenth century, including, of course, the Civil War. Some 114 men from Ancram alone fought in the Union Army. The social scene was marked by the sudden proliferation of both schools and churches—Methodist, Baptist, and Episcopalian as well as Congregational, the latter of which was never the established church in New York State although it was in Massachusetts and Connecticut. Besides the routine free primary schools, several of the towns built academies in emulation of the older and more prestigious establishments in nearby towns of Massachusetts and Connecticut. In newly organized granges, the adult townspeople began to seek cultural uplift of the sort dispensed through lyceum and athaneum programs in which Ralph Waldo Emerson and Mark Hopkins might be featured speakers.

Ancram industry and agriculture flourished remarkably, with agriculture eventually outpacing industry as manufacturing shifted to urban centers. The beautiful rolling hills of the region found their true role as pastures for large herds of dairy cattle with the railways and later on tanker trucks carrying the fine fresh milk and butter to New York City. Although there is little in its subsequent history which lends it special distinction, Ancram did provide the platform on which Franklin Delano Roosevelt made his first public bid for office. On June 3, 1910, in front of Pulver's Hotel (still standing) in Ancramdale, before an audience of a few score townspeople, the young Roosevelt made his first speech as candidate for election to the New York State Senate. It was not the beginning of one of the more memorable Roosevelt campaigns—he lost—but it was the launching of a glorious career on the part of a gentleman of the region in whose veins flowed *patroon* blood.

Ancram emerged into the regional spotlight yet once again during the early 1970s. A pair of young promoters, John-Peter Hayden and Donald Chapin, conceived the project of restoring a cluster of old Ancram village buildings as a center of art, music, and tourism. They were inspired, perhaps, by the example of Mr. Charles Rudnick, a local resident, who had recently renovated and reopened the old Ancramdale hotel, general store, and several adjacent buildings, in one of which he set up a shop for the rebuilding of antique carriages or the construction of authentic copies. Messrs. Hayden and Chapin converted the Ancram Grange into an Opera House in which to stage scenes from light opera and performance by famous personalities. They restored a church as an Athaneum in which to show art films and to hold exhibits. A big old home became an inn advertising luxury suites and gourmet cuisine. An old-fashioned general store became a vintage boutique.

PART II

ONE DAY ITINERARIES

CHAPTER 7

Various Villages of Salisbury Town

"If one has not leisure for detailed exploration and can spend but a week, let him begin, say, at Sharon or Salisbury," wrote Henry Ward Beecher, a connoisseur of the Litchfield-Berkshire region a century ago, and his advice is still sound today.

Salisbury Village, like many others of the mid-Housatonic region, looks very much as it did in the early nineteenth century except that it is now much more attractive. In the very early days the village was denuded of trees; the streets filthy and often all but impassable, were the domain of grazing or foraging cattle, goats, swine, and fowl; the buildings were unpainted and many of them stood almost directly on the street. It was not until about the year 1800 that the townspeople became interested in what would now be called village renewal and beautification. Salisbury, in short, is a much enhanced New England village in which there reside today more simulated than native New Englanders, many in semi or full retirement, who consciously prize the architecture and general ambiance which old-time New Englanders took for granted. They view with trepidation the seasonal tides of tourists, a phenomenon which began in fact a century ago with the influx of summer visitors patronizing the then new Berkshire and Litchfield county resorts.

Salisbury village is the administrative center of Salisbury Town (i.e., the 60 square mile township), which includes also Lakeville, Lime Rock, and Taconic, the ghost village of Mt. Riga (now a summer colony), certain vestigial settlements such at Joycetown, Hammerton, and Amesville, and wide stretches of countryside dotted with handsome homes both old and new.

At the village center stands the *Town Hall*, not, however, facing a green, as in many other villages, for what was originally the green and parade ground was later allocated for the village church and adjacent buildings. The present Town Hall incorporates the first Meeting House-Church, built between 1749 and 1852 at cost of $3,766.67, plus generous servings of rum and cakes to entice volunteers to raise the structural framework. Since then it has been several times modified and expanded, the presently stately proportions and façade dating from 1913. The Honorable Robert Scoville, leading resident and U.S. Senator, donated $17,500 for the job, and the village overshot his generosity by the amount of $500.

Behind the Town Hall is the old *village cemetery*, the earliest grave being that of Dr. Wade Clark, possibly the town's first physician (d.1750). The most impressive of the monuments is a bronze urn cast in Paris in 1874 for the wealthy Coffing family by the American sculptor, R.H. Bartlett. In the yard of the Town Hall are to be found an iron kettle ("kittle" to the natives) of the sort once made in Lakeville for use on farms, a trip hammer and anvil from an early forge, and a marble watering trough into which flows crystal clear spring water. Inside the Town Hall with offices on the first floor and a big meeting room on the second, are displayed fine old maps and the Civil War flag of the Salisbury Company of the Union Army. Salisbury, with population of about 3,000 persons, provided Abraham Lincoln with 353 soldiers of whom 53 died of injuries or disease. At the time of the Revolution, the town, with population of about 2,000 persons, is known to have raised at least 141 fighting men of whom 26 lost their lives. In both wars the soldiers were volunteers, most, however, responding to public pressure and payment of bounties. The most famous of the Salisbury fighters in either war were the revolutionary cavalry detachment known as Sheldon's Horse, whose commander, gentleman farmer Elisha Sheldon, found himself in trouble with the townspeople prior to the war by reason of "lascivious carriage" He was subjected to trial by court martial during the war on charges, of which he was inconclusively exonerated, of being not only "indolent, ignorant, capricious" but downright dishonest in his handling of funds and supplies.

Across the road which leads up the hill from Town Hall stands the one-time *Bushnell Tavern* (1742), now a private home. The building is much bigger and handsomer than it was in the early days, having acquired two centuries ago, for instance, a very stylish second floor ballroom. Here, in 1777, may have occurred an entertainment given by the local gentry in honor of Baroness Riedesel, wife of the commander of King George's Hessian (German) soldiers who had just surrendered at Saratoga. Numerous village "belles" then danced gayly with the Baroness's brilliantly uniformed officer escorts, while just across Fell Kill (Brook) the ordinary Hessian soldiers were encamped with grossly inadequate shelter or provisions.

Across Main Street from Town Hall is the *Congregational Church*, built in 1798 by Salisbury master carpenter Moses Wells at cost of $3,766.67. A severely simple structure the design of which may be based upon one by the famous Boston architect, Bulfinch, the church was drastically Victorianized in the nineteenth century, but the damage has now been undone. The brick building beyond the church is the *Academy* (1888), where, for tuition of $4.00 per eleven week term, young boys could get secondary level education and prepare for Harvard or Yale. Beyond the Academy, the prominent structures are the *Episcopal Church* 1821), the *Ragamount Inn* (originally two or perhaps three separate structures joined together by Greek Revival Portico to serve as Deacon Clapp's Salisbury House Hotel), and at the fork in the road, the *White Hart Inn*, originally two private homes, one of which once housed a school and the other a general store.

The commercial district is of recent and uninspired construction, the early buildings on the site having been destroyed in the Great Salisbury Fire of 1903. The volunteer firemen of Millerton, New York, then galloped to the scene (a five-mile traject) and saved adjacent structures. Important town archives then being stored in the old Post Office were salvaged, somewhat singed, by the alert town clerk. Town records indicate that here and elsewhere in the village—some of them in the big home properties still standing on Main Street—were to be found the makers of clothing, shoes, hats, carts, sleds, wagons, also full or part-time carpenters, bricklayers, masons, cider mill operators, and distillers of cider brandy. The big old homesteads, it should be recalled, consisted typically of a main house and connecting outbuildings—barns, workshops, and offices, not to mention the outhouses, which were commonly built into one of the wings for ease of access during bad weather.

Opposite the one-time Bushnell Tavern is the *Scoville Memorial Library* (1894), successor to what the townspeople claim (other towns dispute them on technicalities) to have been the first public library in the nation. It opened in Town Hall in the year 1771 with a collection of 200 books purchased in England by Mr. Richard Smith, an early proprietor of the Lakeville Furnace, at total cost of £45 subscribed by 34 persons. The readers used to gather once a fortnight to bid for books, a bid of one penny over a competitor conferring two-week reading privilege. Penalties of up to a shilling were imposed for damage, which meant generally either tearing or "greasing," that is, droppings of candle wax. The original collection was strong on sermons, but it included also American and European history, world travels, and works on science and philosophy.

On the edge of the village, beyond the library, stand two early nineteenth century mansions of the Coffing Family, associates of the Lakeville Holleys in the iron industry, and across the street from them the Congregational and Episcopal parsonages. The former probably occupies the site of a log cabin with lookout tower for spotting Indians which was built as parsonage and church for the first pastor, Rev. Jonathan Lee, a few years before the construction of the Meeting Hall-Church, now the Town Hall. Some of the most noteworthy of the early Salisbury residences are located well beyond the village limits, among them Deacon Chittenden's brick house (1773), now Prospect Farm (just off Route 44) and the Camp-Ball House (1746) on Route 41, both distinguished works of architecture. The Chittenden house, it might be mentioned, was the boyhood home of Christopher Rand, *New Yorker* writer whose collection of articles, *The Changing Landscape* evokes the mood of the Salisbury of the early twentieth century. The Camp-Ball House, long the home of an heir to the Gillette razor fortune, is now an antiques gallery.

Mt. Riga village, now a ghost town save for a few old houses restored as summer cottages, was the site between 1781 and 1847 of a major iron furnace and foundry. Located at an elevation of 2,380 feet, it is accessible by a 3.5 mile winding roadway which leads up from Town Hall. In its prime it rivaled Salisbury village in population and affluence. Gone now, however, are the church, the school, and the general store which once stocked an extraordinarily large and select line of merchandise—a $150,000 inventory presided over by four clerks. When ladies of

SALISBURY VILLAGE

RESIDENCE OF LEONARD RICHARDSON, LIME ROCK

CONGREGATIONAL CHURCH, SALISBURY CENTRE

RESIDENCE OF W^M H BARNUM, ESQ. LIME ROCK

RESIDENCE OF MRS. M A HOLLEY, LAKE VILLE

Wm BUSHNELL'S HOTEL

D CLAPP'S BUILDINGS, SALISBURY CENTRE

fashion from the valley went shopping for choice silks they frequently found that an expedition up Mt. Riga was well worth their trouble.

The ruins of the *Mt. Riga blast furnace* are to be seen just below the outlet to Large Pond, one of two big mountain lakes. The overflow from the lake powered the leather bellows which fanned the charcoal flame of the furnace. Iron ore, limestone, and charcoal were poured into the top of the furnace ("the stack") above the roaring fire pit; the molten metal was drawn off at the bottom to be cooled and shaped into pig iron in sand molds. The associated foundry was famous for its heavy iron chains and ships' anchors. The anchors, which weighed up to 20 tons, were tested by being dropped ceremonially from a 100-foot tower at a periodical festive occasion; those which survived undamaged were certified for shipment and sale. Mt. Riga anchors and chains were supplied, for instance, for the ships *Constitution* (Old Ironsides) and *Constellation*, and high military officials from Washington, among them John Jay and Gouveneur Morris, visited Mt. Riga to inspect the works. Local and visiting personages were lavishly entertained by Mr. John Pettee, the ironmaster, in his mansion (still standing) on the ridge overlooking the furnace or in one of several family mansions in Lakewood.

The mountain top site of the furnace made sense in early times when vast quantities of timber were available for processing into charcoal at burning pits scattered all about the neighborhood. But when Mt. Riga forests became badly depleted, it became almost prohibitively expensive to haul not only iron ore and limestone but also charcoal up the rather awful mountain trails, of which there were three, and the finished product down again. So in 1847 when molten metal accidentally "froze" in the furnace and complete rebuilding was indicated, the Mt. Riga operation was abandoned.

On Washinee *Street*, which leads from Salisbury village up Wachocastinook Creek, or Fell Kill, toward Mt. Riga, were built some of the town's early enterprises which were dependent upon water power: a gristmill, a sawmill, a fulling mill, a machine shop, etc. Some of the original buildings have recently been transformed into very attractive private residences with gardens on the swift flowing stream. On Selleck Hill Road, which leads from Washinee Street over high land to Lakeville, still stand several of the homes of the large Selleck family of early landowners. Two of these have now been transformed into especially lavish contemporary residences. At the top of the hill is Mayflower Farm house, a modest home long occupied by Miss Julia Pettee, granddaughter of John Pettee, the famous Mr. Riga ironmaster. Here Miss Pettee, librarian of Union Theological Seminary, labored for years to compile the definitive history of the early Salisbury town, a valuable but densely written work unlikely to appeal to an inattentive reader.

Lakeville village has always been the industrial and commercial center of Salisbury Town. In the village center, at the outlet of Lake Wononscopomuc, stood the famous Lakeville *Furnace and Foundry* which made Salisbury Town the "Arsenal of the American Revolution." The operation began in 1748. In 1762 the colonial hero, Ethan Allan, built the great blast furnace which supplied revolutionary period foundries with high grade iron for casting into cannon and other munitions for the Continental army and navy. On the site of the original iron furnace now stands the much adapted successor structure, converted in the mid-nineteenth century into a factory for production of high grade cutlery, but now occupied by the *Lakeville*

Journal. In the center of what is now known as *Pocketknife Square* (named for the most popular item of cutlery, one which gained a near monopoly on the American market), is the old Central New England Railway Station. Lakeville was once served not only by numerous freight trains but also, three times daily, by deluxe passenger trains which made the journey to New York, Boston, or Albany a matter of a few hours of swift and easy travel. Across from the station is a small house which may have been the home and general store of Heman Allen, brother of Ethan Allen and one of his partners in establishment of the furnace. Ethan Allen too lived somewhere close by, but his house has been moved and altered beyond recognition.

The flamboyant family of five Allen brothers, Ethan, Heman, Heber, Ira, and Levi, all of them interested indirectly if not also directly in the Lakeville Furnace, warrant an extended aside. Born in Litchfield, brought up in Cornwall, several of them lived and worked for a time in Sheffield or Lakeville. All except Heman were involved in Ethan's Ticonderoga caper when, without firing a shot, a few stealthy American infiltrators seized the fort from a sleepy English garrison. All of the Allens were later to become important figures in the creation of the State of Vermont as distinct from the State of New Hampshire. They were not exactly the sort of heroes whose careers are fit, however, for unexpurgated entry in public school history books. Ethan was as much roisterer as patriot; he was frequently in trouble with the law in Lakeville for disorderly conduct, not to mention also an early act of defiance and heroics when he had himself vaccinated against smallpox at a time when such precaution was illegal. All five brothers were such compulsive land grabbers that the entire State of Vermont seemed scarcely to provide ample scope for their skills.

Brother Ira was the richest. He had land enough — 300,000 acres — that he could easily give 4,000 acres to the state for the establishment of a university and carve out an entire township as a dowry for his daughter. But his lands were eventually confiscated and he died an impecunious fugitive in Philadelphia. It happened because he got involved in what many if not most people at the time regarded as a very shady international armaments racket. Commissioned to purchase ordnance in England, he made the acquisitions in France instead on terms which seem to have been unduly advantageous to himself. On his return voyage to America on a chartered ship inappropriately named *The Olive Branch*, carrying 20,000 muskets and 24 big brass cannons, he and his vessel both were seized by the English. Ira's subsequent attempts to clear his name and his record involved his imprisonment first in England, then in France, and upon his return to Vermont, he found himself landless and debt-ridden. But Levi was the real black sheep. When Ethan was captured and jailed by the English, Levi contrived an expensive state-financed scheme for his rescue. The attempt miscarried,and Ethan accused him of having attempted merely to enter into profitable trade relationships with the English enemy. Levi's Vermont properties were thereupon confiscated; Levi fled to Canada and openly joined the English to serve with their armed forces in South Carolina. After the war Levi lived first in Canada, then in England, returning eventually to the American South to engage, naturally, in dubious real estate deals. He died in debtor's prison in Vermont.

On the shore of Lake Wonoscopomuc is a very attractive Lakeville village park, a civic amenity curiously restricted in the apparently uncordial manner of certain other New England towns, which seek to shelter themselves from tourists, to the use of residents only. On the hill across the lake stands the Hotchkiss School, where the scions of some of the wealthiest and most important American families are subjected to an educational and social discipline which is now becoming increasingly difficult to maintain at the announced standards. At various points on or near Lake Wonoscopomuc live persons whose names are well known in public and corporate circles, members of the Buckley family, for instance, and the chairmen of various boards of directors, who seek seclusion in Salisbury and so far as the passing public is concerned, anonymity.

At a point on the hill above the town center which commands an excellent view of Penknife Square stands the Holley-Williams Mansion (1808), now open as a museum, seat of the Holley dynasty of Salisbury Iron Kings who, beginning in the 1790s, dominated the industry and the town for three generations. Beyond the Holley-Williams House in a splendid walled park overlooking the lake stands Holley-wood, the home of Alexander Hamilton Holley, who enhanced the family fame by becoming Lieutenant Governor, then Governor of Connecticut. Alexander Hamilton Holley also participated in very numerous town, county, state, and national affairs, being one of the founders, for instance, of the Iron Bank, one of the sponsors of the Housatonic Railway, and patron of the rather unfortunately named Lakeville School for Imbeciles, a pioneer institution in providing practical training for the mentally retarded. Alexander Hamilton Holley's son, Alexander Lyman Holley, engineer, inventor, editor, and industrialist, is regarded as the town genius, whether benign or malevolent depending upon the individual point of view. Having perfected the revolutionary Bessemer process of steel making, Alexander Lyman rooted the new industry within the domain not of the Holleys but of Andrew Carnegie, thus writing finis to Salisbury as the nation's iron capital.

About one mile from Lakeville on the Millerton Road (Route 44) can be seen *Mine Pond*. This muddy little lake edged in part with trash and garbage dumps which was once Ore Hill or Magic Mountain, a 100-acre property containing deposits of exceptionally high grade iron ore, which supplied much of the Salisbury industry and was exported to neighboring towns as well. Around about Ore Hill stood Ore Hill Village, once a collection of half a dozen mining company offices and numerous company and private homes. Several small surviving buildings standing along the road in the vicinity of what was Ore Hill railway station, have recently been renovated. From Ore Hill two trails led up Mt. Riga and one—now Route 112—across Lakeville Town Hill to Lime Rock, passing the present day site of the Hotchkiss School (and the old Lakeville Cemetery) and numerous fine houses. On what is now the Hotchkiss School playing field once stood Montgomery Mansion, one of the most imposing of the early homes. It was built and occupied during the War of the Revolution by members of the very rich and important Livingston family, *patroons* of Livingston Manor on the Hudson, refugees from marauding English armies who burnt their Clermont mansion.

Lime Rock was the site chosen by Mr. Thomas Lamb, pioneer Salisbury industrialist, for construction along the swift flowing Salmon Kill of the town's first iron furnace, sawmill, and gristmill. His competitors, who had acquired water rights from the Indians at Lakeville, presently built the predecessor to Ethan Allen's blast furnace. Even though the iron ore had to be fetched across the hill from Lakeville, where Mr. Lamb too acquired deposits, Mr. Lamb and his successors found Lime Rock with its abundant water power an advantageous location.

In the early nineteenth century the firm Barnum and Richardson, great rivals to the Holleys and the Cushings, opened a big new blast furnace at Lime Rock, specializing after about 1840 in production of car wheels for the nation's new railways and presently also cannon for the union army. The ruins of the Barnum and Richardson furnace are still to be found along Salmon Kill on private property virtually hidden by the owner's house. Above the furnace site stands a very finely proportioned three-story red brick building in federal style which served as the company headquarters and is now occupied as a private home. Several of the easily identified Barnum and Richardson family mansions survive within Lime Rock proper, one of them occupied by the School of General Semantics founded by Polish Count Korzybski to counsel conferees on effective communications. The rows of minute to medium size houses are Barnum and Richardson company-built houses for iron works personnel, size and style being scaled to the status of the occupant. The company casino (a club, not a gambling joint) is now a private home easily distinguished by its rather gaudy architecture and ornamentation. The schoolhouse is now a private home readily identifiable by its belfry. Various other buildings suggest an earlier company use but most of the commercial section was destroyed in the great flood of 1958. The new Lime Rock is in large part the work of a New York City real estate speculator who bought up badly deteriorated properties very cheaply in the 1930s, more or less restored the buildings, and advertised Lime Rock as a paradisical retreat for artists and aesthetes, no few of whom bought in.

The Honorable William Henry Barnum was Lime Rock's most famous citizen. He once won a seat in the United States Senate in an election contested by Phineas T. Barnum (no close kin) of circus fame, both their campaigns being suggestive of Barnum and Bailey. Like others of the Barnums and the Richardsons, William Henry spared himself no luxuries. He was especially fond of high stepping horses and handsome carriages. The routine evening parade through and about the village of the town's leading personages in their stylish equipages signified also a fancy for horse racing. The very popular motor car race track on the edge of the village · is thus in its way a reminder of times past.

Near Lime Rock are two special curio pieces. One of them, located in a valley about half-way between Salisbury and Lime Rock on Lime Rock Road (unnumbered), is the *Yale Grant.* This one square mile piece of property was assigned by the state as an endowment for Yale College. Having no better idea what to do with such a remote holding, Yale leased it out for 999 years to half a dozen tenants willing to pay a minimum of five cents per year per acre. This was not then an altogether risible figure, not, at least, in comparison with the rental which Yale assessed and collected for a 70-acre property elsewhere. In that instance the fee was one peppercorn per annum, a mere token, to be sure, intended to maintain the legal fiction of receiving something of value in return for use of a property encumbered with restrictions regarding gift or sale. To avoid the inconvenience of carrying peppercorns or the like to New Haven, some Salisbury tenants, like Yale tenants elsewhere, eventually worked quit-rent settlements. But the Belter family, operators of a flourishing 275-acre dairy farm, of which 70 acres are on Yale Grant land, still faithfully pays $27 per year. They remit not to Yale direct, but to the town of Salisbury as agent; and since they also pay town taxes on the land, Yale graciously refunds them their $27, a complicated bookkeeping transaction which some persons find mystifying. When and if Yale repossesses this property upon expiry of the lease on May 26, 2776, it may recover something of its millennial losses.

The other curiosity comes in triplicate—the now all but vanished village of Amesville; the phantom *Falls village*, which apparently found itself evanescently at various locations on both sides of the river before settling into its present site on the east bank within Canaan Town; and the Falls Village Folly, in which both Amesville and Lime Rock actively participated. Amesville was virtually the creation of the brothers Ames, who built and operated a big iron works (1833) close to the site of the Great Falls of the Housatonic. Here they employed 800 men in turning out railroad car wheels, and munitions which rivaled the output of Lime Rock in quantity and quality. Mr. Horatio Ames, the leading partner, was a gentleman of gigantic frame who fancied frock coat and silk hat for daily wear, adopted a paternalistic attitude toward his help, and had an obsession about developing bigger and better cannons to help Lincoln win the Civil War. Horatio determined to manufacture super-weapons which would cast a 50, a 100, indeed even a 125-pound ball a distance of one mile, thus far exceeding the capability of any existing model. He tested out his new cannons by aiming them at Sugar Hill, where peaceful farmers were again and again dismayed to hear cannon balls whizzing past their plows. Mr. Ames perfected his wonderful new 125-pound cannon just as the Civil War came to an end and thus found himself suddenly without a client. The Amesville operation went bankrupt and was not revived; the proprietors had in fact already lost heavily on the Falls Village Folly, in which the Barnums, the Richardsons, and other regional entrepreneurs also collaborated and collided.

The scheme, which went through various fits during the period 1820 to 1865, was to convert Falls Village into a major industrial, commercial, and transportation center serving the whole of New England. By construction of locks and by-pass channels at falls and rapids, the Housatonic was to be made navigable all the way up to Falls Village and perhaps even past the   Great Falls above Falls village, all the way to Pittsfield. Canals were to be dug connecting the Housatonic with the Erie Canal and a projected Boston-to-Albany canal. The village was to become a major junction point of both old and new railways running north, east, south, and west. The Great Falls itself, a scenic wonder which early travelers compared with Niagara, was to be tamed by constructing mile-long stone conduits at three levels on the sides of which would be built new water powered industrial establishments. This fanciful project failed to attract realistic technical or financial backing. It fell apart when it turned out that the expensively constructed water conduits leaked more water than they delivered and that investors in new inns and stores, let alone industrial enterprises, soured on prospects. A monumental stone retaining wall just above the present day power plant constitutes just about the only easily accessible evidence of this Housatonic Bubble. Construction in 1912 of the Berkshire Power Plant, incidentally, involved damming the Housatonic just above the Great Falls and channeling the overflow through tunnels to turn the electrical generators, an operation which leaves the Great Falls almost dry for the better part of the year. The view of the smooth rock terraces over which the 130-foot falls originally plunged is in its way scenically satisfying but scarcely the sublime spectacle celebrated by early travelers, one of them Yale President Timothy Dwight.

CHAPTER 8

Ashley Falls, Sheffield, and Great Barrington

The so-called Lower Housatonics, now the towns of Sheffield and Great Barrington, were the first areas of the mid-Housatonic River valley actually to opened by or to white settlers.Dutch migrants from the Hudson River valley entered the region between 1710 and 1720 to make deals with the Indians for small parcels of land on which to establish farms or trading posts. Then came a few English adventurers from the Connecticut River valley, lured by the vision of rich new lands which, they felt, rightfully belonged to the Connecticut Colony but were being needlessly forfeited to the Dutch of New Amsterdam. Would-be English settlers petitioned the Connecticut General Court (1722), which authorized agents to negotiate with the Indians (1724), who proved to be willing to part with land for the equivalent in baubles and rum of about four cents per acre. The General Court then ordered the six square mile town of Sheffield to be surveyed (1731) and the land to be parceled out among twenty-five of the original petitioners.

The prime mover in the opening and development of Sheffield Town was John Ashley, familiarly known as Captain John (an officer of the colonial militia). Together with his brothers Ezekiel and Aaron and his son John, Jr. (General John, an officer in the Continental Army), the Ashleys dominated the economic, political, and social development of the town throughout the subsequent century. The Ashley clan settled at a rapids on the Housatonic, now Ashley Falls village, about three miles south of Sheffield village. There they devoted themselves less to farming than exploitation of water power, which meant establishment and operation of a gristmill, a sawmill, a cider mill, a fulling mill, and an ironworks. The Ashleys and Ashley Falls flourished phenomenally. Colonel John, who lived to the age of 93 (1709-1802), was so formidable a patriarch that of all the patricians then known as River Gods, he was possibly the most venerable and venerated.

Colonel John built himself a stately home quite in keeping with his means and manners. It has been restored and relocated, standing today — open to the public as a museum — a couple of miles outside Ashley Falls on the edge of the nature reserve known as Bartholomew's Cobble. Here Colonel John entertained the other prominent local personages who helped him draft the so-called "Sheffield Declaration of Independence" as of February 18, 1773, anticipating Benjamin Franklin's document of 1776, which echoed Colonel John's rhetoric, which, in turn paraphrased the French revolutionary philosophers. Here too Colonel John's black slave, Mum Bett, having eavesdropped upon the councils of the freedom-fighters, made her -personal declaration of independence of the Ashley family, General John's wife having just threatened her with a red hot poker for a minor act of disobedience and disrespect. Mum Bett applied to the Ashley family friend, Judge Theodore Sedgwick, who accepted her case and won the historic court decision that she was entitled to claim "the inalienable right to freedom."

The Ashley family home, the oldest and one of the most elegant of the great homes of the region (with General John's handsome residence standing close by), bears no comparison in size and grandeur with the stately homes of Old England, but it is a testimonial to American colonial taste and craftsmanship. The closely adjacent Bartholomew's Cobble bears witness, correspondingly, to the pristine beauty of the early American wilderness in one of its less widely appreciated aspects. It is now a national nature preserve, appropriately described as "a 500-million-year-old glacial outcropping of marble and limestone supporting the largest concentration of fern species and lime-loving plants in America," attracting, incidentally, 235 species of birds and numerous species of bird and nature watchers.

Present day *Ashley Falls village* represents the quintessential elements of the contemporary Berkshire-Litchfield region—retirement retreats and antiques, to which, it seems, the very attractive little cluster of old homes is primarily dedicated. The abandoned railway station is a reminder, however, of the industrial past. In the nineteenth century Ashley Falls was a major center of marble and limestone quarrying, and the flourishing railway lines of the time shipped thousands of tons of the output to eastern seaboard cities. New York City Hall, for instance, was built partly out of Ashley Falls marble. And at least one massive and memorable order was placed by the national government. It involved 100,000 marble slabs at $2.65 each to mark the graves of soldiers fallen during the Civil War.

Sheffield village, which now far surpasses Ashley Falls in importance, with even more numerous and ubiquitous antique shops, has all the customary New England town features   placed on or near the village green, in this case a long parkway lined with splendid old buildings. The following are especially noteworthy:
The *Old Parish Church* (build 1760, rebuilt 1829).

The *Sedgwick mansion*, a porticoed early Greek Revival structure adjacent to a curious duplex of the same genre. Here lived various members of the famous Sedgwick families of Cornwall, Sheffield, and Stockbridge, especially Judge Theodore Sedgwick, one of the drafters of the Sheffield Declaration, the protector and patron of Mum Bett, an army general in the War of the Revolution, one of the most eminent of the region's many lawyers.

The *Don Raymond House*, now the home of the Sheffield Historical Society. Don Raymond, leading merchant and suspected Tory, was accused in 1776 of inciting a servant to chop down the town's Liberty Tree. The servant was tarred and feathered; Don was made humbly to seek the forgiveness of the townspeople and was soon thereafter rehabilitated as supplier of provisions for the Continental Army.

The *Dewey Memorial Hall*. In 1871 Dr. Orville Dewey, wealthy retired Unitarian minister, established the Sheffield Friendly Union for the promotion of "intelli-

Colonel John Ashley House
King House

Drawing Room of Ashley House

gence and cheerfulness." With his son and daughter to assist him in between travels to Europe, he organized a program of lectures, plays, readings, concerts, recitals, study courses, conversational evenings, and other projects of intellectual and moral uplift. The Friendship Society was an early manifestation of the rage for lyceums, atheneums, and granges which swept the region somewhat later in the century and fetched in such distinguished platform performers as Henry Ward Beecher and Ralph Waldo Emerson. It was indicative also of a special Sheffield predilection for social and cultural improvement.

In 1849, for instance, the ladies of the town organized a W.C.T.U., which gave drinking men a bad time, and in 1880 they demanded and got the right to vote in town meetings. A male-dominated Society for the Detection of Horse Thieves, however, persisted forlornly from 1869 to 1913 without a single case of successful detection and expired only when automobile thievery became more modish. A Sheffield Society for promotion of the welfare of Indians was organized, unhappily, only when there were virtually no more local Indians to protect. But a Sheffield Village Improvement Association worked wonders of beautification by planting trees and creating parks, thus undoing some of the damage done by the pioneers, to whom nature's own vegetation seemed a threat. The Association was unable, however, to save the Great Elm, a gigantic tree more than 100 feet high with a trunk 20 feet around which somehow escaped the axes of the early woodsmen, probably because it provided shelter for early town meetings and church services. The Great Elm was destroyed by lightning in 1926 and thus did not fall victim to the Dutch Elm blight which has recently killed many of the elms planted by various other village improvement associations.

Great Barrington was settled at about the same time and in much the same manner as Sheffield and Salisbury but was distinguished in early days at least for its wickedness and in later times for its industrialization and extravagance. The reputation for wickedness traces to the fulminations of the Rev. Samuel Hopkins, the town's first pastor (1743-1769), against the sinfulness and ingratitude of his congregation. The townspeople seem in fact to have been inattentive to the good pastor's lengthy Calvinistic sermons about damnation and to have encouraged him at last, by suspending his salary, to seek a brighter career elsewhere. Rev. Hopkins is honored in Great Barrington today, however, as a profoundly learned divine and the progenitor of the local Hopkins line which numbers Mark the forty-niner and Mark the teacher among its famous personages. Industrialization meant the construction of very numerous factories built to take advantage of water power along a stretch of Housatonic River rapids, enormous nineteenth century textile mills, for instance, of which the skeletons still stand in Housatonic Village. Two prime examples of the extravagance were the Congregational manse, built in 1895 at cost of $100,000, more luxurious, it was said, than a bishop's or even an archbishop's palace, and the Searles Castle, a pseudo-chateau built at cost of well over a million 1888 dollars. Both these monuments were financed by Mark Hopkins' money, the manse as a memorial to the above-mentioned Rev. Samuel Hopkins.

The places of special interest in Great Barrington today are:

The *Town Hall* (1876), built on the approximate site of the original town hall, court house, and jail which featured in the history of the revolutionary period. Here on August 16, 1744, there assembled a crowd of 1,500 patriots from various parts of the Berkshires, armed with pitchforks, scythes, and a few muskets, determined to prevent the sitting of the King's Court. This was a post-Boston Tea Party act of defiance of King George which other towns presently emulated, much to the dismay not only of the British but of the local gentry, ofttimes members of the courts, whose sense of propriety was outraged and whose persons were subjected to indignities. Here on September 12, 1786, a band of Shays' rebels again prevented the sitting of a court, this time an independence era court which was about to order the confiscation of the properties of impoverished and delinquent taxpayers who happened to include many revolutionary war veterans. And here on February 27, 1787 occurred the penultimate act of Shays' Rebellion.

A couple of hundred armed but indisciplinary tockbridge, where a hundred of rebels—demobilized soldiers of the Continental Army protesting unemployment and impoverishment—had already raided Stockbridge, taken "blue stocking" hostages, and renewed their spirits on a cold winter night with deep drafts of grog by enforced courtesy of the Widow Bingham, proprietress of the Red Lion Tavern. They next raided Great Barrington before heading off pell-mell, by sleigh, on horseback, or afoot for legal sanctuary across the New York State line. They were intercepted, challenged, and captured by the belatedly alerted General John Ashley and the unenthusiastic Sheffield militia, whose members, by and large, sympathized with the rebels. This last battle of this forlorn immediate postindependence uprising of the proletariate occurred at a point between Great Barrington and Egremont on present day Route 41, where an inconspicuous marker can sometimes with some difficulty be discerned in a roadside cornfield.

The *Dwight House* (now called the *Bryant House*). This especially large and handsome saltbox house was built in 1759 by General Joseph Dwight, famous soldier of the French and Indian wars. It was designed to the specifications of his stylish wife Abigail, widow of John Sergeant, missionary pastor of Stockbridge, who had built her an almost equally splendid Stockbridge residence 20 years earlier. Here in 1777, after the battle of Saratoga, Abigail's son, Colonel Elijah Dwight, extended most hospitable entertainment to defeated English General John Burgoyne. Here in 1821, William Cullen Bryant, town clerk, lawyer, and poet, married Frances Fairchild, sister-in-law of the then owner.

The *Stevens Funeral Home* (1815). This was the house in which William Cullen Bryant took up residence with his bride, paying $30 per annum in rent, plus 17 cents per week for pasturage for his cow.

Wainwright Hall (built in 1766, Victorianized in 1890). Ralph Pope and William Stanley, two early experimenters in electrical engineering, associates respectively of Thomas Edison and George Westinghouse, lived and worked in this house. On March 20, 1886 William Stanley both literally and figuratively electrified the town by switching on lights in 26 business and residential properties along Main Street, the first such feat of modern urban lighting.

The *Congregational Church* and *Manse.* The original wooden church (1742) in which Rev. Samuel Hopkins preached was located just east of the present bridge across the Housatonic on Route 7. It was replaced in 1860 by a stone building which was in turn replaced, after a fire, by the present structure, built in 1882 of local blue dolerite at cost of $100,000. The church is most famous for its splendid $40,000 organ, the gift of Rev. Timothy Hopkins, adopted son of Mr. and Mrs. Mark Hopkins, in memory, naturally, of Rev. Samuel Hopkins. The memorial manse was the later gift of Mrs. Mark Hopkins, after she had claimed a few millions as the widow's portion of Mark's estate, over which other heirs engaged in litigation so lengthy and costly that relatively little was left to divide.

The *Searles Castle* (1886), also known as the Sherwood-Kellogg-Hopkins-Searles Terrace, is an opulent 40-room extravanganza of the Gilded Age, one of a hundred such follies perpetrated in the region. It was originally the domain of Mrs. Mark Hopkins, nee Mary Frances Sherwood, in her youth a belle of Great Barrington and a teacher in a private school conducted by the spinster sisters Kellogg. Mark Hopkins the forty-niner—the great-nephew of Rev. Samuel Hopkins, the great grandson of John Sergeant, the grandson of Mark Hopkins the teacher—woed and wed Miss Sherwood on a return visit to his home town and took her back to California with him to share his railroad and real estate fortune. Upon being widowed and inheriting not only from Mark but also the Kellogg properties, Mrs. Hopkins herself returned to Great Barrington along with a certain Mr. Edward F. Searles, by profession an interior decorator, her constant companion and adviser, soon—although 20 years her junior—her new husband. Mr. Searles persuaded Mrs. Hopkins to build herself an appropriate Berkshire mansion on the site of the old Kellogg house; they opened it with lavish entertainments during the Christmas season of the year 1886; they married in early 1887 and presently went to live in yet another mansion, this one Mrs. Searles's, in Meriden. Upon the death of his wife in 1891, Mr. Searles inherited all of her properties— having to make a generous settlement, however, with outraged relatives who took him to court for exercise of "undue influence." Mr. Searles was never very happy thereafter in Great Barrington, which, he felt, did not truly appreciate such gestures of his as the gift of a fine new school. He said that the town was gouging him on taxes, and he objected to the new street railway which routed noisy cars around a bend just outside the music room in which he liked to practice on the organ. Upon his death in 1920, Mr. Searles left the chateau to his own secretary-companion, a certain Mr. Walker. The new heir promptly protested the town's appraised tax value ($650,000) and petulantly offered to sell the property for one tenth that figure. An impromptu syndicate of investors, thinking to make a killing on quick resale, promptly offered him cash and he accepted. But pseudo-French chateaux, however lavishly built, furnished, and decorated commanded a very thin market, the expense of maintaining any such establishment having already become almost prohibitive. So the castle was run for years as a girls' school and then fell vacant. It was purchased by a New York real estate investor who owns also the Berkshire Inn across the street; he leases it out to another operator who is trying to convert it into a major tourist attraction.

The *Wheeler House* (1771). Truman Wheeler, the builder, was the proprietor of a general store which occupied the ground floor front. As a colonel in the Continental Army he fought in the battle of Saratoga, and after that great American victory he escorted many of the captive British soldiers, via Great Barrington, to Boston. In Great Barrington, where the soldiers camped for a time, he administered home remedies to the ill and the injured. At the time of the Shays Rebellion, the Wheeler House provided shelter for Deputy Sheriff Ezra Kellogg, who managed to escape from Stockbridge and alerted Sheffield's General John Ashley to the emergency. The Wheeler House remains today in the hands of the Wheeler family.

The *Knox Trail* Marker. Colonel Henry Knox, 26-year-old Boston book dealer, was commissioned during the winter of 1775-76 to transport 59 big brass cannons, military booty taken by Ethan Allen and his Green Mountain Boys when they seized British Fort Ticonderoga, for delivery to the revolutionary army then assembling in the neighborhood of Boston. Colonel Knox succeeded in dragging the cannon by ox cart and ox sled through ice and snow over virtually trackless mountains; on his hazardous trek seaward, he passed through North Egremont, South Egremont, and Great Barrington, the cannon and the feat attracting enormous admiration on the part of the general public. The sensation caused by the Knox caravan was topped after the great American victory over the English in the Battle of Saratoga when units of the defeated army were then marched through Great Barrington on their way to prison camp on the eastern seaboard, the ordinary soldiers being required to drag their cannons along with them. But the greatest sensation of all was the vivacious Baronness van Riedesel, wife of the commander of the Hessian mercenaries, who rode along with her two children in her great gilded carriage with parade dress guard attending her.

The *Indian Battle* Monument. This marker memorialized an August 1676 battle between palefaces and redskins, but historians are at a loss to reconstruct the exact circumstances. It may have occurred on the river bank at about the point where the marker is placed; it may have occurred at about the present day line of demarcation between Massachusetts and Connecticut; it may have been two separate events. Major John Talcott, with a party of English soldiers and Indian guides then on a reconnaissance mission at the end of the war against King Philip, may have attempted to surprise an Indian village at dawn and thus have provoked a pitched battle. Or Colonel William Whiting may have been in command and it was not a battle but a massacre of inoffensive Indians then disporting themselves in the river somewhere below Sheffield. In either event it was the one and only serious confrontation, early or late, between white men and Indians in the entire mid-Housatonic region. The Indians, some 75 of whom were killed or captured, were probably invading Mohawks from the Hudson River valley, whose disaster the Housatonic Indians applauded rather than deplored.

The Green River Mill (Route 23), built as a fulling mill in 1760, converted into a textile mill in 1835 and later into a gristmill which remained in operation until 1928. The mill is typical of the early structures designed to take advantage of Housatonic River waterpower.

TERRACE PLACE. Residence of Miss N. KELLOGG, Great Barrington, Mass.

RIVERSIDE. Farm and Residence of G. W. LESTER, Great Barrington, Mass.

The Rising Paper Mill (1873), noteworthy for its elaborate architectural design, the most important surviving monument of nineteenth century industrialization, remains in operation today.

Housatonic village, where these mills are located, was a typical nineteenth century company town, or rather, a multicompany town. It was built up with rows of identical company houses for employees and stylish mansions for the owners, specimens of both these genres being still preserved.

Van Deusenville was also an industrial town with an important ironworks. It is best known today for the building which was once the Congregational Church and is now a private residence. Here lived Alice Brock, the proprietress of Alice's Restaurant (in Stockbridge), the patroness of Arlo Guthrie and his clique of dramatically alienated youth.

The Fair Grounds. An annual fair used to be an important feature of New England village life, the fair at Millerton (New York) being especially celebrated for its exhibits, competitions, and other entertainments. The Great Barrington Fair, albeit much more grandiose, is now the closest approximation of such old time events; livestock shows and horse racing are its most popular attractions.

CHAPTER 9

Stockbridge, Lenox, and West Stockbridge

The original Stockbridge in 1736 was an Indian town in which, rather than being sequestered and protected on a reservation, the Indians were exposed to model whites and encouraged to emulate them. The town had the standard New England institutions — town meeting house, church, school, homes, and farms, but agriculture, commerce, industry, and society were expected to develop under Indian proprietorship. Over one hundred Indian families were actually initiated into this arcane community community, and four white families were invited to join them as apostles of enlightenment. Chiefs Umpachenee and Konkapot obligingly led their tribes into this promised town and themselves became selectmen and deacons. The London Society for the Propagation of the Gospels in Foreign Parts appointed and paid John Sergeant, a dedicated young Yale tutor, to be preacher, teacher, and mentor, and the eminent divine Jonathan Edwards was his successor. Ephraim Williams of the ubiquitous and accomplished Jonathan Williams clan, father of the stylish Abigail, bride-to-be of John Sergeant, was the first white settler, and the others were his relatives and friends, all of them people of quality.

There were exactly three fatal flaws in this arrangement. The first was the fallacy of expecting the process of development to proceed in accordance with the vision or the plans of the not necessarily omniscient developers. This fallacy has persisted, of course, throughout the present century with regard to Third World lands inhabited by people as unpredictable as the not altogether noble savages who was regarded, even by the benevolent John Sergeant, as "a Miserable and Degenerate Part of our Race." The second was rum, for which the thirsty Indian would tipsily mortgage his property. The third was the example set by the model whites — not how to uplift the red man but rather how to do him out of his land and yet otherwise do him in.

The visitor to present day Stockbridge should bear in mind that the handsome early nineteenth century Town Hall and Church replace the original and much plainer Indian school-church-meeting house built on approximately the same site. The picture postcard Main Street scene (fixed for all time in the world celebrated Norman Rockwell paintings) was originally a panorama of some 50 little Indian houses (not wigwams) built and furnished in the white man's manner. Just about all that remains today of the original Old Stockbridge are the Indian cemetery and the John Sergeant memorial Mission House (strictly speaking, the Abigail Williams Sergeant house), which stood originally on the ridge above the town, where the white families lived in sheltered isolation from the savages.

Contemporary *Stockbridge village* is no more Norman Rockwell's Stockbridge than it is John Sergeant's, but the omnipresence of the Rockwell image creates certain misapprehensions in the minds of many visitors. To be sure, Norman Rockwell lived and painted here from 1953 until his death in 1973. He occupied the Old Corner House, originally a Field family residence. It was the childhood home of the famous author, Rachael Field, whose *All This and Heaven Too* traces the story of the Field clan, especially that of Henry Martyn Field and his Parisian bride, the petite Mlle. Desportes, the accused in a sensational French trial for the murder of the Duc de Praslin. A visit to the Old Corner House, now a Rockwell museum, seems inevitable. A rival in fame only a few years ago was Alice's Restaurant (now the Village Restaurant under quite a different management), which launched Arlo Guthrie and a generation of flower children on a guitar-strumming, hair-growing, jeans-wearing quest for what it was perhaps that the Indians had and lost. But contemporary Stockbridge is not in fact a relic of the Indians or Norman Rockwell or Arlo Guthrie but rather of the extended Stockbridge intellectual-literary-cultural community of the nineteenth century, a community which stretched from Great Barrington to Pittsfield. It was dominated by the Sedgwicks—Theodore Sedgwick the lawyer and revolutionary patriot, his daughter, Catherine, "the American Jane Austin," and others of the Sedgwick, Longfellow, Field, Hopkins set which included, for instance, outsiders such as Herman Melville, Nathaniel Hawthorne, Henry Wadsworth, and Fanny Kemble).

The visible evidences of the Stockbridge legacy of several centuries past is best viewed on foot and at leisure, with visits to at least four museums and one mansion. In addition to the *Rockwell Museum*, one should view the displays of memorabilia, antiques, and collectibles in the basement of the *Stockbridge Litrary*, and then carry on to the *Merwin House*, a repository of New England Victoriana, and Mission House (1739), a revelation of colonial taste and refinement. One can sight in passing the Sedgwick mansion, still owned and occasionally occupied by members of the family and not open to the public. On the ridge above the town one can inspect Naumkeag, built and furnished according to the standards of one of the more discriminating of the very wealthy nineteenth century Americans, Joseph Hodges Choate, onetime ambassador to the Court of St. James.

The walk down the town's Main Street is best done with historical briefing notes fresh in mind. In the cemetery across from the Town Hall are the graves of the Salisbury great—the Sergeants, the Williams, the Sedgwicks, the Fields, and miscellaneous others. Next to the Mission House is the parsonage built by Rev. Dudley Field, long-time town pastor. The site of John Sergeant's original home in what was then the Indian town, a home occupied later by Jonathan Edwards, is now the grounds of the Austin Riggs Center (a psychiatric hospital). In the inconspicuous little corner house adjacent to the Center Timothy Edwards (son of Jonathan) once ran a general store, Jaheel Woodbridge (son of Sergeant's assistant) had a law office, and Cyrus Field rigged up a telegraph office to connect with his Atlantic cable. Catty-corner from it, at the main intersection, is the *Red Lion Inn*, successor to the Widow Bingham's modest tavern of revolutionary days. At the Widow Bingham's the patriots of 1774 drafted a Sheffield declaration of defiance of King George II and the Shays' rebels of 1787 warmed themselves with hot toddy while their "blue stocking" hostages shivered outside in their nightshirts.

Stockbridge and the nearby region lend themselves to excursions on the part of persons especially interested in art, theater, music, literature, or just the wonders of nature, a combination of two or more of these tastes being recommendable. The more vigorous outdoors person might well begin with a climb up *Laurel Hill* to admire the work of the Laurel Hill Association in preserving the town's natural beauty. One can continue to *Ice Glen*, a narrow rocky gorge in which ice persists even in summertime, the scene each Halloween of a torchlight procession with variety show entertainments. Next might be a climb to *Laura's Tower* to view the panorama from a 1,488 foot elevation. The climax should probably be a visit to *Monument Mountain*, where William Cullen Bryant once gave a reading of his famous poem in celebration of the mountain's majesty to a party of picnickers which included Melville, Hawthorne, and Holmes.

For those with literary bent, a brief side excursion northward into the Lenox and Pittsfield region brings one first to Edith Wharton's white marble mansion (within the Foxhollow complex) in which she wrote, inter alia, the grim New England tale called "Ethan Frome." Next comes the site of The Perch (just across from the Bellefontaine mansion), home of the famous English Shakespearean actress Fanny Kemble, now a Catholic girls' school. Then comes a replica of Hawthorne's *Little Red House* (at the back gate of *Tanglewood*), where he wrote *The House of Seven Gables* and fretted that the magnificent lake view was no Boston seascape and that the winters were much too cold for anyone with a delicate constitution. Just outside Pittsfield is *Arrowhead*, now a museum, where Herman Melville wrote *Moby Dick*;close by is Oliver Wendell Holmes's *Holmesdale*, where the urbane Autocrat of the Breakfast Table wrote the Cavinist-teasing fable of the wonderful one hoss shay.

As pre-conditioning for any such literary ramble one should sample a few of the Berkshire writings by native Berkshireans, beginning with those of Catherine Sedgwick, who presided over a salon of early nineteenth century writers and artists. It takes a dedicated reader, however, to make much headway against prose such as this in a letter from Catherine's heroine to the hero: "Some months have elapsed, dear Alsop, since we parted, and parted with a truly juvenile promise to keep up an unremitting epistolary intercourse." It is best, perhaps, to turn to the deliberate humorists. Nathan Torrey, for instance, who, being asked for a verse for the dedication of a new church, tossed off: "Flat roof, tall steeple, blind guide, ignorant people." And David Hitchcock characterized the local gentry as "That dear distinguish'd few, who claim as their inherent due, All merit, ministry, and

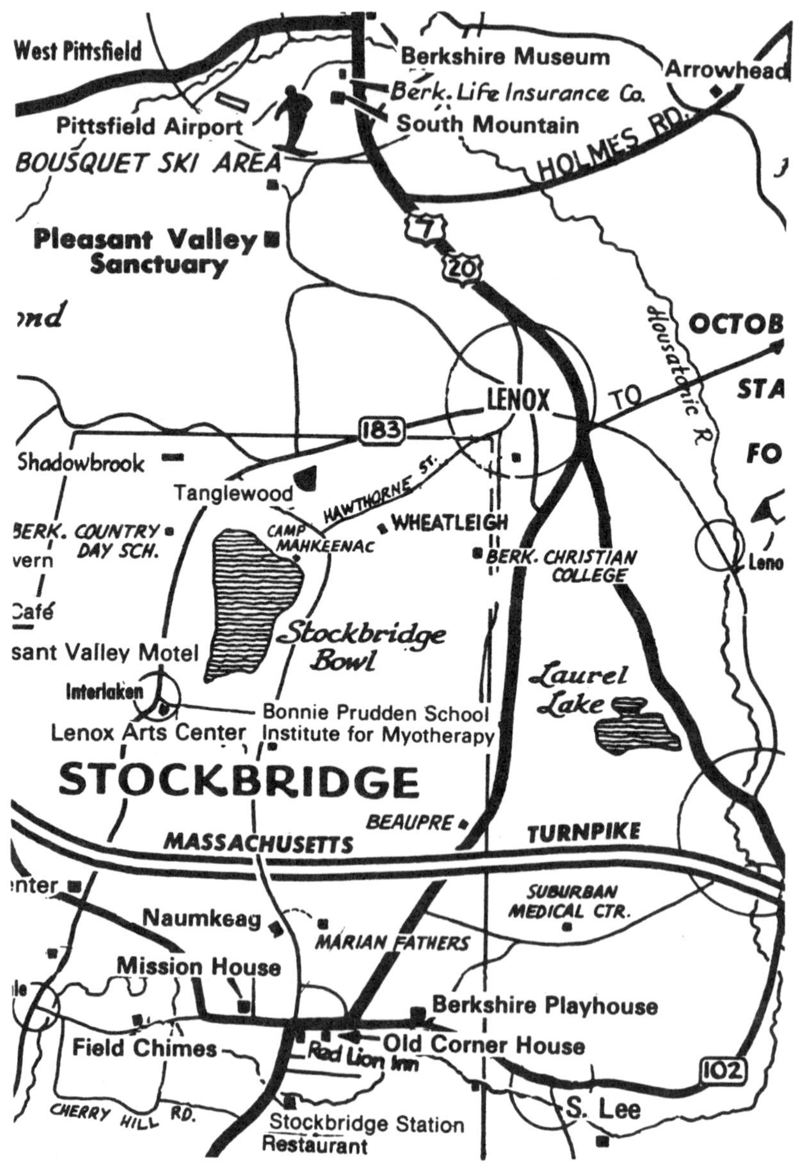

West Pittsfield
Berkshire Museum
Berk. Life Insurance Co.
Arrowhead
Pittsfield Airport
South Mountain
HOLMES RD.
BOUSQUET SKI AREA
7
20
Pleasant Valley Sanctuary
OCTOB
Housatonic R.
STA
nd
LENOX
TO
FO
183
Shadowbrook
Leno
Tanglewood
HAWTHORNE ST.
WHEATLEIGH
BERK. COUNTRY DAY SCH.
CAMP MAHKEENAC
BERK. CHRISTIAN COLLEGE
vern
Café
Stockbridge Bowl
sant Valley Motel
Laurel Lake
Interlaken
Lenox Arts Center
Bonnie Prudden School
Institute for Myotherapy
STOCKBRIDGE
BEAUPRE
TURNPIKE
MASSACHUSETTS
SUBURBAN MEDICAL CTR.
nter
Naumkeag
MARIAN FATHERS
Mission House
Berkshire Playhouse
Field Chimes
Old Corner House
Red Lion Inn
102
CHERRY HILL RD.
S. Lee
Stockbridge Station Restaurant

Stockbridge Main Street

money, Like drones that smuggle all the honey." American literature had far to go from such beginnings, but Herman Melville, among others, sped it on its way.

The art, music, theater tour means:

Chesterwood, the summer home and studio of Daniel Chester French, celebrated for the "Seated Lincoln" in Washington and the Concord "Minute Man," a Victorian mansion with splendid gardens and models of some of French's works.

Gingerbread House in Tyringham, home and studio of Sir Henry Hudson Kitson, sculptor of Lexington's "Minute Man" and Plymouth's "The Puritan Maid." A deliberate grotesquerie with support structure contrived of 80-ton chestnut beams and grottoes strewn with massive boulders, this melange now houses an art gallery in which may be found on sale the works of regional or world artists, deservedly known or unknown.

The other Berkshire cultural attractions are too well-known and well advertised to require more than bare mention: *Tanglewood* (Lenox) and its summer concert season with the Boston Symphony, the *Berkshire Playhouse* (Stockbridge) and its Theatre Festival with plays and players from Broadway and other dramatic milieu; *Jacob's Pillow* (Becket) for ballet; *Music Mountain* (near Canaan) for chamber music.

Lenox has been called the jewel of the Berkshires and not without good reason. For the connoisseur of architecture every village in the region is a temptation to loiter, but Lenox offers an especially choice set of three public buildings, plus a collection of other famous structures which range from the arresting to the appalling. The greatest architectural gem is the *Lenox Church* (Congregational), a structure of such perfection that it has been more or less authoritatively attributed to Boston's master architect, Bullfinch. The fact is that the design came right from Plate 33 of Asher Benjamin's *Country Builder's Assistant*. This popular handbook, which provided detailed specifications for construction of both public and private buildings, does much to explain the very high level of New England taste and craftsmanship. The Lenox church was built in 1805 by Benjamin D. Goodrich of nearby Richmond at cost to the congregation of $4,833.33 and could not be duplicated today for less than one million. On February 20, 1806, just seven weeks after its January 1 dedication, this serene edifice was the scene of a macabre service especially memorable even within the context of Massachusetts Calvinism. Rev. Samuel Shepard that day addressed a two-hour sermon to an almost singularly attentive congregation of which one member, at least, must have wished it would never terminate. He was Ephraim Wheeler, seated upright in his casket, condemned to death for rape of his daughter, exposed in advance as living example off the wages of sin. Only the pastor's excruciating sermon then interposed between Ephraim and the gallows, to which, with fife and drum corps escort and the congregation ghoulishly trailing him, he was about to be borne, still in his ready-to-be-closed casket.

The second gem of Lenox is the *New Court House* (now the library), built in 1816 at cost of $20,059.11, somewhat modified but by no means damaged by increasingly expensive later restorations. The old courthouse and Town Hall (1788-1791), which had already passed through several not altogether happy transformations as post office, general store, etc., was moved to another site nearby (Housatonic Street) where it now seems just a nondescript commercial building. The new Town Hall is handsome but lacks historic patina.

The third gem is the *Academy* (1803), now a Visitor's Information Center, an institution originally of great educational as well as architectural merit, having been a model for comparable schools in other towns. The early curriculum included mathematics, history, geography, English, Latin, and Greek and involved frequent "declamations" and exhibitions of penmanship. The most famous teacher was John Hotchkin, who, according to his students, managed somehow to make learning contagious even though he habitually "wore a severely solemn expression" and tolerated no nonsense about indiscipline. The tuition was $7.00 per 14-week term; room and board with private families cost $1.25 to $1.50 per week. Among the famous graduates were Alexander Hamilton Stephens (Vice-President of the Confederacy), Anson Jones (last president of the Republic of Texas), Mark Hopins (the famous educator, president of Williams College), and Henry Wheeler Shaw, otherwise known as Josh Billings, of nearby Lanesboro, the nineteenth-century Housatonic Will Rogers, who contributed witty poetry and prose to the press and shone on the lyceum circuit. Lyceum, it should be mentioned, was the rage of the intelligentsia, and the Pittsfield-Lenox region was avid for educational and cultural institutions of many types. Pittsfield, for instance, had one of the nation's first medical schools, which rivaled Harvard's in enrollment and curriculum. The students, unfortunately, robbed graves for fresh   cadavers, and so did not really set an example of piety and sobriety such as would have become aspirant professional men.

In the 1880s and 1890s Lenox went through a period of architectural frenzy when millionaire settlers from metropolitan areas built "summer cottages" of royal Graustarkian style and proportions and tried to lead lives to match. *Shadowbrook*, built in 1892 by Anson Phelps Stokes, banker and industrialist, was reputedly the largest private home ever built in America. A 410-foot long architectural pastiche with fittings and bric-a-brac intended to match size with splendor, Shadowbrook was reminiscent of a Roman bath with medieval facade and renaissance furniture. It was the home of Andrew Carnegie in his later years and then passed to the Jesuit Fathers, who converted it into a theological seminary. Shadowbrook burnt to the ground in 1956, at no great loss artistically, but also at no special gain, for it was replaced by a new seminary of modernistic design which, perhaps for aesthetic reasons, stands empty today. The townspeople have vetoed a perfectly plausible scheme to convert it into a penitentiary.

Mr. Giraud Foster who, it was widely said, made his fortune in a single day—by marrying it, built *Bellefontaine* (1890) for $2.5 million as a   replica of Le Petit Trianon. Here he resided until his death in 1945 at age 94, the last of the barons of the Gilded Age. The chateau and its contents were auctioned off in 1946 at prices which curdle the blood of today's collectors. The building and grounds went for $70,000, but even then, of course, they would have cost another $70,000 per annum to maintain. A set of 20 perfect Lowestoft dinner plates fetched $65. The Veronese marble fountainhead which Mr. Foster purchased in Italy for $10,000 was bid in at $125. The property soon passed to the Fathers of Mercy, but after a disastrous fire in 1947, it was restored in part as a seminary of the Immaculate Heart of Mary.

Lenox Village
Settled in 1767
WEST ST. RT. 183
STOCKBRIDGE RD.
MAIN ST.
HOUSATONIC
ST.
RO

Lenox Academy and Library

Wheatleigh, built in 1893 by H.H. Cook as a wedding gift for his daughter, Mrs. Carlos de Heredia, generally referred to as Countess, a misapprehension she did nothing to correct, required 60 servants to keep up house, gardens, and stables. It functions today as a deluxe inn.

To the itineraries already suggested should be added a visit to one of the most important of the nineteenth century perfectionist communities—the Hancock Shaker Village in Richmond. Shaker farm complex has been painstakingly restored and guides provide an illuminating commentary upon what was an amazingly successful experiment.

Hancock Shaker Village is worth a leisurely visit and attention to the presentations of the guides for the insight it gives into one of the most successful of the perfectionistic movements of former times. The Shaker homes and farms were models of architectural and agricultural rationality. Shaker religious practices startled more orthodox sects but would probably seem like minor deviations today. They involved much marching about and singing, speaking in tongues, and achievement of state of ecstasy induced by or resulting in physical contortions (hence the name Shaker). The Shakers stressed although they did not demand celibacy, and the membership gradually diminished until in 1960 the last two surviving members at Hancock turned the property over to a nonprofit organization to maintain as a museum and crafts center. The Shakers are now best remembered for their handsome furniture and their mechanical inventions which include the rotary harrow, the automatic spring, the turbine water wheel, the threshing machine, the circular saw, the washing machine, and the screw propeller.

The village of West Stockbridge (just off the Massachusetts Freeway and Route 41) neatly encapsulates the economic history of the region right up until the present time, with tourism as the new key industry. Here in about the year 1762, at the outlet of Williams Lake (later Furnace Lake, still later Shaker Pond), created by damming Williams Creek, Elijah Williams, scion of the Stockbridge Williams clan, built a home (1763), an iron furnace, a sawmill, a gristmill, a fulling mill, and a general store. All of this spelled almost instant growth and prosperity for a new village known successively as Williamstown, Queensboro, and West Stockbridge. The Williams ironworks, repeatedly modified and expanded, continued in operation until 1905, when it seemed more profitable to ship the ore to a more modern establishment being operated in Richmont by Salisbury iron kings, Holley and Coffing. The ironworks were then sold and converted into a gristmill, which flourished for the next century, especially during the period 1830-1867, when it was owned and operated by the Shakers (hence the name Shaker Pond) and drew upon the extraordinarily productive Shaker farms. Meanwhile two new industries developed to boom proportions—the quarrying of high grade marble, of which the town had inexhaustible deposits, and the exploitation of the limestone for the making of lime. A score or so of operations gave employment to up to 250 men each, and a new Gay and Woodruff Blast Furnace, built when vast new deposits of iron ore were discovered, gave employment to as many more.

West Stockbridge industrial output made the village the logical target for the first regional railroads. In 1831 the Hudson and Berkshire Line linked West Stockbridge with Hudson, New York (distance 34 miles; passenger fare $1.00); in 1842 the Housatonic Valley Line linked it with Bridgeport. Within a very few years the extensions of the earlier lines and the new Albany-Boston line gave the townspeople quick access to all major urban markets of New England, including, of course, New York City. The Gay and Woodruff blast furnace (which closed down in 1872) and the marble quarries (which remained open into the present century) signified a proliferation of hardware stores with the Baldwin family emerging as dominant in the business. The Baldwins acquired the Shaker gristmill (ex-Williams ironworks) to convert into another hardware outlet and to operate also as an electric power plant which provided the townspeople at a very early period with electric lighting. But twentieth century West Stockbridge was not destined to remain a significant industrial center. It went into a period of gradual but prolonged decline from which just about a decade ago it suddenly emerged as a much advertised Old Yankee Marketplace catering to tourists lured in off the Massachusetts Turnpike or from nearby Tanglewood. The Old Shaker Mill is now an antique shop and almost the whole of the business district is being redeveloped for crafts shops, boutiques, general stores, supermarkets, eateries, and other such presumed conservators of the Yankee heritage, among them a Vietnamese restaurant and the "Whistle Stop Market" at the old railway depot. The new West Stockbridge is the project of a wealthy young developer whose activities have created no little dismay among the more conservative townspeople.

The visitor interested in more than "shop-hopping," the most highly touted possibility, may care to take notice of Elijah Williams' surprisingly modest home (1763), located on the hill above the pond, the two Greek revival homes of the Baldwin family at the end of Main Street, the old Congregational Church, the Westbridge Inn, and the very numerous fine old homes of the nearby region. One one-time monument which has somehow got misplaced in the recent shuffle is the home and shop on Albany Street (just beyond the Shaker Mill) of Anson Clark, an ingenious Yankee tinkerer who improved upon many devices, including the daguerreotype, but somehow failed to achieve either fame or fortune.

West Stockbridge, it should be mentioned, was a stronghold of Shays' rebels, who provoked frequent street clashes with more orthodox villagers. West Stockbridge was also an early stronghold of Mormonism. A Mormon Society of about 30 members was organized here in 1840, much to the scandal of the rest of the community; the converts migrated in 1945 to Nauvoo, Illinois, and later to Utah.

North Egremont offers a pleasing spectacle of general store, inn, church, and gracious homes clustered about the town center. It also has a few other modest tourist attractions. An old gristmill survives in almost operable shape. A marker commemorates the emergence out of the trackless mountains in the winter of 1776-77 of Colonel Henry Know transporting by ox cart and sled the 59 big brass cannons which Ethan Allen took as booty at Fort Ticonderoga for delivery to the Boston patriots. Just outside town there is a "Shun Pike," a deviation from an old-time turnpike which enabled thrifty Yankees to by-pass a toll gate at which they would have had to pay four cents for a man on horseback, ten cents for a horse or ox-drawn cart, and four cents per dozen for herds of cattle, swine, or sheep, these being fairly standard charges for each ten-mile stretch.

South Egremont offers more, bigger, better, more commercialized buildings, no few of them purchased in the countryside by an early twentieth century real estate developer and moved to town for resale to incoming city folk. Just outside Egremont on the road to Sheffield is the Shays Rebellion marker, designed and placed almost deliberately, it would seem, to be inconspicuous.

The four karat *bijou* of the Berkshires is miniature *Alford village* with its perfect little church, school, town hall, and mansion, all tastefully grouped and displayed against a scenic hill once mined for marble, and an inviting little cemetery into which the early population (see the life spans as indicated on certain tombstones) seemed indisposed to hurry. It may be a disservice even to invite attention to secluded little Alford; but the vulgar visitor is unlikely to find anything over which to loiter, and the appreciative will wish the simulated Alfordians of today all success in their studied effort to ward off pollution in all its aspects.

CHAPTER 10

Cornwall, Litchfield, Kent, and Sharon

The Cornwall-Litchfield, Kent-Sharon circuit is an exercise of sheer self-indulgence in bucolic and parochial serenity. It is not unmarred, of course, if one seeks out the blemishes, and certainly it is no scene of naive simplicity now that urbanites have largely displaced the rustics. But it is pleasurable to a degree that may soon be gravely menaced by the very spring verdure, summer breezes, autumn colors, and winter skiing which fetch in increasingly dense relays of visitors. The numerous and rather bewildering Cornwalls (Cornwall Bridge, Cornwall Plains, Cornwall Hollow, Cornwall Center, West Cornwall, North Cornwall, etc.) are pleasant enough to get lost in — the road markings being sometimes misleading. But one would do well to concentrate upon *the* Cornwall bridge (not the village of Cornwall Bridge but the historic covered bridge at West Cornwall), and Cornwall Plains (not the original Cornwall village — now vestigial, but settled not much later and always in its miniature way much grander.

The Cornwall bridge, spanning the Housatonic at a point where especially swift rapids (fine for kayak fanciers) show up very nicely on a color photograph taken against the backdrop of a scenic hillside dotted with old houses. It is therefore a routine stop for visitors traveling along an extraordinarily agreeable stretch of riverside highway. But Cornwall Plains, a village today of only about a score of houses, is the primary objective of any visitor even mildly knowledgeable — or willing to become so — about Pastor Hezekiah Gold, Henry Obookiah, and the Generals (father and son) John Sedgwick I and II. The commingled ghosts of these local celebrities may still walk the quiet little churchyard at Cornwall Plains, but their bones rest under appropriate markers elsewhere — the old general's at the site of his home in Cornwall Hollow, the young general's and Obookiah's in the old town cemetery not far from the church. Obookiah's modest marke paid for out of charitable donations, is especially touching. This young "native of Owhyhee" (Hawaii), a one-time acolyte of an island shaman, later a trainee for Christian missions, who died very painfully of pleurisy at age of 26 in the icy Cornwall winter of 1818, passed on, according to the epitaph, "with a heavenly smile upon his countenance and glory in his soul."

Pastor Gold was the second incumbent (1755-1787) in the pulpit of the Cornwall Church (Congregational). As such, his predecessor having forfeited the right by early resignation, he was the proprietor of one-fifty-third share (725 acres) of town land, from which, by sale of very desirable home and farm plots to later comers, he became very rich. But Pastor Gold proved to be excessively arrogant and avaricious; despite his command of powerful Calvinistic hell's fire homiletics, the majority of his congregation eventually rebelled against him. They attempted to bar him from the church and called for the engagement in his place of a "serious, pious, godly, orthodox, learned minister." Pastor Gold, who had been a chaplain in the Continental Army rought back with a ferocity perhaps unbecoming a divine and on one occasion had to be placed under arrest for physical assault upon an insolent parishioner. He did have allies, however; one devout lady of the congregation, perceiving one Sunday morning that a deacon was about to pre-empt the pulpit upon which he and the pastor were converging with unseemly speed, either conked the rival on the head with her footstool or swatted him with her fan (accounts vary). In either event she sufficiently slowed him down so that the pastor could resume temporary command. Pastor Gold and his irate parishioners both resorted to the law. Finally, in 1787, the pastor settled for £100 in cash and appointment to alternative position as town representative in the state assembly at salary of 140/12/0 per annum, a not inconsiderable raise. His descendants have been prominent among Cornwall residents right up until the present time.

Obookiah of Owhyhee (Hawaii) found himself in New England   by courtesy of a certain Captain Brintnall, a Yankee trader who purchased furs in the Pacific Northwest and sandalwood in Hawaii to exchange for silks, teas, and porcelains in Canton. Orphaned in earth youth when his parents were killed in the course of local wars, apprenticed to his uncle, who tutored him in the prayers and incantations of the Hawaiian priesthood, Obookiah welcomed Captain Brintnall's invitation to sail with him to Canton and onwards to New York. Somehow the boy made his way to New Haven where he tearfully implored the authorities for admission to Harvard. Obookiah's earnestness and industry gained him various patrons, among them students, clergymen, and farmers. Reports of his plight, not unlike that of other young Hawaiians and Chinese then beginning to appear in America, gained widespread circulation in church circles. The newly created American Board of Foreign Missions, which was just then beginning to send missionaries overseas, determined upon the establishment of a Mission School in the States. The intent was to educate and convert promising young boys from "heathen lands or tribes" is company with pious American boys studying to become missionaries. The town of Cornwall, in which wealthy patrons promised to provide facilities and subsidies, was chosen as the site; the Mission School was established in the year 1817 and remained in operatin until 1827. During the decade of its existence, the school enrolled approximately 100 boys, among them 42 American Indians (from 13 tribes), 18 Hawaiians, 5 Chinese, 3 Marquesa Islanders, 2 Tahitians, and 2 Malays (one in fact a Dutch Eurasian from Sumatra, the other a Chinese-Malay from Malacca). Obookiah, one of the first of the Hawaiians, was an exemplary student and convert who helped raise money for the school by traveling with his sponsors and testifying to the Christian joy which he experienced. He died in his first year of formal study, but his *Memoirs*, published posthumously in English, Hawaiian, and Cherokee, sold briskly in ecclesiastical circles at home and abroad and went through various editions with total sales on the order of 50,000 copies.

Obookiah was certainly the most famous of the Mission School students, but it is difficult to say who was the most tragic. Two other candidates for that distinction were John Ridge and Elias Boudinot, sons of Cherokee chiefs, who created near riots in Cornwall by marrying local girls (one a Gold) and were victims of murd   after they returned with their brides to their people. At first, on the Cherokee Reservation in Georgia, the lives of these Indian-American couples seemed blissful and even inspirational. John and Elias worked to improve the lot of the Indians, but they acquiesced presently in the disastrous white man's scheme of moving the tribe from George to Arkansas — a long march on which 4,000 died. The young braves then turned against their former mentors, killing them, and expelling their wives and children from the new reservation. By that time the Mission School had already been closed. Too many of the students had had to be expelled for "indolence," "drunkenness," "irreverence," or "immorality," the record of the Chinese being especially dolorous. The sponsors had come to the conclusion that it was preferable to convert and educate young heathen in the lands or social milieu of their origins. The curriculum vitae of William Tennooe, as compiled by Edward C. Starr, historian of early Cornwall, is especially revealing:

"Tennooe, Kanui, *William Tennooee* (student) 1817-1819; came to Boston about 1809; lived as a servant; was on a privateer in the War of 1812; his brother died at Providence; he was a barber in New Haven; 1815 went to Goshen; to North Guilford, 1816; First Church, 1818; returned, 1819; excommunicated for intemperance and Sabbath breaking (the first record on the church book there); employed in a saloon; went to California; reformed and taught school about 1840; church in Honolulu; again in California during the gold fever, he made and lost a fortune; was found an irreligious bootblack in 1860, at San Francisco, by Rev. Mr. Rowell; Mariners' church, there; became blind and later was sent to his early home where he survived all the Hawaiians of the Foreign Mission School, and when he died, a monument in his memory read, . . . In the life and death of Kanui God's Providence and Grace were wonderfully manifested."

General John Sedgwick II (son of General John Sedgwick I, who fought with distinction in the War of the Revolution) was one of the top commanders of the Union Army during the Civil War and according to many of his admirers should have been named Commander-in-Chief. A graduate of West Point, a veteran of Indians Wars in the West and campaigns in Mexico, General Sedgwick performed heroic services at Bull Run, Antietam, and Gettysburg, but his troops, unfortunately, took extremely heavy losses. At Antietam, the General himself had two horses shot out from under him and was carried unconscious from the field of battle with three grievous wounds from which he was long in recovering. In the disastrous Chancellorsville Campsign he manated to save most of his troops, whom he led later in forced march to Gettysburg, where his timely arrival and brilliant strategy turned the tide of Battle. At Spottsylvania, where he was boldly exposing himself to snipers while directing the artillery fire, reassuring the men that confederate sharpshooters could not hit an elephant at that distance, he was shot dead on the spot. In the Cornwall Historical Society are preserved the general's dress uniform, his sword (gold, scabbard, jeweled hilt), and numerous letters, photographs, and other memorabilia.

Litchfield, said the eloquent Henry Ward Beecher in the mid-nineteenth century, is a village built on "two old-fashioned, lovable, livable, grass-ribboned streets of double width, crossing at right angles, on a lofty plateau, crowned by many an elm. Give or take a few trees, for many an elm has died from the Dutch elm blight but other species have been planted, the somewhat precious Beecher description still fits what is in fact a precious town. Litchfield remains both serene and shady; it has what is undoubtedly the biggest, finest collection of early American homes of any New England village and is frequently nominated as the most beautiful village in the United States.

Litchfield exercises what is known as "The Lure of the Litchfield Hills" (the name of a magazine of the 1920s and 1930s devoted to regional history and culture), which has resulted in something of a cult among residents and visitors. The true Litchfield connoisseurs deplore what they term the commercialization and vulgarization of other Berkshire towns and hold (it would be ill-bred to boast) that Litchfield remains basically unscarred. Despite the heavy traffic of swiftly transient tourists, there really is very little in the town to appeal to the action-oriented set. It is still the cultured and leisurely holiday-maker, just as it was in the 1890s, who feels himself and is made to feel sufficiently at ease to stay over and to return.

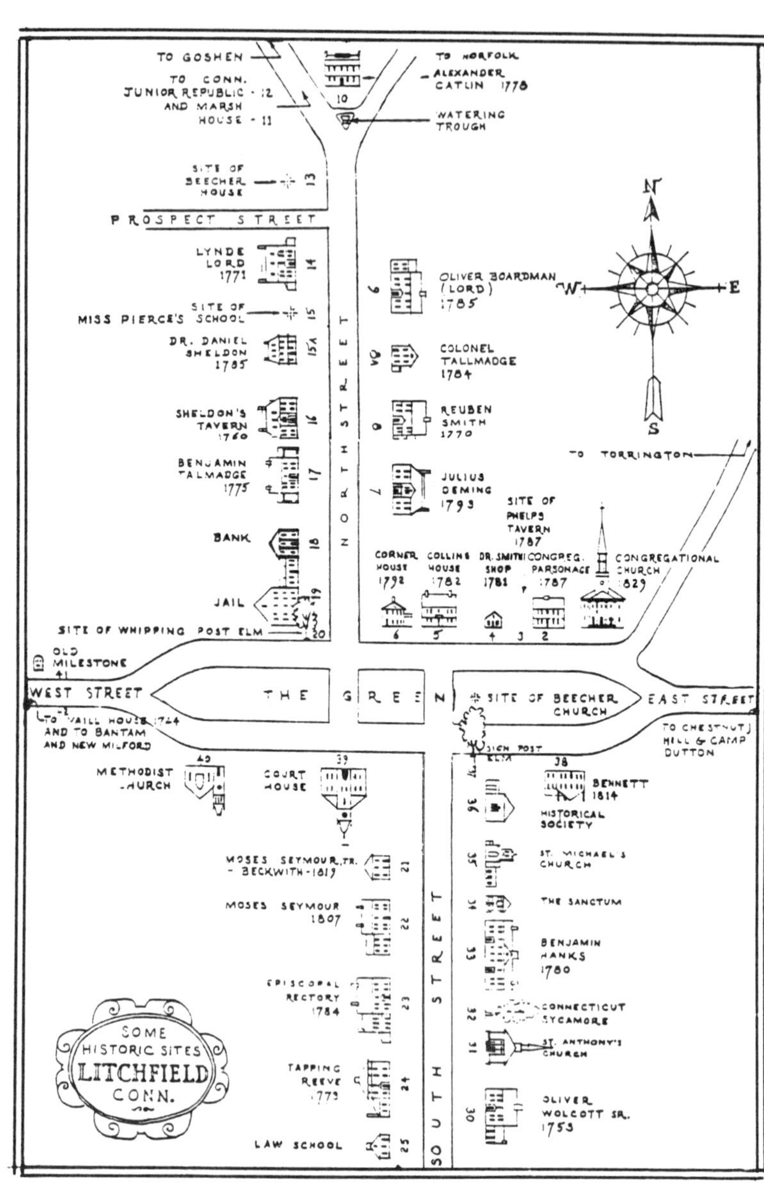

TO GOSHEN
TO CONN. JUNIOR REPUBLIC - 12 AND MARSH HOUSE - 11
TO NORFOLK
ALEXANDER CATLIN 1778
WATERING TROUGH
10
SITE OF BEECHER HOUSE 13
PROSPECT STREET
LYNDE LORD 1771 14
OLIVER BOARDMAN (LORD) 1785 6
SITE OF MISS PIERCE'S SCHOOL 15
DR. DANIEL SHELDON 1785 15A
COLONEL TALLMADGE 1784
SHELDON'S TAVERN 1760 16
REUBEN SMITH 1770
BENJAMIN TALMADGE 1775 17
JULIUS DEMING 1793 7
SITE OF PHELPS TAVERN 1787
NORTH STREET
BANK 18
JAIL 19
SITE OF WHIPPING POST ELM 20
CORNER HOUSE 1792
COLLINS HOUSE 1782
DR. SMITH SHOP 1781
CONGREG. PARSONAGE 1787
CONGREGATIONAL CHURCH 1829
6 5 4 3 2
OLD MILESTONE 41
WEST STREET
THE GREEN
SITE OF BEECHER CHURCH
EAST STREET
TO VAILL HOUSE 1764 AND TO BANTAM AND NEW MILFORD
SIGN POST ELM
TO CHESTNUT HILL & CAMP DUTTON
METHODIST CHURCH 40
COURT HOUSE 39
38
BENNETT 1814
36
HISTORICAL SOCIETY
MOSES SEYMOUR, JR. - BECKWITH - 1819 21
35
ST. MICHAEL'S CHURCH
MOSES SEYMOUR 1807 22
34
THE SANCTUM
SOUTH STREET
33
BENJAMIN HANKS 1780
EPISCOPAL RECTORY 1784 23
32
CONNECTICUT SYCAMORE
31
ST. ANTHONY'S CHURCH
TAPPING REEVE 1773 24
30
OLIVER WOLCOTT SR. 1753
LAW SCHOOL 25
N W E S
TO TORRINGTON
SOME HISTORIC SITES LITCHFIELD CONN.

West Cornwall & Covered Bridge

Even the touristical visitor to Litchfield would be well advised merely to let the village quietly impress itself upon him as he strolls aboutse along its two "grass-ribboned streets of double width" and admires its gracious architecture, duly impressed, perhaps, by the obvious wealth of the colonial gentry. With an excellent sketch map (provided free at the Tourist Kiosk, one can easily identify the historic spots, and assuming a modicum of background reading, one can associate them with the historic personages.

In Litchfield in early days, it must be remembered, the streets generally seemed less like thoroughfares and more like thickets, quagmires, or snowdrifts. Houses were unpainted and commonly set right on the road. It was a rare woodsman or townsman either who spared a tree, but early Litchfieldians made three exceptions: One was the indispensable Whipping Post Tree in front of the jail on East Street; one was the equally utilitarian Sign Post Tree in front of what is now the Historical Society; the third was the Beecher Tree, cooling the church in which Rev. Lyman Beecher's fiery sermons at times raised both temperatures and tempers. The re-greening of Litchfield began during the War of the Revolution when young Oliver Wolcott, Jr., scion of the town's most important family, planted 13 commemorative sycamores, of which only one, the Connecticut Tree, survived and survives today in front of the Catholic Church. The magnificent elms, of which Litchfield preserves proportionately more than do other New England towns which followed its example, were planted mainly during the latter half of the nineteenth century.

Litchfield town, which now seems tranquilly somnolent, was a center of great regional activity in its early days and in the year 1790 rated as the third largest town in the United States, its 20,342 population comparing with New York's 33,131, Philadelphia's 28,522, and Boston's 18,320. In the village center, on about the site now occupied by the Court House (a replacement of two successive earlier structures of very much greater architectural merit), once stood a palisaded fort and watchtower for protection against marauding Indians, who, in this particular region did remarkably little marauding. Here, during the War of the Revolution, stood huge depots for collection and distribution of munitions and foodstuffs, Litchfield being regarded as reasonably safe from British invasion and the location being conveniently close to the Salisbury ironworks and regional farmlands.

The most famous name to be associated with Litchfield is that of the forbiddingly sober and erudite Beecher family—fittingly memorialized in Lyman Beecher Stowe's *Saints, Sinners and Beechers* (1934), and immortalized by Harriet Beecher Stowe's *Uncle Tom's Cabin*. Litchfield itself, unfortunately, lacks Beecher memorials or memorabilia. The Congregational Church at the end of the village Green is a later replica, not the actual structure in which Harriet's father, Rev. Lyman Beecher, transfixed his congregation with near-heretical exegesis of orthodox Calvinism and impassioned denunciation of such popular—and many thought indispensable—stimulants as cider brandy.

The Beecher family home and barn have disappeared—removed, some say, to the site of the Spring Hill School. In them the precocious early teen-age Henry Ward Beecher practiced pulpit homiletics before more or less attentive audiences of children, horses, and cows, before going on later so to transport his congregation in Brooklyn that it forgave him his alleged dalliance with a pretty young choir singer.

The once nationwide fame also of sons Edward, Thomas, and James (preachers all) and daughters Catherine and Isabella (feminists, educators, writers) proved to be so evanescent even the thoroughly documented Litchfield Historical Society is hard put to produce the evidence. The name Beecher nevertheless carries a Litchfield cachet. Although some Litchfieldians may associate it, mistakenly, with the Great Stove War of 1816, most, if not all of them are aware that it was the Civil War which Harriet helped to induce, and that her father's sermons heated up the Congregationalists on various causes, not so much the abolition of slavery as the abolition of drinking and duelling.

The other Litchfield names most to be conjured with are Wolcott, Sheldon, Talmadge, Reeve, and Pierce. All their homes (except that of Miss Pierce) are still standing today, probably in better state of maintenance and certainly more convenient than when they themselves were in residence. Some can be visited; all can be admired from the exterior in the course of a brief and pleasant stroll along the town's two broad avenues.and the kind people in Town Hall, the Historical Society, and the Visitor's Kiosk provide such good maps, flyers, and illustrated booklets that no one need tax his memory with dates and facts or add a camera to his accoutrements.

Very briefly to rehearse the record, the Oliver Wolcotts, father and son, were town and state officials, army officers, and dedicated patriots during the revolutionary period, who later became yet more important and wealthy in industry and commerce, being, inter alia, pioneers in the China trade. The Sheldons were inn keepers and landed gentry, Colonel Elisha Sheldon being the recruiter and commander of one of Washington's very few cavalry brigades. Major Benjamin Talmadge , one of Sheldon's officers, was the very model of patriot and soldier. An especially handsome, dashing, and daring cavalryman, he was the hero of a dozen raids on British forts and the man who exposed and later befriended Major Andre, the gallant British spy. The husband of Litchfield's most beautiful and charming hostess, the father of a family of irreproachable children, the founder of the nation's first chain store, a partner of the Wolcotts in trade, Tallmadge was as prominent in peacetime as in wartime.

Mr. Tapping Reeve was the founder and chief teacher of the nation's first law school—his little one-room schoolhouse in which he instructed scores of men later to become high national and state officials still stands in his side yard. Miss Sally Pierce was the founder and chief teacher of a very famous Young Ladies Seminary which stressed learning as well as gentility. With the Wolcotts, the Sheldons, the Talmadges, Mr. Reeve's young gentlemen and Miss Pierce's young ladies—many of them from very wealthy and prominent families of the North, East, or South—the Litchfield social season was as dazzling as that of Boston and the intellectual climate as rarified.

A visit to Litchfield should include a prolonged stop at the Historical Society with its splendid museum exhibits and its collection of documents relating to town history. No visitor should miss the room of early American paintings or the Treasure Chest (on the stair landing) with the curious explanation of its origin and contents. The chest, which contained bags filled with Spanish doubloons, was sent to the society by an anonymous donor and was left lying about for years before it was opened and examined.

From Litchfield Village the visitor should proceed along Bantam Stream and around Bantam Lake to view what is now mainly a nature reserve, public park, and resort area. In or near Bantam village once stood numerous small industries— among them the Litchfield Carriage Company, which produced prestige vehicles and managed up until 1917 to compete with the automobile manufacturers. On Bantam Lake the Berkshire Ice Company used to cut 75,000 tons of ice per year for local consumption and export.

In the early parsonage (long ago moved to the property of the Spring Hill School one half-mile north of the village), which Rev. Beecher purchased for $1,350 and resold to his successor, were born and brought up a few of the very numerous Beecher children, among them Henry Ward Beecher and Harriet Beecher Stowe. Henry Ward Beecher, precocious, as were others of his clan, in his very early youth delivered practice sermons in the barn and garden and acquired the techniques which made him in later years the enormously popular pastor of the Brooklyn Plymouth Church. His dazzling personality was doomed to be somewhat dimmed by scandal—of which he was formally cleared—regarding improper relations with a pretty young choir singer and Sunday School teacher. The lady in question was the wife of his clerical assistant, a gentleman who advocated as a contributor to church papers but did not always personally endorse the practice of free love. In her Litchfield home little Harriet Beecher absorbed her antislavery principles, in part from her father, in part from an aunt, whose husband had taken a slave mistress and fathered mulatto children.

The Second Litchfield Church, not Lyman Beecher's, was the chief battlefield of the Great Church Stove War of 1816, between warmth-craving parishioners, whom others considered sinfully sybaritic, and the more frigid Calvinists, who regarded comfort as conducive to perdition. The pro-stovists prevailed and one brisk November Sunday morning just after its installation, warmed themselves gratefully fore and aft at the stove as they entered the church. The anti-stovists shunned this contrivance of Satan and the especially godly Mrs. Peck, almost swooning from the hellish heat, had to be assisted into the open air. The stove was as yet unlighted.

If heating caused a battle, seating started community feuds. Occupancy of the front pews constituted incontrovertible evidence of status, and there were never enough pews in the front or near the front to satisfy the status-seekers. The deacons drew up elaborate criteria based upon age, wealth (as measured by taxes), office (deacons took precedence over selectmen), piety, charity, and accumulation of other merit points. One formula called for calculation of the property taxes paid by the head of the family over a period of 20 years, then the addition of 20 shillings for each year of his age, plus other sums for public services in order to establish, as it were, his net spiritual worth. The computers of the period were not quite up to the task, nothing served to defuse animosities, and those who occupied the front pews did so by reason of such total self-assurance that interlopers wilted and withdrew.

The Litchfield names most to be conjured with in the period of the town's greatest glory, the late eighteenth century, were Wolcott, Sheldon, Talmadge, Reeve, and Pierce. In the Wolcott family mansion first lived Oliver Wolcott, Sr., revolutionary patriot who caused George III's gilded statue to be hauled by ox cart from New York City to Litchfield, there to be melted down for bullets for return via minute men's muskets to the king's military proxies. Here also lived Oliver Wolcott, Jr., Washington's Secretary of the Treasury. After being badly scarred in the already vicious bureaucratic in-fighting of the nation's capital, where he was accused, for instance, of trying to burn down the treasury to destroy evidences of defalcation, Oliver, Jr., recouped his fortunes in the China Trade and re-established his personal prestige as Governor of Connecticut.

The present day village of *Kent* dates from the 1820s but some of the choicest buildings of the original town, now known as the *Flanders Region*, still survive in a remarkably happy state of preservation and renovation. On the west side of the road stand homes originally built and occupied by owners of gristmills who exploited the waterpower of Cobble Brook. One of them, Mr. Jonathan Morgan, was also a shoemaker and in his spacious basement he operated a very popular tap room. Another building, the largest of the group, was once Flanders Arms, an inn very highly thought of by travelers of the revolutionary wartime period. On the east side of the road the very distinctive building with the double entryway housed simultaneously a general store, a fur trading station, a butcher shop (basement) and a ballroom (second floor). The old meeting house has vanished, as has the original school, but a small schoolhouse dating from the early 1800s still stands, occupied now as a private home, also half a dozen other old buildings, several of them the homes of early artisans. Flanders provides prime examples of the very best in early American architecture of the three important genres, colonial, federal, and neoclassic, or Greek Revival.

Kent town once had an ironworks which rivaled that of Salisbury in importance; the fine stone furnace now stands within the grounds of the well-known *Sloan Museum* of early American Tools, close to a model of an early settler's cabin. To introduce the distinctive aspects of town history, however, it is necessary to recount something of the story of the Schaghticoke (or Scatacook) Indians, and that also of Bull's Bridge, an authentic although frequently and extensively rebuilt covered bridge which is still in service.

The Schaghticoke Indians, who sold Kent to the early white settlers, suffered an even more wretched fate than did those of Stockbridge, whose community some of the Kent tribespeople joined. Almost as soon as the English town of Kent was settled, the Indians petitioned the townspeople for assignment of a missionary who would bring them "the sweet words of Jesus." Receiving no reply, they applied to the Moravian Brothers, German missionaries from Saxony then active in New York State, where Count Zinzendorf and his daughter Benigna had just begun to preach and teach at Shekomeko in what is now Dutchess County. In 1743 a Moravian missionary and his wife settled in Kent, where they encountered much hostility, especially on the part of the pastor, Rev. Cyrus Marsh. Charged with being agents of the French and inciting the Indians to massacre the English, the Moravians were soon expelled. In 1749 others settled in the town and within the next several years they opened a school and a church, baptized 150 Indians, and made noteworthy progress ineducation. Again in 1763 the **Moravians** were expelled and this time many of their converts followed them to their new field of endeavor in Pennsylvania.

The remaining Kent Indians, a mere score or so of families, were resettled on a minute Indian reservation, some 200 acres of land on the west bank of the river just below Kent village and another 2,000 acres as hunting reserve in the hills, which were set aside in 1752 for their use. The Kent census of 1774 showed a population of 74 Indians. Revolutionary wartime records indicate that some of the braves (there is mention of an improbable total of 100) served as scouts for the continental army. Others manned the signal system—drums and fifes—which transmitted official messages up and down the Housatonic valley in a matter of hours. During this same wartime period, however, the Kent Indian reservation was drastically reduced, much of the land being leased out to pay off Indian debts. In the course of the next few years the Indian population virtually disappeared from the town, the few remaining acres of reservation land being occupied today by persons of mixed blood.

Bull's Bridge, three miles south of Kent village, was not the earliest of the town bridges (chronologically it was the fourth), but the most important. It carried the main traffic between Hartford on the Connecticut and Fishkill and Poughkeepsie on the Hudson, thus linking the important regional river ports. The bridge was built in 1771 at their own expense by the wealthy landowners William Johnson and David Lewis, who were authorized by the General Assembly to charge a toll of two pence for a man mounted on horseback and three pence for a driver with a cart. It took its name from the Bull family—Isaac Bull and his four sons, John, Jacob, Thomas, and Abraham, owners and operators of a nearby iron furnace, gristmill, and sawmill.

Jacob Bull, the second son, built an inn at the foot of the bridge—possibly the building which now stands in the northeast corner of the road intersection. The inn prospered from the first, and upon the outbreak of the War of the Revolution it was always crowded with travelers and carters. But Jacob Bull, unfortunately, aroused the resentment and hostility of the townspeople; as a Quaker, he refused to volunteer for military service and he may have harbored deserters, or even, it was whispered about the town, fugitive royalists. Relations between the villagers and the brothers Bull became especially tense when John and Abraham, who had yielded to public pressure to volunteer, refused to obey orders to march with their regiment to Fairfield. To make matters worse, Jacob's young son, Jeremiah, did "breke the Saboth by going a whortelberrying (blueberrying)," almost as grave an offense against God and man; the boy was apprehended and put on trial for his crime.

Jacob and his wife Mary were presently taken to court, charged most specifically with passing counterfeit money but guilty, according to public opinion, of "atrocious crimes" adding up to "high treason." They were both convicted, but only John was held in jail. He was faced with the probability of being sentenced to ten years of hard labor in the infamous Newgate prison (now restored as a museum), a copper mine near Winsted where royalists and criminals were confined in dank underground cells and worked like slaves. Jacob escaped from jail and disappeared for over a year. Upon being apprehended he was lodged in the Litchfield jail—much to be preferred to Newgate since it catered to VIP royalists. In October 1778, having posted £300 bond and pointed out that his brothers were then actually serving in the army, Jacob was released. He resumed the management of his inn, which served as a collection point for the grain, beef, and pork that Kent provided in abundance for the army.

Bull's Bridge, it may be noted, was the scene of a mysterious misadventure obliquely but provocatively referred to in certain historical records. George Washington, mounted on horseback, was traveling with his entourage through Kent when at the Bull Bridge someone, or something important—was it George, or his horse, or George and his horse, or perhaps just a horse-drawn goods wagon?— slipped off the bridge and was pulled out only with very great difficulty. At any rate it seems to have cost $215 to recover a horse, perhaps also a rider and/or a vehicle, from the river currents, a very pricey operation by the standards of the times even though the new national currency was by then badly depreciated.

Sharon, like Litchfield, is to be savored. It is remarkably like Litchfield in appearance and has been populated by people of distinction and discernment. Curiously, however, the town history has never been compiled save for a very sketchy early work by Charles Sedgwick, one of the less gifted members of the very important Sedgwick clan, and few of its personalities have been publicly celebrated. A certain Mr. Joseph Bostwick, however, built a simple household contrivance so much better than that of any of his competitors that the world duly beat a path to his door and Sharon enjoyed fame as the Mousetrap Capital of the Universe. Another inventive genius, young Andrew Hotchkiss, virtually paralyzed from birth, first fashioned himself mechanical aids to muscular control and then perfected numerous other devices which made the fortunes of Hotchkiss and Company of which his brother Benjamin Berkeley Hotchkiss was the head. Andrew designed, inter alia, the adjustable wrench, the double-headed ox-bow pin, the locomotive snow plow, and various improvements relating to projectiles which resulted in the Hotchkiss repeating rifle and air cooled machine gun. Hotchkiss and Company, which started in Sharon at the site of an old Indian burial ground on Webotuck Stream, presently established branches in New York, Bridgeport, and Hartford and sent its agents around the world to sell armaments to international warmakers and peacekeepers well in advance of Dupont de Nemours.

Sharon was known also a century ago for its manufacture of superior and very stylish hats, clocks, cabinets, and satinets, but one finds its industrial products today only in antique shops. Rev. Henry Ward Beecher suggested that Sharon (like Salisbury) would be a good location in which to engage in leisurely exploration, but no one has as yet really explored the town's potential or given it the multiple star Baedecker billing which it deserves. No doubt many of the townspeople prefer such obscurity and anonymity, but the collections in the Hotchkiss Library, the historical society, and Town Hall constitute lures which some historian some day will be unable to resist.

The one most memorable historical event relating to the region was a curious revolutionary wartime engagement which occurred in Washington Hollow (south of Milbrook) between patriots and Tories. At the time of the approach of General Burgoyne and his army out of Canada, a body of 200 armed Tories, most of them from Dutchess County, moved through the countryside with intent, it seems, to join the invaders. A force of 100 patriots from Sharon and Amenia marched off to intercept them. Just as the Tories were drilling and parading one morning in front of a public house near Bloom's Mills, the patriots advanced upon them, opened fire, and dispersed the band. Apparently there were no casualties, but the patriots took 40 Tory prisoners who were confined for 2 years in the old English church in Sharon (then used as a barracks) and for 2 more years in Exeter, New Hampshire.

CHAPTER 11

Through Ancram and Mt. Washington to the Hudson

New York State's Columbia Country has so significantly impinged upon and deviated from the adjacent towns of Berkshire and Litchfield Counties that the New York border region warrants at least a brief survey and visit on the part of the Berkshire-Litchfield devotee. The history of Columbia County as a whole and Ancram Town in particular is inextricably involved in that of Livingston Manor. So an excursion into New York cannot logically stop short of the Hudson River site of Clermont Mansion, the secondary seat of the *patroons*, that is, the Lords of Livingston Manor.

To drive through Ancram town and immediately adjacent areas is to retrace the one-time itineraries of the now almost traceless "Ancram Screechers," alias the Tin Horn and Calico Indians. These were irate tenants of the Hudson River Valley *patroons* masquerading as Indian braves to harass sheriffs bent upon evicting them for their refusal after two centuries to go on paying rents on the lands and enterprises which they themselves and their ancestors had developed. One center of defiance—but of none of the numerous scenes of terrorization and violence—was Ancram village, the site of the first of the important Livingston industrial operations. The Lords of the Manor (of English, not Dutch descent) built here on Roeliff Jansen Kill (stream) an iron furnace and foundry, which richly supplemented their income from farms, forests, and trading in furs with the Indians.

Roeliff Jansen (RoeJan) Kill (Stream), which flows North-South through Ancram Town, is named for an early Swedish settler who, when once traveling by boat between Fort Orange (Albany) and Nieuw Amsterdam, was caught in the winter freeze and marooned on shore at a spot where an important stream joined the Hudson—a stream which he presumably explored. Jansen's life story warrants an aside as a revealing episode in the history of the region and the state. Originally a migrant from the Swedish island of Marstrand to the city of Amsterdam in search of his fortune, Jansen, accompanied by his wife, Anneke, their two daughters, and Anneke's mother, Tryn, soon traveled onward to Nieuw Amsterdam. In America he rose rapidly in status from that of tenant farmer to that of *sehepens* (sheriff) on the manor of Killian van Rensselaer and became a prominent figure at Fort Orange. Falling out eventually with the van Rensselaers, Jansen transferred himself and his family back to Nieuw Amsterdam, where he entered the service of the Dutch West India Company on its Manhattan Island farmlands. Presently he acquired personal title to a very great deal of Lower Manhattan real estate, which, upon his death, he left to his widow. Anneke later married Dominie Everhard Bogardus, pastor of the Dutch church, by whom she had several more children. Upon the dominie's death by drowning when his ship foundered off the English coast, Anneke inherited his considerable properties to add to the Jansen-Bogardus descendants discovered a flaw in the Bill of Sale to Lovelace. The signature of one of the heirs, it seems, had been omitted. The subsequent lawsuits tied up the New York courts for 150 years. Trinity Church won the lands, but the Jansen-Bogardus case broke all previous records of protracted litigation.

Present day *Ancram village*, scenically located on a ridge above the iron furnace site, is a monument to the successful modern manufacturing enterprise of Kimberly Clark (a cigar wrapper factory where the iron furnace once stood) and the recent unsuccessful venture of a pair of New York city aesthetes who sought to create an elite tourist attraction with art and culture as the lure. This involved the conversion of the old time church, grange store, tavern, and Livingston family lodge into an opera house, an art gallery, a boutique, a deluxe inn with gourmet cuisine, and proprietors' residence. The residue is still on view and on sale.

Nearby *Ancramdale* is worth driving to and through as an example of a smaller village—once known as Hot Lands for its rich and presumably earth-heating deposits of lead, now mined out—which has been more modestly restored for more utilitarian purposes. And Gallatin warrants at least a pause long enough to read the village historical marker cataloging the railways, inns, taverns, and stores which once serviced a population ten times as large as today's. But the primary target of the visitor interested in ties to the Berkshires should be Clermont.

There are two convenient points of entry or exit into or out of Ancram Town. The first is Millerton, a Litchfield county village manque which, in the early days, was almost a dependency of Salisbury. The second is Boston Corner (or Corners), a once infamous scrap of real estate in the tri-state triangle at the tip of the oblong— a narrow fifty-mile strip of land over which the states of New York, Massachusetts, and Connecticut long quarreled. Boston Corners in particular was at once claimed and disclaimed by each of the three states, which wished to clarify and extend its boundaries but hesitated to accept responsibility for policing what came to be called Hell's Acres.

The visitor need budget no time for an actual stop either in Millerton or Boston Corner. Millerton is said to have some fine homes, which require some hunting. It has little, however, in the way of local lore unless one places even token credence in the implausible tale of a certain Sarah Reynolds, whose home still stands just north of the village. One night during the winter of 1776, said Sarah, three Tories climbed down her chimney and got themselves cremated in her log fire. Sarah produced neither buttons nor bones in corroboration of her fable, but for lack of a better, it has become part of the village annals. And Boston Corners has nothing except a very inconspicuous market to remind one that here, on October 12, 1853, there occurred, among many other events of highly dubious propriety, let alone legality, the famous Sullivan-Morrisey prize fight. This distinctly unsporting event, for which the railways laid on special trains out of New York City and Albany, was witnessed by mobs of shady sporting types, who converted a totally unQueensburyian match into an almost equally bloody and bruising public riot. They thus managed, as most people thought to be impossible, still further to blacken the reputation of this long isolated sylvan retreat of horse thieves, smugglers, counterfeiters, and other unsavory characters. Boston Corner today is a little resort and retirement community which has buried and forgotten its past.

Boston Corner is most highly to be recommended at present as a point of entry to or exit from Ancram—or, to be more precise, since this one-time junction of important railroads now lies on no marked highway, one should travel via nearby Copake Falls (not Copake village). To do so is to get a glimpse of the ruins of the Copake Iron Furnace and to make a scenic drive up or down Bash-Bish Gorge. It might even allow for a hike along a mile or two of not very rugged trail to view Bash-Bish Falls, a favorite resort of nineteenth century picnickers which might appeal even to more blasé moderns. And beyond Bash-Bish Falls and Gorge lies the town of Mt. Washington.

Mt. Washington is a beautifully scenic curiosity—an incorporated town with year round population of less than 100 persons occupying the highest and most isolated part of Western Massachusetts. From early colonial times until the mid-nineteenth century some part at least of the Mt. Washington real estate was under dispute between New York and Massachusetts or Massachusetts and Connecticut, the definitive boundaries being difficult to determine, in part because of over-lapping claims, in part because of faulty surveying.

Mt. Washington's earliest settlers were Dutchmen who came in from Rensselaer and Livingston Manors in the 1750s, in order to escape from the onerous conditions of land tenancy imposed by the Hudson River Valley *patroons*. The *patroons*

Livingston Manor (Ancram)

Hamlet House

Shaker Family Village & Arrowsmith

attempted to project their authority into this remote region, thus provoking the settlers to acts of retaliation which, in turn, stirred up minute and sporadic border warfare. The settlers, for instance, several times raided Livingston lands, creating disorders, seizing hostages, and defying the authorities. The leader of the settlers was John Hallenbeck, and "Hallenbeck's Hubbub" had loud repercussions in Albany and Boston. Mt. Washington eventually acquired status as a Berkshire County town and a population of a hundred or so farmers who provided it with the standard fixtures—town hall, church, school, gristmill, sawmill, forge, general store, etc., some of which structures still survive. The year-round population has dwindled, but summer residents and other visitors have multiplied to the point that traffic on the twisty road up from Bash-Bish Falls calls for an alert driver. The falls, it should be mentioned, is one of the scenic wonders of New England, and the climb (or ride) to the peak of Mt. Everett (2,624 feet) is rewarded on a clear day with a stunning view out over Massachusetts, Connecticut, and New York.

The Mt. Washington town hall is a reminder that for many years Mt. Washington residents turned out at break of day to cast their votes in presidential elections in order that the town returns might be the first in the nation to be reported, the town thus gaining a reputation not precisely as a bellweather, but undeniably a leader.

Mt. Washington was once well known for its potato crop. The crop today is blueberries, not wild, but cultivated. Visitors who seek to "go a whortleberrying," as in former times, will commit trespass upon state or private land; they had best content themselves with viewing birds, butterflies, and foliage, the latter especially to be recommended in spring and fall.

Clermont, a Livingston family mansion set in a 15,000 acre park high on the bank of the Hudson, gives some clue to the one-time magnificance of the greatest of the river valley *patroons.* The property was given by old Philip Livingston, founder of the line, to Robert, his second son, when the manor proper passed to the eldest son in what amounted to entail. The original manor house at Hudson was long ago destroyed by fire, as was a secondary mansion on the same property; but Clermont, which was burnt by marauding British soldiers in 1777 but promptly rebuilt in much the same style as before, remains intact as example of family style and taste. It remained in the hands of Robert's direct descendants up until the year 1962, when the survivors turned it over to the State of New York to open to the public. It is fitted and furnished as it was for the Livingstons; family portraits adorn the walls; family heirlooms, antiques of museum quality, are in their accustomed place. From Clermont one can gaze out today, as did the Livingstons, over one-time Livingston properties stretching as far as the Catskills on the West Bank of the Hudson; just as the Livingstons ruled the lands, so too they virtually ruled the waters, for Hudson River sail navigation in the early days and for several decades even steam navigation later on were subject to their control.

Lacking more extensive personal properties to supervise, Robert Livingston I devoted himself to his profession as a lawyer, and so too did his son and heir, Robert II. Robert II was one of the drafters of the Declaration of Independence; he administered the presidential oath of office to George Washington; he served for ten years in Washington's cabinet as Secretary of Foreign Affairs. The most glorious episode of his career was his negotiation of the Louisiana Purchase. Rather than settling, in accordinace with his instructions, merely for New Orleans and the Mississippi delta, he got Napoleon's consent to the purchase of the whole enormous American Southwest. The French, to be sure, were so apprehensive that the English would take these lands by force and not by bargaining that they were eager to offload and would probably have settled for less than Livingston offered. Nevertheless, his coup of acquiring 885,000 square miles of prime real estate for

$15,000,000 far surpassed even old Philip's feat of acquiring his original 800 square miles of Hudson River Valley land for an investment of about $20,000. It was a coup for which he never got full credit, for a newly appointed American Ambassador to France arrived at just the moment that the papers were to be signed and accepted the felicitations.

In certain respects the most inglorious aspect of Robert II's career related to his claims to virtually exclusive rights of navigation on the Hudson River. While in Paris consorting with Talleyrand and Napoleon, Robert II met Robert Fulton, later to become his partner and the husband of his niece, who was then trying to sell French investors a steamship for operation on the Seine, a deal which did not come off. Livingston and Fulton joined forces. With the former's money and the latter's engineering skills, they designed, built, and put into the operation, not on the Seine, as originally planned, but on the Hudson, the steamship, appropriately named the *Clermont*, which introduced a new era of waterborne transportation. On August 11, 1807, with Robert II entertaining a party of V.I.P.s on board to caviar and champagne, the *Clermont* made the 150-mile run between New York City and Albany in the mind-boggling time of 32 hours. Well in advance of this triumphant excusion, Livingston had thoughtfully obtained, in partnership with Nicholas Rossevelt (who presently dropped out), the exclusive rights of steam navigation within the State of New York. The *Clermont* was the first of a small fleet of vessels which, for the next 17 years, plied the Hudson to the very considerable enrichment of the Livingston and the Fulton families.

Competitors became interested, naturally, in breaking the Livingston-Fulton monopoly. Cornelius Van Derbilt, captain of a rival steamship, the *Bellona* introduced service between Elizabethtown, New Jersey, and the Battery, thus trespassing, according to the Livingston lawyers, into restricted New York State domain. Van Derbilt managed artfully to dodge the process servers who boarded the *Bellona* each time it put in at the Battery, and in retaliation he caused the New Jersey courts to prohibit the Livingston packets, for whatever reason, be it winds, currents, obstructions, or faulty navigation, from crossing the invisible New Jersey-New York state boundary line drawn down the exact middle of the river. Further to publicize his case he somehow outfitted himself one day with valid New York State papers and then submitted to arrest, only to prove in court that the Livingstons were subjecting him to undue harassment. He then engaged the incomparable Daniel Webster to carry his cause all the way to the United States Supreme Court, which pronounced monopoly "repugnant" to American democratic society and thus opened the Hudson to free competition.

The Livingstons (not Robert's descendants, who held no patent, but the main family line) were soon to lose their monopolistic control over lands and the installations thereon which, for generations, they had refused to sell. In the mid-nineteenth century, as noted above, the "Tin Horn and Calico Indians" forced the Livingstons and other Hudson River valley *patroons* to "emancipate their serfs." There had been prior cases of parting with property but relatively few and insignificant in comparison with the vast family holdings. As a special favor to his brother-in-law, M. Peter de Labigarre, an aristocratic Frenchman, Robert II himself, for instance, made a grant of 150 acres of prime real estate on which de Labigarre built himself the stately Chateau de Tivoli to serve, presumably, as the center of a new

Clermont

Robert R. Livingston

Map of Clermont

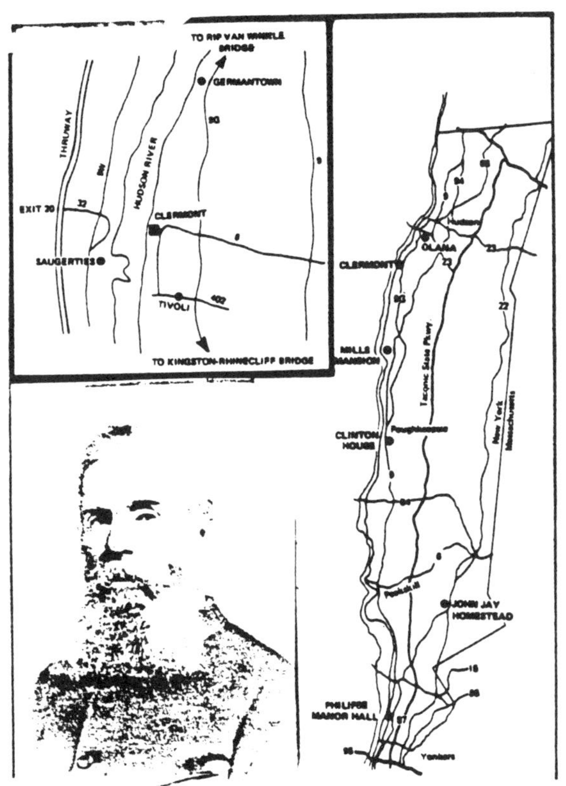

Herman Melville

community to be created by other royalist refugees from the French revolution. Tivoli attracted numerous aristocratic visitors but no settlers willing to work with their hands. The one really serious settler was Madame de la Tour du Pin who rented a farm not far off and actually worked it in person, more to the amazement than the admiration of certain exquisite callers who found her new style of living unbecoming the chatelaine of extensive properties in Europe, which, in fact, tiring of the frontier, she eventually returned to postrevolutionary France to reclaim. There seem to be no extant traces of the Chateau de Tivoli and the people of present day Tivoli are mystified if one asks about it.

Across the river at present day Athens the Livingstons patronized one of the mid-nineteenth century perfectionistic experiments to the extent at least of selling off home sites to utopian settlers on streets named Liberty, Equality, Love, Happiness, Beer, Cider, Art, Science, and also, of course, Livingston. The Hudson River valley was the scene of other Nirvanas, most of which flourished only momentarily. At Haverstraw, for instance, the Franklin Community Owenite experiment persisted for just six months (1825) before the members decided to desist from shared labor and to discriminate between thine and mine. Shalom, the New Zion, founded in 1838 by 11 New England Jews, lasted all of 4 years. The founders bought 500 acres of land and hired builders to put up a synagogue, a museum, an art gallery, a store, two factories (one for quill pens, one for fur hats), and 11 houses. They later conceived the ingenious scheme of buying up used clothing cheap in New York City, reconditioning it in Shalom, and peddling the produce to the upriver rustics as the latest in urban fashions. But even recycled fashion could not effectively fashion a viable new town.

The visitor to Clermont House will probably wish to extend his itinerary to see how other prominent American families of a later era also managed to achieve a style of living appropriate to their means and condition. The tourist brochures advertise a wide choice of targets. The two nearest to Clermont are the Mills and the Vanderbilt estates, each in its way overpowering although not necessarily in quite the manner which the owners fancied. It need scarcely be mentioned that the mansion of another distinguished American family in whose veins flows *patroon* blood is located at Hyde Park.

The more mobile and resolute visitors to the Berkshire-Litchfield area will no doubt extend their explorations up and down the Hudson River valley and for that matter that also of the Connecticut, for here, as in the less traveled mid-Housatonic region, the roots of American history are always and ofttimes agreeably manifest. And the visitor who confines himself basically to the Housatonic may wish to travel northward at least through Pittsfield and onward to Williamstown, if only to enjoy the superlative scenery and to visit, in Pittsfield, the Berkshire Museum, and in Williamstown, the **Clark** Art Institute. He would be well advised, however, to avoid industrial Adams and to proceed only with reduced expectations through decreasingly inviting territory southward to Long Island Sound. The more adventuresome can accomplish much of this itinerary by bicycle, canoe, kyak, or even, in stretches, by hang glider, with side excursions on foot along the Appalachian Trail. This is a part of the United States into which the influx of tourists of all varieties is becoming ever more modish and massive. But it is one also in which the resourceful traveler can readily seek out as yet serenely beautiful and untrampled enclaves where the one-time "hideous, howling wilderness" has been tamed and garnished and endowed with an abiding sense of a benevolent human and national destiny.

BIBLIOGRAPHY

Atwater, Francis, *History of Kent, Connecticut*, Meriden, 1897.

Bellamy, Edward, *The Duke of Stockbridge: A Romance of Shays' Rebellion*, Cambridge, 1962.

Berkshire: The First Three Hundred Years — 1697-1979, Pittsfield, 1976.

The Berkshire Hills (Federal Writers' Project), New York, 1939.

Birdsall, Richard Davenport, *Berkshire County: A Cultural History*, New York, 1959.

Brooks, Van Wyck, *The Flowering of New England 1815-1865*, New York, 1936.

Carmer, Carl, *The Hudson* (Rivers of America Series), New York, 1939.

Christman, Henry, *Tin Horns and Calico: A Decisive Episode in the Emergence of Democracy*, New York, 1945.

Church, Samuel, and A.H. Holley, *Historical Addresses Delivered by...*, Litchfield, 1842.

Crossman, Joseph W., *A New Year's Discourse, Delivered at Salisbury*, Hartford, 1803.

Dangerfield, George, *Chancellor Robert Livingston of New York, 1747-1812*, New York, 1960.

Davis, Ann Soper, ed., *Kent 1776: A Connecticut Town Two Centuries Ago*, Kent, 1976.

Deming, Dorothy, *Settlement of Litchfield County*, New Haven, 1933.

Dewey, Chester, *A History of the County of Berkshire, Massachusetts*, Pittsfield, 1829.

Fales, Edward D., *The Story of Falls Village*, Lakeville, 1972.

Garnett, Edna Bailey, *West Stockbridge, Massachusetts*, West Stockbridge, 1976.

Gladden, Washington, *From the Hub to the Hudson*, Boston, 1869.

Gold, Theodore S., *Historical Records of the Town of Cornwall, Litchfield County, Connecticut*, Hartford, 1904.

Hard, Walter, *The Connecticut* (Rivers of America Series), New York, 1947.

Hart, Albert Bushnell, *Commonwealth History of Massachusetts*, New York, 1927.

A History of the Roeliff Jansen Area, Ancram, 1975.

Holland, Josiah Gilbert, *History of Western Massachusetts: the Counties of Hampden, Hampshire, Franklin, and Berkshire*, 2 vols., Springfield, 1855.

Jones, Electa F., *Stockbridge, Past and Present, or Records of an Old Mission Station*, Springfield, 1854.

Kilbourne, Payne Kenyon, *Sketches and Chronicles of the Town of Litchfield: Historical, Biographical, and Statistical*, Hartford, 1859.

Kimball, Richard A., ed., *Commemorative Guide: Bicentennial Celebration*, Lakeville, 1976.

Leder, Lawrence H., *Robert Livingston, 1654-1728, and the Politics of Colonial New York*, Williamsburg, 1961.

Lockwood, John H., ed., *Western Massachusetts: A History 1636-1925*, 2 vols., New York, 1926.

MacCracken, Henry Noble, *Old Duchess Forever: The Story of an American County*, New York, 1956.

McHugh, Jeanna, *Alexander Holley and the Makers of Steel*, Cambridge, 1980.

MacLean, George Edwin, *History of Great Barrington (Berkshire)*, 2 vols., Great Barrington, 1928.

Middlebrook, Louis F., *Salisbury Connecticut Cannon: Revolutionary War*, Salem, 1955.

Miller, Perry, *The New England Mind*, New York, 1939.

Obookiah, Henry, *Memoirs of...*, Elizabeth, N.J., 1819.

Olcutt, Samuel, *The Indians of the Housatonic and Naugatuck Valleys*, Hartford, 1882.

Osborn, Norris Galpin, ed., *History of Connecticut in Monographic Form*, 5 vols., New York, 1925.

Palmer, Charles J., *History of Lenox and Richmond*, Pittsfield, 1904.

Perry, Clay, and John L.E. Pell, *Hell's Acres: A Historical Novel of the Wild East in the 50's*, New York, n.d.

Pettee, Julia, *The Rev. Jonathan Lee and His Eighteenth Century Salisbury Parish: The Early History of the Town of Salisbury, Connecticut*, Salisbury, 1957.

Preiss, Lillian E., *Sheffield: Frontier Town*, North Adams, 1976.

Rand, Christopher, *The Changing Landscape: Salisbury, Connecticut*, New York, 1968.

Rome, Adam Ward, *Connecticut's Cannon: The Salisbury Furnace in the American Revolution*, Hartford, 1977.

Rudd, Malcolm D., *A Brief Military History of Salisbury, Connecticut*, Salisbury, 1910.

    An Historical Sketch of Salisbury, Connecticut, New York, 1899.

Sedgwick, Charles. F., *History of the Town of Sharon*, Hartford, 1842.

Sedgwick, Sarah Cabor, and Christina Sedgwick Marquand, *Stockbridge 1739-1974*, Stockbridge, 1974.

Shepherd, Henry L., *Litchfield:Portrait of a Beautiful Town*, Litchfield, 1969.

Smith, Chard Powers, *The Housatonic: Puritan River* (Rivers of America Series), New York, 1946.

Smith, Joseph Edward Adams, *History of Berkshire County, Massachusetts*, Pittsfield, 1872.

    , *The History of Pittsfield* (*Berkshire County*), Massachusetts, 2 vols., Boston and Springfield, 1869-1876.

Starr, Edward C., *A History of Cornwall, Connecticut*, New Haven, 1926.

White, Alain C., *The History of the Town of Litchfield, Connecticut*, Litchfield, 1920.

Wood, David H., *Lenox: Massachusetts Shire Town*, Lenox, 1969.

Woodruff, George C., *History of the Town of Litchfield, Connecticut*, Litchfield, 1845.